Finding the Bunny

A Memoir

SAMANTHA PARIS

FOREWORD BY
PETER COYOTE

Voice Haven Productions
Sausalito, California

Finding the Bunny
by Samantha Paris

Voice Haven
PRODUCTIONS
Published by
Voice Haven Productions
1207 D Bridgeway
Sausalito, CA 94965
415-331-8800
www.findingthebunny.com
findingthebunny@gmail.com

Finding the Bunny is my life story, as I recall my memories and experiences—although, at times, some timelines had to be changed for storytelling purposes, and some names had to be changed for legal purposes. I chose to insert the names of friends and loved ones whenever possible.

Publisher's Cataloging-In-Publication Data
(Prepared by The Donohue Group, Inc.)

Names: Paris, Samantha. | Coyote, Peter, writer of supplementary textual content.
Title: Finding the bunny : a memoir / Samantha Paris ; foreword by Peter Coyote.
Description: Sausalito, CA : Voice Haven Productions, [2018]
Identifiers: ISBN 978-0-9993121-0-0 (softcover) | ISBN 978-0-9993121-1-7 (POD) |
    ISBN 978-0-9993121-2-4 (ebook)
Subjects: LCSH: Paris, Samantha. | Voice actors and actresses--United States--Biography. |
    Voice-overs. | Self-actualization (Psychology) in women. | LCGFT: Autobiographies.
Classification: LCC PN2287.P37 A3 2018 (print) | LCC PN2287.P37 (ebook) |
    DDC 791.43028092--dc23

Library of Congress Control Number: 2017952319

Editors: Terry Bisson and Gail M. Kearns
Book and cover design: *the*BookDesigners
Book production coordinated by To Press & Beyond.

Printed in the USA.

DEDICATION

I dedicate this book to my beloved students, past and present. During my thirty-year teaching career, I am convinced that you have taught me far more than I ever taught you. Namely, what love, devotion, and family are all about. I am so proud of each you and I am proud to say that *because of you*, I was able to "find my bunny."

To my Voicetrax team, Vicki Baum, Roni Gallimore, and Chuck Kourouklis, you exemplify every day how great teamwork makes the impossible, possible—helping our students realize their dreams, and helping me realize my own.

For my chosen mother Janet Mann, Andre, and Graziano. I am where I am today because of your unconditional love and support. I know that down to the *deepest parts of my soul* and will remain forever grateful.

FOREWORD

If you picked up this book because you think it's about voice acting and that it might help you polish your chops and pick up extra income, you're sadly correct. Because by concentrating so intensely on your personal career, you're missing 90 percent of the value of what Samantha Paris can teach you. But let's start at the beginning.

I know something about the art of voice acting. After forty years of voice-overs; ads; 150-something documentaries; two Emmys; having been the "voice" of General Motors, Tylenol, Oracle, Brita, Chiquita Banana, Mazda, Claritin, lots of other brands; and doing seven, long-form Ken Burns documentaries, perhaps my initial resistance to a "voice teacher"—even one as lovely and charismatic as Samantha Paris—might be excused as an overdose of arrogance and self-importance.

It's not that I thought that I knew it all, or had nothing to learn or to teach, when Samantha approached me to teach a class at her school, Voicetrax, but I have a particular way of working, and I just "knew" that she would never get it, because if she did, I thought it would render her and her school superfluous.

In the first place, I *never* rehearse. I never even read the copy before I enter the studio to record. I read everything in the recording studio for the first time, because I have a kind of mystical belief that the first time I read something is when it makes the deepest impression on me, and that somehow my voice will transport that information to the listener. When I first met Ken Burns, and he entered the room carrying pads, pens, DVDs, and enormous scripts so that I could "prepare" for the National Parks series that he wanted me to narrate, he was horrified to learn that I never prepare. Startled, he blurted out, "That will never work." Seven films later, we're still working together.

So, when Samantha (did I mention, "quick," "sharp," "dazzling," and "charming"?—and, as I soon learned, brilliant) first came to see me, I was polite, because there's never a reason to be hurtful to others. I tried gentle dissuasion by explaining—in escalating detail—why my "method" would never work at her school. She kept smiling (did I mention "dazzling"?) and laughing and saying, "That's what I teach." Finally, at the edge of exasperation, I remember saying, "Samantha, I'm not about *technique*, I'm about *authenticity* and you can't—" And she interrupted me by laughing again and saying, "That's what I teach." And she does.

It turned out that Samantha has a few mystical beliefs of her own. She fervently believes that the power of possibility is pre-programmed in a person's internal life, and that he or she can be inspired to *give voice* to it. As a naturally gifted teacher, an accidental but nonetheless brilliant entrepreneur, and an indomitable force of nature (did I mention the difficulty of "Just saying 'no'"? Think "very attractive boa constrictor"), Samantha can wring expressiveness from a stone. She inspires the best in her students, nurturing their growth and transformation in ways that so far supersede voice acting, that she should put a warning sticker on her forehead that reads, "inspirational teacher."

Her mentorship begins with learning how to be six again, when each of us was perfect in our imperfections and completely believable in whatever we did. We've already transcended "voice acting" at this point, and if you're beginning to get the idea that her idea of voice acting might help you be a better businessperson, parent, coach, or human being, you're getting warm.

Samantha has trained more than *10,000* aspiring and working voice actors since she founded Voicetrax San Francisco in 1988. From corporate executives, realtors, and attorneys, to belly dancers, soccer moms, and police officers, Samantha's students represent all walks and status potentials of life—a Whitman's Sampler of backgrounds, professions, personalities, and vocal tones. She has made a tremendous impact on her students' lives, and, as proof, I offer the innumerable career successes and personal victories she can claim on their behalf.

But the process does not (or has not) stopped there. So many of her students go on to stay "to train" with Samantha for years—even after their careers are established, probing, going deeper, and expanding themselves in the process—that lunch at her school sometimes feels as if you've been plunged into the world's largest, warmest, Italian family. (Did I mention that her husband, Graziano, is an Italian chef who supplies the lunch, and that I had suspicions that several people in the room might have materialized just for his food?)

Finding your voice is such a simple idea, but, like a Japanese tea ceremony, it is far easier said than done. Questing after your *true voice* in your work and in your life can be your epic journey: learning to be who you really are—an unrepeatable expression of nature with as much integrity, power, and beauty as a hummingbird, a dolphin, a panther, or a bear—is a thrilling, captivating, elusive, frustrating, humbling, enlivening, and deeply fulfilling path to explore. The ultimate reward is coming to respect and accept yourself, which then becomes the motive force for becoming all that you might have hoped to be.

Irish author Oscar Wilde once said, "Be yourself; everyone else is already taken." For those of us who make our living in the self-expressive arts as actors, writers, entertainers, artists, and the like, that is even more true. Once we've found our true voices, our authentic, in-the-moment truth, we have control (in the same way a kayaker utilizes the energy of a river) of the process of bringing mindfulness and authenticity to our lives and work at every turn.

Finding *your* true voice marks a turning point in life, bringing greater self-understanding, meaning, and purpose to it. When we're fortunate enough to find that true voice, we've essentially discovered the key that opens the lock to the gates that have prevented us from reaching the open ranges and plains of possibilities within us.

Finding the Bunny is an entertaining, edifying, and inspiring story of Samantha's life and career, set in the rather fascinating (but not widely understood) world of voice acting—a world that is, as the book's description announces, "America's most influential yet invisible art." The story peels back the curtain on the art and craft of voice acting, but if that's all you take out of it, that's akin to eating the icing and leaving the cake. The deeper, nourishment is in the cake, for anyone who feels that they've lost touch with their original energy, authenticity, and joy, and now desires to seek new paths, break old habits, and make the most of the cards they've been dealt. Learn how to enjoy the ride you've actually bought a ticket for, even if it appears to be far from what you might have envisioned for yourself.

Finding the Bunny is about *transformation* more than anything else—offering ideas that might challenge or freshen your thinking, enrich your life, and light your own path. Through her engaging, cleverly told tale, you'll understand the depth behind her charming phrase "finding the bunny." You'll be inspired and believe her when she espouses her deep understanding that—contrary to popular practice and opinion—*talent can be taught* and *"safety lies in the risk."*

Her reputation preceded her, but when we finally met in person in 2016, and she invited me to speak at Voicetrax's "Inside the Voice Actor's Studio," despite my long-standing habit of warning aspiring voice actors *not* to go to school, I agreed (did I mention "persuasive," "charming," and "dazzling?)" to "check it out." I was duly impressed by what she had created and assembled and deeply moved by the remarkably warm and supportive culture and community she has created. Voicetrax is a creative haven, offering world-class training, camaraderie, and support, and, as of today, it's the *only* school of voice acting I've ever encountered in which I have absolute confidence.

Read this book. It will be an eye-opener, a thought-provoker, an education, an adventure, and an inspiration. (Did I mention "more fun than a bucket of kittens"?) You might even surprise yourself and "find the bunny" in your own life.

Peter Coyote
Sebastopol, California
May 2017

Part 1

1966

WOODLAND HILLS, CALIFORNIA

It's hard to fall asleep when you are afraid of being murdered. Maybe when I turn seven, I won't be afraid. It's also hard to sleep with my mom and dad down the hall screaming at each other. Are they saying my name? Is it my fault they are fighting? It's hard to hear, because their room is so far away and the door is closed.

"Gene, stop. *Just stop!*"

"No, *you* stop!"

I hear something break.

"You bitch!"

I'm so scared and I squeeze my eyes tight. I try to put my mom and dad out of my mind, because I must protect myself from the murderer who I know is just outside my window. He's there almost every night. To keep him away, I make a magical shield. I tuck all my sheets tightly around me, so none of my body parts are showing except my head. Not a foot, not a hand. It's hot and uncomfortable, but I *must* survive.

So far, it's working, but I'm still scared, because I'm whispering what I always whisper: "When you die, you sleep forever." I really think about those words, what each word means, even every letter. *When I die, I'm going to sleep forever . . . Okay, so I'm going to* die *. . . and then I'm going to* sleep forever . . . *sleep* forever . . . f-o-r-e-v-e-r.

As I'm thinking about just how long forever is, the tears roll down my cheeks. Am I never going to wake up? Ever? But I'm going to Disneyland for my birthday next week. My daddy says I actually get to meet Walt Disney. I can't die. I don't want to die. Please God, don't let me fall asleep.

I wake up the next morning relieved that my super-duper sheet shield has worked again. My baby sister, Lori, is in the kitchen taking the Hostess Twinkies and pink Sno Balls out of the bottom drawer where Mom keeps them. In the living room, I turn on the TV to watch cartoons.

The house is silent, but I know the murderer will be back again tonight. He's always outside my bedroom window, waiting.

Forty-Four Years Later

FEBRUARY 19, 2010
VOICETRAX, SAUSALITO, CALIFORNIA

"Okay, Steve, we're done. That was the *best* private lesson we've had to date. Have you lost weight?"

"Huh?" Steve opens the door of the voice-over booth and walks toward me.

"Not to be nosy, but have you lost weight?"

He grins. "Forty-nine pounds. Thanks for noticing."

"How could I not? Jesus, I have a hard time trying to lose five. How are you doing that?"

"Easy," he says. "Thanks to you and this place, I quit drinking."

"I thought bartenders weren't supposed to drink."

"That's on the job," he says. "Has nothing to do with what I was doing after work."

"What do you think you were doing today that you haven't been doing in the booth up to this point?" I ask him.

"You mean aside from all the other stuff you're always telling me to do?"

I smile. "I think you know what I mean."

"I think I'm finally learning to let go and just be myself. Be me. I think—I'm discovering I kind of like myself now, so it's easy."

The Kleenex box is always within arm's reach. I take two and pass them to him.

"Samantha Paris, no one has ever made me cry. Ever!" Steve shakes his head and chuckles. "Look what you're doing to me. I'm crying and I love it. I fucking love it!"

"Listen, Steve, you keep crying. Just keep letting go and embracing who you are, because who you are is exquisite." I cross over to him and give him a hug. "Now let's talk turkey here for a minute, because I want to remind you of something. Your growth has been off-the-charts fantastic, but it's going to get harder now. You are definitely at a place where if I *tell* you what to do, how to feel, who you're talking to, et cetera, you can go there. But at the end of the day, I'm not going to be with you when you are auditioning. For the majority of the time, you are going to be at home with your computer, your microphone, and standing in a closet or something. You're going to be directing yourself. That means we have to start working on your self-direction. I'm warning you now—it's not easy, but you'll get it. Just remember, a year ago, you couldn't even act! Hell, you could barely get two sentences out without stumbling."

"Yeah, I know. My dyslexia was getting the best of me."

"And now look at you. So, we got past that hurdle together, and we'll get through the next. Got it?"

"Got it, chief. Thanks."

"Good. Now get outta here."

And with that, Steve smiles, turns, and walks away, shutting the studio door behind him. I look at the clock: 12:01 p.m.

My life is so intensely structured into seconds, minutes, and hours, not to mention days, weeks, and months. As a voice-over performer, I am told to bring the copy in at 28.5 seconds—not 28, not 29—28.5. As a voice-over teacher, I must stay on time with my private lessons. If I have six in a row, I can't go over even five minutes for each one, or I'll be running twenty-five minutes late for the last.

As a business owner, running an incredibly bustling voice-over academy, I am also the keeper of more than fifty other instructors' schedules and their time constraints. And speaking of time (which I never have), it's only February, yet I have my entire teaching schedule set in stone for all of 2010. It's nearly impossible for me to be spontaneous. It makes for one rigid Samantha at home, and it's not anything I'm proud of.

It's 12:02 p.m. Yikes! My next student is new to me, and it's his first private lesson. He attended my "Finding Your Voice" lecture, but didn't volunteer to try any of the exercises, and he took one beginning-level class at my school, one that I didn't teach.

"Nick, hi! Come on in." He gets up from the couch and extends his hand.

"Nice to finally be working with you," he says.

"And you." I shake his hand and we enter the studio. "You know, when I saw your name on my sheet, I giggled. Nick Stratton sounds so strong. So tall." I drop my voice two octaves. "Nick Stratton, private eye."

"How can a name sound tall?" he asks.

"I don't have the slightest clue, but yours does, and anyway, I'm right. What are you, about 6'3"?"

"6'5", last I looked."

"See? I rest my case." I give him a pointed look. "So," I enter a lower register again, "Nick Stratton, tell me about yourself. What brings you here?"

"Well, I spent the last decade working my way up the corporate ladder, starting as an executive assistant to one of the most powerful real estate executives in the country. I was promoted along the way and finally made my way to become the vice president of a multi-billion-dollar brokerage. I worked incredibly hard, like sixty to eighty hours a week, and helped build the company from scratch."

Dude, this is not a corporate job interview.

Nick continues, "My boss held me up to my other colleagues as an example of how they should all be. You can imagine how that went over with my coworkers."

"I'm guessing not so good?"

"Well, I was the shining star and they knew it. It made for really resentful, jealous feelings, but I persevered."

I'm feeling like a kid listening to the adults in a Charlie Brown cartoon.

"So, after a decade—"

Wah, wah, wah.

"of devotion to my vision—"

Wah, wah, wah.

"and earning six figures—"

Wah, wah, wah.

"I reached the top of the mountain."

Who ever says, "reached the top of the mountain"? Who is this guy? I resist the urge to stifle a yawn.

"My stress level—" Nick continues.

Wah, wah, wah.

"huge bank account—"

Wah, wah, wah.

I start dreaming about taking a nap with Linus' blanket.

"I'm living in Mountain View and sitting on my sofa drinking whiskey at 9:00 a.m."

"You're drinking at 9:00 a.m.?" I ask.

"I was lamenting what had become of my life and wishing—"

"Whoa, whoa, whoa." I hold up a hand. "You've gotta loosen that tie of yours. Honestly."

He looks at me funny and checks his collar. "I'm not wearing a tie."

I roll my eyes heavenward. "I can see you're not wearing a tie, but you *sound* like you are!"

"Oh, like my name sounds tall?"

"Well, not exactly. You're just so stiff. Relax. I simply wanted you to tell me a little about yourself and why you're here. A normal response to this question would have been, 'Well, I've been in the corporate world—real estate, to be exact—for a long time, and even though I have been really successful and made a lot of money, I haven't felt fulfilled or happy. I'm here because I've always been interested in this line of work and I loved performing as a kid.'"

"Who the fuck are you, Samantha Paris?" Nick doesn't actually say this, of course, but the expression on his face does. But I don't care. I pride myself on my honesty, and I know that one day we'll both look back on this conversation and laugh. He will become a successful voice actor, and I will have done my job. That is, if he sticks with this, which at this moment, I'm not so sure about. I'm sure he feels hurt, insulted, or more likely both.

"Nick, look. I know you are serious about this. When you took the beginning seminar, Al shared with me how you did. He said, 'The guy has a lot of voice,' and he could tell you were determined to succeed. He admired your drive."

Nick nods his head.

"Tell me a few things you learned in the class."

"That this stuff is really hard, and that there's a lot more to it than I thought," he admits.

"And what else?" I prod.

"That you have to know who you are talking to."

"Yes, but I'm sure you learned something even bigger."

He takes a moment to think before he answers. "That I have to let go and just be me."

"Yeah. You've gotta get rid of that tie. Do you want to give it a go?"

As I adjust the mic in the booth, Nick scans his script.

"You know, you didn't disappoint. I was told you can be tough."

"I like to think of it as tough love, with an emphasis on love."

And with that I close the booth door, and Nick's lesson begins.

As I work with him, I find myself agreeing with Al's assessment. He's clearly determined to be successful. That's a great quality to have, but it can also get in the way of the learning process. I'm always telling my students that you have to enjoy the journey; you have to enjoy the *process* of learning something new. If you are constantly looking down the road, in this case, to earning a full-time living doing voice-over, then you're not in the moment, and the journey is going to be harder and take longer.

My first impression of Nick is that we are going to be in this for the long haul, but I have learned to not put too much stock in first impressions, at least not here. Throughout the years, I have had so many tightly wound types eager to impress on their first lesson. What they all don't realize is that it's ridiculous for them to put so much pressure on themselves. How can they possibly expect to be brilliant at something they've never done before? I have zero expectations about someone's skill level when they first walk in the door. I assume they are going to suck, and anything more than that is shocking.

He's clearly determined to be successful. That's a great quality to have, but it can also get in the way of the learning process. I'm always telling my students that you have to enjoy the journey; you have to enjoy the process of learning something new.

"Okay, my new friend, we're done for today. You can come out of the booth. You did a good job."

Nick has worked up quite a sweat. His button-down collar has wilted.

"Listen," I say, "this was your first private lesson, and you did really well."

He shakes his head. "Man, that was really hard. I can't believe I'm sweating. I was just standing behind a microphone."

I smile. "That's why they call it voice-over *work*. We don't refer to it as voice-over *play*."

Nick laughs.

"It will get easier, but not for a while. Just do me a favor and keep laughing. Embrace being not-so-good at something and getting better. I promise you will. It's my job to make it happen."

I cross over and give him a hug. Man, he is wet. "I'll see you around, okay?" I look him right in the eyes. There's a beautiful soul in there that's locked up so tight.

"Yep, Miss Paris, I will definitely see you around. This was great, thanks."

And boom. He's gone. The clock reads 1:07 p.m. Damn, I'm seven minutes late for class. In this case, it's not the end of the world, as my students are all out in the lobby nibbling away. The class is "Lunch with Punch." The students and Voicetrax take turns providing the lunch each Friday; I provide the "punch."

I close my eyes for ten seconds of glorious breathing. Then I step out into the lobby and address the class.

"Okay, guys, grab your stuff and come on in. Today we're not going into the booth to record. We're going to sit out in the studio and analyze a whole bunch of copy. So, fill your plates up again and let's get going."

The lobby counter is filled with homemade food.

"Yum! Who made this gorgeous frittata?" I ask, picking up a plate and fork.

"I did!"

"Oh, Susan, of course. How could I be so stupid? Your food is always so amazing! And I *know* who made the Caesar salad—thank you, Bill. Jesus, how many years have you been making this for me? I know it's been at least ten years now."

"Actually, Samantha, I've been coming here since 1997."

That stops me dead in my tracks. "You've been coming here thirteen years and you still haven't figured out how to do all this voice-over stuff?"

Bill smirks and I wink. We both know he's a terrific voice actor now, but he simply likes coming to class. For a few hours, he can escape being a lawyer and also a caregiver for his beloved wife, who has been ill for years. This Friday afternoon, "Lunch with Punch" is fun for him.

As everyone gathers their stuff and starts filtering into the studio, Vicki, my office manager, motions me over. "Just for a sec," she says.

"What's up?"

"Natanya called and you have a cartoon audition in LA on Monday. It's a new series and you're up for three different characters. Also, Jeff said that as you're coming down, he'll also have five or six commercials for you to read on."

Jeff and Natanya are my LA voice-over agents from DPN Talent, which is Jeff's agency, and Natanya is a senior vice president.

"Can't I record them here and MP3 them?"

"Nope. Natanya said the director is insisting on doing live auditions, and you were a client request."

My eyes glaze over. "What's my schedule on Monday?"

"You don't wanna know." She crosses back to her desk and pulls out the huge binder with the schedule. "You have six privates, and we all have a PR meeting with Nancy."

"Well, at least I don't have an evening class too. Can we reschedule the privates anytime soon?" I have years of experience informing me that this is a ridiculous question, but I ask it anyway.

"Not really. We just finished booking all of your private lessons for March, so it will be April for these guys. And you have cancelled on Christian twice. I'm going to hate having to call him."

"I would hate having to call him too. What time is the actual audition?"

"Natanya scheduled you for 10:00 a.m., so that you will have time to also audition at DPN before you fly home."

I sigh. That means up at 4:00 a.m., leave at 5:00, and arrive at the airport at 6:00 for a 7:00 flight. Then I'll be in Burbank by 8:30 a.m., if the flight is on time, rent a car, and make it to West Hollywood by 9:30 a.m.-ish.

"I don't know, I can't think right now. I've gotta start class."

"Sam, I really think I should call her back."

"Nah, she can wait." I enter the studio and close the door behind me, trying to soften the click. "All right, guys. So, script analysis. Script analysis is hugely important because if you don't **get** the script . . . you're not going to get the job. It's that simple."

"Don't they give you the script?"

"Not get, Roni, **get**! You've got to *get* what the copy is saying. Now that might seem obvious, but I know for a fact that nine times out of ten, when you go into the booth to record, you have no clue what you're saying. You're reading the words, you're saying them, but you're not really *internalizing* them. You know when you hear a song on the radio and sing along while you drive? And then one day, maybe years later, you hear the song again and you *really* hear the lyrics? And you think, 'Holy shit! *That's* what they're saying? I've been singing along for years without really thinking about what I've been singing!'"

I look at my twelve students sitting there. Some are still eating.

"I'm right, *right*? Of course, I'm right—I'm always right!" They laugh because they know I'm not kidding.

"I know that's what you do with your copy. You're saying the words without knowing the meaning. I mean, you're not stupid, you *do* know the meaning, but I mean the m-e-a-n-i-n-g."

Everyone but Bill, who's heard this a zillion times, is staring at me blankly. "Okay, let me tell you a story. Actually, I'm going to tell you two personal stories today, so you will learn that I am just as *meshuga* as all of you." They laugh.

"These two stories pertain to what I still do to this day when I'm analyzing a piece of copy. I have been staring at voice-over copy for thirty-something years now." I pause. "Wait, let me figure this out. I started when I was fifteen, and I'm about to be fifty, so that's—"

"Thirty-five years," Gary yells out.

"Thanks, Gary. Thanks for pointing out that I can't add, and that I'm getting old!" Laughter erupts again.

The room quiets. "Okay, so my point is, in all my thirty-five years of doing voice-over, no one ever told me, 'You have a great voice.' I don't. I never heard, 'Oh, I love your voice. Have you ever thought about being on the radio?' Fact is, I have an average voice, and it's okay. I sound like the 'girl next door.' I used to, anyway. Now I sound more like the 'mom' or 'gal' next door. Same difference. I'm not going to sell luxury cars or French perfume, but I *am* going to sell the toilet bowl cleaner, or talk about the ready-mix I found that helps me feed my family of four."

Okay. They're listening, putting their plates aside.

"My point is that when I first started studying voice-over all those years ago, I *knew* that because I didn't have an amazing voice, I was going to have to do something different to stand out from all the other actors. I was going to have to act better than *anyone*. Period. I knew my job would be to really bring the writers' words to life; to see everything in the copy that each writer intended and, sometimes, see even more! So that's what I did. And I made a career out of it. On countless occasions, I was told by producers that I was cast because my interpretation was better than anyone else's. I really took pride in that. It felt good knowing that I booked jobs because I had a brain; because I could act and I didn't just have a pretty voice. So, let me share with you what I used to do when I first started out, and what I still do to this day when I'm looking at my script."

My students are hanging on every word. Be mindful, Sammy . . .

"I come from a highly dysfunctional family," I confess. "My parents divorced when I was about ten. When I was really little, maybe five or six years old, I would hear my parents screaming at each other in their bedroom with the door closed. I was scared and would lie in bed and worry that I was going to be murdered. But I had a solution. It was to hide. I figured that if I tucked all the sheets around me really tightly so that none of my body parts were showing, nobody would come in and murder me. It was uncomfortable, and I was really hot, but that's what I did. Not even a foot, not even a finger stuck out. And I would lie there and think this really creepy thing. I would think, *When you die, you sleep forever.*

There is a twittering of nervous laughter rippling around the room, but most people remain quiet.

I press on. "Anyway, I would lie there and keep repeating those words: 'When you die, you sleep forever. When you die, you sleep forever.' And I would really frighten myself as I absorbed the meaning of each and every word. Die . . . sleep . . . forever . . . And finally, I would fall asleep. And guess what?"

Blank looks.

"It worked," I say. "Here I am today, unmurdered."

|| When you die, you sleep forever.

Laughs replace the blank looks.

"So, what's the point of this story? Well, after I got into voice-over, whenever I looked at a script, I would remind myself of that phrase. I would say to myself, 'Okay, Bobbi, remember, when you die, you sleep forever,' and that would remind me to absorb each and every single word of the copy."

A couple of the students look perplexed.

"I changed my name from Bobbi to Samantha about twenty years ago. In case you haven't read it, it's in my bio, in the Voicetrax brochure."

"Why did you change your name?" Roni blurts out.

"The full answer to that is a story for another day. But the short answer is, although I had an alcoholic stepfather, he did actually say one profound thing to me when I was a teenager.

He said, 'The only thing you really own in this life is your name. It is the one thing that's yours.' I lived for thirty years with a name that I was absolutely ashamed of. I was born Roberta Lynn Block. Bobbi for short. Oh, my God, I hated it."

"Why?" Devin blurts out. "What's wrong with Roberta? It's my mother's name."

"Well, I'm happy for her, but to me, no offense, Roberta sounds more like a wicked pull toy than an actual person. So, I changed it."

I let them chew on that for a few silent seconds.

"Let's look at your packet of copy. The first script is for Acme Clean & Flush. Go ahead and read it to yourself. I'll be back. Time for a pee break."

I walk out the studio doors and Chuck and Vicki are both at their desks, busy answering phones. Outside and around the corner is the bathroom. When I first built this place back in 1992, I hated that I had to go outside to go the bathroom. But I quickly became grateful for that, because I realized that if it weren't for that walk, I would never see the light of day. I would never know that I actually work in Sausalito with all the boats and the bay right outside my front door.

I cannot keep doing this anymore. Twenty-two years of teaching. I cannot do this anymore.

But how can I not do this anymore? I think about those twelve wonderfully exquisite human beings in my studio right now. I love them more than I love myself. Tears well up in my eyes as I enter the stall.

Samantha, pull yourself together.

I wash my hands and look in the mirror.

Where has my life gone? My career? Am I about to pass up yet another acting job for a teaching schedule?

I spend all day helping these beautiful people realize their dreams, but I'm not living mine. I feel like such a hypocrite.

I will myself to stop, dry my eyes and snap out of it.

Vicki is off the phone when I return to the office. "Well, are you going to LA?" she asks.

"Vic, I'm not going to do it. I just can't. Please call DPN and apologize to everyone. Tell them how much I appreciate everything they do for me, and that I will call on Monday."

Vicki gives me that disappointed nod she's grown accustomed to giving me a lot in the past year. This is nowhere near the first time I have turned my agents down. Meanwhile, my class is waiting.

"Okay, Susan, read it aloud for everybody's benefit."

:30 ACME Clean & Flush
TWELVE LITTLE BOTS

AVO: Never. Ever. Touch that disgusting toilet brush
again.

Introducing new ACME Clean & Flush.

The toilet brush, you flush.

Just snap on the tip. It already contains the
cleanser...

...so, you're scrubbing with the power of ACME...

The bristles begin to drop off...

...for safe flushing.

Then eject.

And flush the germs away. It's completely septic safe.
Nothing cleans...

...like new ACME Clean & Flush.

THE SPECS

The voice-over should be thirty-ish male or female
(have yet to decide). Our voice should be conversa-
tional, powerful, yet friendly and generally pleasant. No character voices.

"So, Susan, let's review the obvious voice-over basics. Who are you talking to?"

Susan's no newbie. She knows better than to say the sponsor or the consumer.

"My daughter, who is living away at college and I'm visiting her."

"Good! Ding, ding, ding. Now, *why* are you saying this?" I ask her.

"I don't know. Because she has to clean her toilet? Because I'm selling Acme Clean & Flush?"

"What?" I yell. "How many times have I told you guys: When you are doing commercial voice-over, you are *never* selling a product! Voice-over is the biggest no-sell sell. Get it out of your heads that you are selling anything! You must genuinely believe for thirty or sixty seconds that this product is great, or helpful, or whatever. You're *not* selling! Oy. Okay, Susan, what does this product do? What makes it special?"

"Well, I'm not going to have to touch a toilet brush again. That's really special."

The class laughs and agrees.

"But what does it *do*?" I ask.

She's smiling, but looking at me blankly. "Guys! This is a toilet brush that you flush. They've invented this actual toilet brush that you flush down the toilet! Isn't that incredible? Isn't that just absolutely amazing?"

The whole class is looking at me like I'm certifiable.

"Look, I'm going to say something right here. You can *never* judge the copy. I mean, for today's discussion, I will share that, yes, I think this product is fucking ridiculous. I don't believe for one second that it is completely septic safe, or that it is okay for our environment. I mean, it's stupid! If you have to clean your toilet, just use a basic toilet brush, some cleaner, and be done with it. However, when my job is to perform this piece of copy, my head doesn't go to that adult, cynical place. Thinking like that isn't going to do me any good. So, back to this script. You have to really visualize these words. Susan, put down your script for a second and just paraphrase the copy. Tell me all about it."

She's silent. She shakes her head.

"It's okay," I say. I walk over and give her a hug. "You might not know what this product does, but you sure make a mean frittata."

She smiles and the class cracks up.

"I've proven my point. So much of the time, we read the words, but they don't stick. We don't *internalize* them. You can read a piece of copy, but sometimes you have other things on your mind, or you're in a hurry—you don't notice your attention is divided. It happens to me too. So, when it does, I will immediately think to myself, 'Okay, Samantha, remember, *when you die, you sleep forever.*' It reminds me to slow down and drink in all the words." I can see the gears grinding in their brains.

> So much of the time, we read the words, but they don't stick. We don't *internalize* them.

"Let me share another story," I continue. "How many of you have heard the expression 'finding the bunny'?"

A couple of timid hands go up, but they're not really sure. I smile at Bill. He knows.

"Most of you haven't heard it before, because you're just now taking this class. You might ultimately never use my 'When you die . . .' expression, because it's depressing. Maybe you'll come up with your own phrase that will work for you. But, I assure you, you *will* use this technique. I don't know an advanced Voicetrax student who doesn't."

They are sitting up straight. Maybe it's the word "advanced."

"Here is my dysfunctional story number two. I was the middle child. My siblings and I are each three years apart. There is my younger sister, Lori; then me; and then my older brother, Larry. Before my parents' divorce, my brother was about eleven-ish and

I was eight-ish. My father used to subscribe to *Playboy*."

I look around the room. "For the articles, right?" Everyone laughs.

"My brother was allowed to take out the centerfolds, and he had Miss January through Miss December plastered on his bedroom walls. Larry taught me that on the cover of the magazine, there was always a small *Playboy* bunny hidden somewhere. You know, their logo, with the big ears and all. Larry would test me to see if I could find it, and sometimes I would spend what seemed like hours staring at the cover, trying to find the bunny. I loved it when I found one! So, what's my point? I started to learn voice-over when I was fifteen years old. I didn't have a lot of life experience to use. So, looking at my scripts back then and knowing I didn't have a special voice, I knew I had to try to see as much as I could in the copy. In other words, I was looking for the bunny. I'll show you exactly what I mean. Look at this script for Shopper Bee."

CLIENT: Shopper Bee Supermarkets
JOB: :60 Double Coupon Discount Radio (4 a.m.)
NUMBER: 267840
REVISION: 1

(SFX: Crickets at night)
(SFX: Door opens)
MAN: Honey?
WOMAN: Yes?
MAN: Are you okay?
WOMAN: What do you mean?
MAN: Well, it's four o'clock in the morning and you're on the front porch with a pair of scissors in your hand.
WOMAN: I'm waiting for the paper.
MAN: I see...Why?
WOMAN: Because Shopper Bee is offering double the value of any manufacturer's coupon up to fifty cents. And I want those coupons.
MAN: Mmhmm. But it's four o'clock in the morning.
WOMAN: That's when they deliver it.
MAN: Okay. Honey, I know you love saving money, but...
WOMAN: Shh! Did you hear something?
MAN: Unh-unh.
WOMAN: I tell you what. I'm gonna walk to the corner and see what I can spot from there.
MAN: Honey, we don't even have a newspaper subscription.
WOMAN: We do now. I signed us up yesterday... twice.
(SFX: Music under)

THE SPECS

WOMAN: Female, thirty-five to forty. Her character should be excited and determined. A bit out of left field, but not too crazy. She is single-minded in her mission.

MAN: Male, forty-five-ish. His character goes from confused and a little worried to a sense of ridiculous disbelief when he finally figures out what's going on. He should not be overly dramatic.

"Devin and Diane, please read it out loud."

They quasi-perform the script and we begin to discuss.

"Who are you guys?" I ask.

"I guess we're married, and my wife is a little crazy," Devin says.

"Wait a minute. Are you crazy, Diane?"

"Well, I am outside at 4:00 a.m. waiting to get a paper so I can cut out some coupons; so, yes, I guess I am crazy."

I make a "sorry, you lose" buzzer sound. "No, you're not crazy. What crazy person thinks they're crazy? What makes you crazy is that you don't know that you are! What makes a dorky person dorky? Same thing. They don't know they're a dork. Get it? So yes, you guys are married, and you, Diane, are anxiously waiting for the paper on the front porch, with a pair of scissors in your hand. You, Devin, are in bed since it's four o'clock in the morning, and you wake up and realize your wife is not in the bed with you. What do you do?"

"I guess I get out of bed and go look for her."

"Exactly. So, you go look for her, you find her out there and you say . . . "

They begin the script again. When they are done, everyone thinks they were really good. They say they were believable.

"Really?" I say. "You think that was good? Do you think if there are twenty or thirty other groups performing this, Devin and Diane would stand out and book the job?"

The students are nodding their heads and Gary yells, "Yeah, why not?"

"I'll tell you why not. Because they read this script like every other actor would read it. Look where it says SFX, for sound effects. The sound effects are crickets. It's four in the morning. How do we talk when it's the middle of the night and we're hearing crickets?"

There is dead silence in the classroom. It's so silent that I could insert the crickets the script mentions.

"Guys, the 'bunny' in this script is the crickets and the fact that it is four in the morning! We talk to each other in a slight whisper. We are trying to keep our voices down, because it's still the middle of the night. Every other actor is not going to think to do that. They're going to use their normal voices, and I am going to book the job. I *did* book the job."

They grin and shake their heads. They like it.

"Okay, next script. Look at Aunt Mary's."

Aunt Mary's
Radio
:60 "Weather Report"

WEATHERMAN: This is your News Channel Five Day Forecast

For Wednesday, we have cloudy skies with 50 percent chance of <u>Beef Stir Fry with Asian-Style Teriyaki Rice</u>.

Clearing up Thursday with sunny skies and a large band of <u>Marinated Rotisserie Chicken with Rice Pilaf</u> coming in from the northeast.

As the weekend approaches, expect up to 8 inches of <u>Kabobs on a Bed of Chicken-Flavored Rice</u>.

As the expected low front of <u>Mushroom Sauté on Whole-Grain, Brown Rice</u> barrels in from the Atlantic.

ANNCR: If only great meal ideas came this easy. Well, actually, they do. With Aunt Mary's Insta-Rice you can go from microwave to a more inspired meal in just ninety seconds. No prep, no cleanup. And because it's available in both plain and flavored varieties, adding rice to your menu has never been easier. So, try Aunt Mary's Insta-Rice in the pouch. Great, delicious rice in just ninety seconds. Bring more to the table.

THE SPECS

Weatherman: Mid-forties to mid-fifties. Deep voice, A little folksy, midwestern, fatherly like delivery.

Announcer: Female, early to mid-thirties. Down-home, friendly voice. Should have a common-sense delivery, like a good friend giving advice.

I notice Vicki entering at the back of the classroom.

"Again?" I moan.

"I have some administrative things for you after class, and Nancy needs five minutes of your time. It's about a pitch she's doing for the *San Francisco Chronicle*."

I look at her with dread, as I know I only have a thirty-minute break before my next class, and I need that time to finish prepping for it. I sigh, "Okay," and she slips back out the door.

"All right, Aunt Mary's. Frank, you be the weatherman, and Cynthia, you be the announcer. Let's do it."

They begin. Frank and Cynthia are actually a bit more advanced than most of the other students. Their cold read goes darn well. Or so they think.

"All right everyone, let's look at the specs. Like a lot of specs, these are fairly stupid, or they don't make sense, and they can often be misleading. The best thing to do is ignore them. Look at the copy. What do the words say? Act the words that are on the paper. Let's take it from the top and, Frank, really take to heart what I just said. It says you're a weatherman, right? Do the copy."

He performs it exactly the way it is on the paper, emphasizing "Beef Stir Fry with Asian-Style Teriyaki Rice," because it's in bold and it's underlined. The same with "Marinated Rotisserie Chicken with Rice Pilaf."

Frank can tell I'm not happy.

"What?" he protests. "You said act what's on the paper and I am. These words are underlined, so I'm emphasizing them!" He laughs weakly. He knows he's doing something wrong and I'm going to nail him for it.

"God, I love you!" I tell him. Now he's really laughing.

"Yeah, I know you do and I'm waiting for the *but*." He's referring to my most famous expression, "You know I love you, *but* . . ."

"I *do* love you, Frank, but that was fucking awful! You're a weatherman. A meteorologist. How do these people act on TV?

When they start their weather report and talk about a cold front coming in, they shiver a little when they say it, or when it's going to clear up and get sunny, they start to act all sunny. I know you know what I'm talking about."

Jerald calls out from the back of the room, "But what if you don't watch television? I don't. I do Netflix."

"Oh, really?"

Jerald is fairly new.

"Are you some elitist trying to impress me with the fact that you never lower yourself to watching TV? First, I'm not impressed, and second, if you don't like TV, why are you here studying voice-over?"

The energy in the room has changed.

"If you don't like TV or you're not going to watch TV, then there's the door. Get out."

I turn back to the class. Jerald's ridiculous comment has at least led us to a teachable moment.

"If you want to do this, you've got to watch TV. You have to watch the commercials and listen to them. There's no DVR-ing or TiVo-ing or any of that crap. You also have to actually watch television. Advertising is always going to reflect what's popular on TV. It always has and it always will. You've got to watch the popular shows and know the actors. What's going to happen if, at the bottom of the script, it says it should be performed à la Elaine, and you've never watched *Seinfeld*? Guess what? Your ship just sank. You're not going to get the part. You've got to know what's out there! You've got to go to museums and put on the headphones and listen to the audio tours. You have to listen to audiobooks and watch documentaries. You need to play video games. Watch cartoons. Shit, you've got to pay attention when a voice is telling you, 'Press one or press two.' I'm not kidding, guys. You have to read God-awful celebrity magazines. You've *got* to know pop culture!"

I pause to catch my breath and realize I'm ranting. I step down off of my soapbox. "Sorry, guys, but you've got to be aware. Now, where were we?"

"You were about to tell me why I sucked," Frank says.

The class laughs a little and I know they will recover.

"Frank, you were emphasizing what is written, but the 'bunny' is that because you are a weatherman, you should be emphasizing all the *weather* words, not what is underlined! I auditioned for this exact same script, except the character was "Libby Lye in the Sky." I was a traffic reporter, but otherwise it was the same thing. All the traffic expressions, like being 'backed up for miles,' and all the Aunt Mary food parts were underlined. The 'bunny' was going against the way it was typed."

I ask Frank to do it again and play up the weather words.

"Al Roker me to death," I say. Frank does it and he's brilliant. I give him a hug.

"Guys, look for the bunny. Look for it every time. There might not always be one, but look for it anyway. Cynthia, your part isn't that there's a bunny there, but you do have to internalize what you're saying, like we talked about with the Acme script."

We have three hours left in this intense, four-hour class, and then I have another three hours of teaching after that.

How can it be that I feel so utterly inspired, yet completely drained and depressed at the same time?

I've been carrying this conflict around with me since the time I taught my first student, Tom Appelbaum.

"All right guys, we're done for the day. Don't forget your homework assignment for next week. You did great and you know I love you."

With that, everyone packs up to go. Jerald approaches me. I can see from the slightly sour look on his face that he still feels the sting of my rant.

"Hey, Samantha," he says.

"Wow! I'm impressed. I tell you to get out of my classroom, go on a rant, and now you want to talk." I give him a hug and, surprisingly, he hugs me back, hard.

"I just want to say thanks. I know how passionate you are and you're right. I do want to do this, so I know I have to watch TV."

"I know you want this too. That's why I'm going to be tough on you. Now, get out of here and have a good weekend. I've got to get ready for my next class." I give him a kiss, a hug, and a shove. He starts to walk away.

"What happened with him?" Vicki says as she approaches.

I know she's all too familiar with people who boast that they don't watch television, like it's some badge of honor. She heard it when she was a student. "Oh, Jerald dropped the 'I don't watch television' bomb. You'd think, after all these years, it wouldn't piss me off, but it still does."

"Well, hopefully he'll figure it out. Here, I've got checks for you to sign," she says, handing them to me, "and a couple of things to go over with you."

Feeling like a beaten warrior, I bow my head like Rafa Nadal, my favorite tennis player, when he's down two sets in a major. I'm drained and exhausted but cannot give up.

"Are we going to have to rob a bank to pay for all this?"

"Don't worry," she says. "We still have $15K in the bank, and I'm going to be making another big deposit next week. We'll be back to a more comfortable cushion. Remember that in that stack you are signing are the payroll checks, so we won't have that for another two weeks."

I sigh in relief, remembering the days when my mother was the office manager, and we were always on the verge of financial disaster. Vicki is sensitive to that. She knows my mother nearly ruined my company.

"I have also paid some checks early because next week I'm out of the office for bookings on Tuesday and Friday."

I'm proud of Vicki and wish I had her life. She knows how to set boundaries, unlike me. I finish signing.

"Now, I know this is going to piss you off because she's done it again." She hands me my class list for the evening. "Mindy just called ten minutes ago and dropped out of class."

"You gotta be kidding me. I told you the last time she did this I wanted to kick her out of the program. She pays for class, doesn't show up, but in the meantime, we have a waitlist a mile long of students really wanting the class!"

"I know, Samantha. I explained to her that it's not fair to the other students, but she did it again anyway."

"Well, not anymore. She's out. I don't care that she has a boat-load of money and can afford to pay for classes she's not going to take. It's simply not right."

"I agree, and I'll draft a letter to her on Monday that you can look at. And speaking of letters, you have a couple of thank-you notes here."

"Thanks, put them on my desk, and I'll read them later. I don't have any more time. I've got twenty minutes to get ready."

"Samantha, no," Vicki says, giving me her evil eye. "I will not put them on your desk. You will sit here and read them now. You have the time and you need to do this. You need to be reminded of why you do all this."

I roll my eyes. "Okay, okay, I'll read them."

"Thanks, Samantha, for all the . . ."

"I can't believe how supportive you were . . ."

"You and your amazing faculty of guest directors have made my dream of . . ."

As heartfelt as they are, it's difficult for me to absorb the love and appreciation these students have for me when I'm so damn conflicted about what I do.

If only they knew my painful little secret. That I swore I'd never EVER become a teacher, let alone run my own school.

"There, I'm done." I hand the notes back to Vicki and look at my watch.

She glares at me.

"What?"

"You didn't read these. You glanced at them. Like you tell your students, you didn't *internalize* all the words," Vicki scolds.

"Yes, I did, Vicki. Julia is really happy with her demo, and she thanked Chuck too. She was also really touched that we told her she didn't have to pay for it right away. By the way, thanks for setting up some kind of payment thing for her. And yes! Rebecca's transformation is so touching. Did *you* read these? You know I'm always saying that I think it's more important that you and Chuck read these notes. You guys are the ones who are dealing with the students on the phone all the time."

"I like for you to read them first," Vicki says. "But I will too, of course. And I'll *internalize* the words!"

"Very funny. Just file them in the box or whatever after you and Chuck read them."

"Samantha," she says in an accusatory voice, "do you even know where the infamous box is? Where all your love letters are kept?"

I don't. I give her another vacant stare. There are now only fifteen minutes left before my next class.

"Nancy's on line two," Chuck says, walking in.

I give him a thumbs-up and turn back to Vicki. "Duty calls, babe, and please don't be mad at me."

"Hey, Nancy," I say, picking up the phone. "How are you?" Nancy's not only my publicist, she's my dear friend.

"I'm good, Sammy. Do you have a few minutes?"

"Can this wait until our meeting Monday afternoon?" I

growl, trying unsuccessfully to mask my frustration.

"Well, I'd like to finish this pitch, so I can send it out Monday morning."

"Okay, shoot."

"I want to confirm that we are changing the name of the voice-over competition from 'LA Idol' to 'T.O.P. Voice.'"

"That's right, and remember, the T.O.P. stands for 'Truly Outstanding Performer.'"

"And Jeff Danis is coming, in addition to Natanya?"

"Yep, and you know what, Nancy? Far be it from me to tell you how to do your job, but may I humbly suggest that you really build up the fact that Jeff is *the* most successful voice-over agent in the country, and that Natanya Rose is a huge animation agent? I want the damn pink section of the *Chronicle* for once."

"I know you do, Sammy. We're going to try."

"Well, shit, Nancy. Every year Jeff comes and provides this amazing opportunity for the winner, or shall I say winners, because last year he picked not just one, but *four* to fly to LA for a week, where they got to audition every day alongside the biggest names in the voice-over industry. I mean, it's incredible, and I've always felt that this is a pink section story."

"Sammy, you have to remember that the *Chronicle* has already done two or three stories on you."

"I know that, and I appreciate it, but it's never been the Sunday pink! You know, I don't want to sound like I have my head up my ass, but during these past twenty-two years, Voicetrax has trained so many people and turned actors and non-actors alike into successful voice actors who make *money*, unlike people who train at the American Conservatory Theater, which is always in the damn pink sect—"

"Well, A.C.T. has been around a long time," Nancy interrupts. "It's a San Francisco institution."

"What the hell are we at Voicetrax? Oh, gee! 'Come learn stage acting at A.C.T., where when you graduate you'll become a stage actor and starve for the rest of your life!' Why are you laughing?"

"Because, Sammy, I just love your passion, and you're adorable when you're mad. You know I'll do my best. Are we still set for four o'clock on Monday?"

"That we are. Now I have to run."

I hang up and walk out into the lobby, where I see that my next batch of students has arrived.

"Hi, guys. I'll be right with you. I have to get a couple of scripts from the other studio." I push open the door and breathe in a mixture of fog and fish smells swirling in the air, as I cross over and enter Studio C. I'm frantically searching for the scripts when the sadness sets in again.

I cannot keep doing this anymore. I feel trapped and have nothing left to give. My well is running dry, but I have to keep feeding the monster I created. I have no choice.

There's no time for tears. I find the scripts, take a deep breath, and it's showtime once again.

Three Hours Later

I faked it tonight, and I feel guilty, as in dishonest, empty. I'm glad I didn't have an engineer to run the board tonight. I need the alone time. I clean the coffeepot, empty all the trash, and realize I haven't been alone in my own studio in years—maybe even a decade. The students laughed a lot in tonight's class, but I was faking it; not the love but the laughs.

I wasn't in the mood to teach an animation class—I actually don't enjoy teaching animation acting all that much. People assume I love it, because I voiced so many cartoons back in the 1980s in LA. But I don't. I've always preferred the creative challenge of doing commercials.

To help guide my students who "hate commercials," I must first get them to look at commercials in a different light. They're simply little thirty-second or sixty-second plays, each one with a beginning, middle, and end. In many of my classes, I make the students write ads. I say to them, "You try to write a commercial. It's not that easy! You have to take a product and somehow make a thirty-second story out of it."

I also love the challenge of commercial acting. Let's face it, as the performer, I am performing for an audience that hates me. Unlike in a play, movie, or TV show, where the audience members are all willing participants, in a commercial, the audience doesn't want to watch me or listen to me, and there are high-tech inventions that can cut me out. So, when I can grab my audience and connect with a group of people who don't want to connect with me, I find that to be such a super-sexy creative challenge. I could go on and on about great commercials. I did try to stay mindful, however, that tonight's class *was* the true passion of many of my students, so I know that in the end, I did an important job.

"God, it's so quiet," I say to myself. If these walls could talk, what stories they would tell—stories of transformation. So many thousands of people have entered this studio with a need to express themselves—a need to find their voices. Many have come in pursuit of the dream of becoming a successful voice actor, and many of them have. I look to the right and see the bar. The neon pink "Sam's Place" sign is still on. I'm shocked it still works. It's never burned out. I find that rather ironic.

I go back to the lobby. The mural of the talking cows holding scripts in their hands still makes me smile. Especially the one that says, "It's selection, not rejection." Back when I opened the studio, I used to do a lot of casting. The mural depicts a "cattle call." At the bottom is the artist's signature: "A Paris '92." Andre.

A small lump forms in my throat. I sit on the sofa. I'm always in such a rush to get out of the studio and get home. The problem is, I'm not going home. I'm going to a small apartment I've rented in Sausalito, because Andre and I are separated. He's at our home.

|| It's selection, not rejection.

I take in a deep breath and close my eyes. I hear Rabbi David's voice blessing the studio the day before it opened. And then I snap out of it. This is silly. I've got to go. I might not be going home, but I am going to the place where I have a bed, and I need to rest. I'll be back here tomorrow morning to do the same thing all over again.

Friday, 9:45 p.m.

SAUSALITO, CALIFORNIA

I'm shivering in this freezing cold apartment. It seems to have been built with cardboard and popsicle sticks, and that mythic, big bad wolf could easily blow this house down.

I feel a heightened appreciation and longing for my insulated home in Petaluma, where Andre must be relaxing, all cozy and warm.

I turn on the heat and head into the living room to turn on the tiny gas fireplace. I think it's there more for mood lighting, as it certainly doesn't produce any substantive warmth. I pour myself a glass of wine and turn on the TV. Nothing is registering, even though I'm staring straight at it. Before I know it, half an hour has vanished. What did I just watch? What was the storyline? I'm doing exactly what my students do—not absorbing.

Sam, look at all the love you give to others. You should give it to yourself also.

I hear Andre's gentle voice in my head and my eyes suddenly

well up with tears for the third time today. This time, I don't fight them. As they fall, I am more than well aware of the fact that these tears are not pity-party tears, as I have no right to feel such things. I have been extremely fortunate. I just feel utterly overwhelmed, like my life has been a runaway freight train I am powerless to stop. I had been holding onto the rails for dear life, while Andre sat in the first-class cabin and occasionally called out to me that everything was going to be fine.

"Just enjoy the journey!" I can hear him calling out to me from his cushy first-class seat.

Andre pushed me, encouraged me, and believed in me from the beginning, and, yes, some of it was genuine, but a lot of it was selfish on his part, even though I am where I am today because of his influence. The tears keep falling, but they are fewer.

"Okay, Andre," I whisper. "I promise to give it a try."

I check my phone and it's nearly eleven o'clock. I need to eat a little something, wash my puffy face, and get horizontal, so I do. As I crawl into bed, I remember what I shared with my class about being little and having to tuck the sheets all around me. Thank God, that's not the case anymore. Now I allow one foot to stick out. I pray I'll sleep through the night. Exhaustion makes me fall asleep, but stress and anxiety wake me up most nights.

The next thing I know, I'm screaming at the top of my lungs, but nothing is coming out. I feel like I'm moving in slo-mo—I'm trying to run, but my legs are heavy, as if they're made of stone. My thighs burn.

Why won't my legs work? I must run. I have to get away!

"Be like YOU?" My throat is on fire. "You're a liar! You're pathetic! You are nothing but a "has-been," I shout, except the words aren't coming out.

Johnny Truffa is rushing toward me. He grabs me by my ankles. I am back in Van Nuys at his studio, in the back room where he made me work. I am tangled up in something. Is it audiotape?

"I don't need you! I hate you! Let me go!" I struggle, trying to yell in his face, but still my mouth won't move. I'm kicking frantically.

Johnny throws something at me, and then I finally find my voice and scream. It wakes me up.

My scream is the only sound in my pitch-black bedroom. I'm sweaty and out of breath. I haven't dreamed or even thought about Johnny, my first "teacher," in ages. He died several years ago. I can still feel his cold hands on my ankles; I know it was a dream, but it felt so real.

I switch on the light and tear up yet again because I feel so alone. I am alone, it's not just a feeling. I wish I had someone who really loved me, someone I could turn to and wake up and share that I just had a nightmare. I grab my phone. It's 2:45 a.m. I see that I have a new text message from Chris. It reads, "Are you still tits on sticks?"

I can't help but give a weak laugh. I should expect messages like this, given that one of my closest friends is a guy. I realize that Chris just became the person I can wake up, because he lives in London. I start dialing overseas.

"Good morning, sir," I murmur when he answers.

"Ah, Samantha Paris, as I live and breathe. Why on earth are you calling me now?" he asks in his super-sexy English accent.

"Because you just sent me a text, you dipshit."

"Well, I figured you'd see it in the morning. Are you still having trouble sleeping?"

"Yep. Actually, I just woke up from a horrible dream. And to answer your question, no, I am not tits on sticks. I have gained four pounds, if you really want to know."

"A whole four pounds. Quick, let's alert the paparazzi and have them snap photos!"

I giggle. Chris can always make me laugh in a way no one else can.

"Do you want to talk about your dream?" he asks.

"God, no. I really want to forget about it."

"Okay, love, so, how are you? Are you feeling a wee bit better now that your mum is out of the office?"

"A *wee* bit better, Chris? How about lightyears better? I don't know why I didn't fire her sooner."

"Well, firing one's mum can't be easy."

"That's true, and also having to face leaving a twenty-year marriage at the same time. My timing sucks. Anyway, going to work sucks less than it used to, and actually, it's a lot better now. The phones are answered pleasantly, there's zero negativity, and the office feels so light. I even changed the alarm code to 'free,' as that's how I feel with her gone."

He pauses for a moment. "That's 3-7-3-3."

"Wow, you really are a numbers guy."

"Have you spoken to her?"

"No, I haven't. And I told you I won't."

"I guess I was hoping you would soften a little. After all, she is your mum."

"Chris, we've been over this. When you discovered all the money she was taking without my knowledge, well, that was just the final straw. I'm actually glad it happened, because it forced me to look in the mirror and finally say, enough is enough. I have been living with a cancer called 'my mother' all my life, and now I'm cancer-free! Do you honestly think I would want that cancer back?"

"No, darling, of course not. Did you hire anyone to replace her?"

"Nope. I didn't have to. Chuck and Vicki, along with a reasonable accounting firm, can do it all, and I am now saving about $70,000 a year. I owe you." I hear him chuckling through the phone. "Honestly, Chris, you did me such a huge favor when you came out here and pored over all the books. You taught me so much."

"Well, you needed to wake up and accept the fact that, like it or not, you own a business. You are the CEO of Voicetrax, and you had to start looking at the bottom line."

"I know. You were 100 percent right. Just because I never wanted a business has nothing to do with the fact that I have one."

"Exactly. And you know, you should be proud of it. I mean, my God, there's no other school like yours. I had no idea what you built and the complexity of it all until I started in with the financials. It's not a little voice-over school. That is for sure. It's insane!"

"You mean I'm insane for running all this."

"You know what I mean." His tone changes. "What's going on with Andre?"

I let out a deep sigh. "It's okay, I guess. I mean, it's sad. I'm really sad. I love Andre. I know I'll always love Andre, but I also know that I deserve better."

"That's the bottom line, isn't it?"

"Yeah, it is. It's crazy that I busted my ass to support us and put up with him smoking pot all day in his studio, creating ceramics and sculptures he was never going to sell. Did I ever tell you my 'paint it blue' story?"

"No, I don't think so."

"Well, a couple of years ago we were really struggling. As you know, house prices had started to drop dramatically, and the bank was trying to pull our home-equity line.

"Oh, I do remember that," Chris jumps in. "I believe you fought them and won."

"Yeah, but it wasn't easy. Anyway, Andre had made these beautiful, large, ceramic, serving plates with beach scenes painted on them. They were fantastic, and I encouraged him to take them to this high-end kitchen/home shop in Sonoma, where I actually shopped a lot. The owner knew both of us. Anyway, she really liked them but didn't want them for the shop."

"Why wouldn't she want them if she liked them?"

"Because the plates were white and the beach scenes he painted were of people playing, reading, and eating but there was very little blue in them. The owner said she would love some, if he would paint them with more blue in the scenes. They were going to sell for five hundred dollars apiece."

"Well, that's a handsome sum."

"I know. But Andre refused to do it. We walked out of the store and he started telling me he was not that kind of artist. That he refused to be 'commercial' and would not sell out."

Chris sighed somberly, adding, "Even though you guys were struggling."

"Yeah, I was crushed. It crystallized in me that I didn't really matter to him. My well-being didn't matter. I had sacrificed my entire acting career to take care of us, and he couldn't even make a few damn plates the way somebody asked for them."

"You mean, he couldn't paint them blue."

"Yeah," I said flatly. "I did always tell Andre that I didn't care if he ever made a penny with his art, as long as he was really *trying*. And I meant it. Unfortunately, that moment was my 'wake up and smell the coffee' moment, and it was crushing."

There is a moment of silence with only the faint sound of international static on the phone.

"Speaking of plates, you have a lot on yours right now, dealing with both your mum and Andre. I don't know how you handle it all. I really admire you."

I burst out laughing.

"What's so funny?"

"I cannot believe how many times a day I still reflect on our conversation in that London taxi two years ago—that philosophy of yours that people fall into one of two categories, 'radiators' and 'drains.'"

"Ah, yes, and you, Samantha Paris, radiate."

"As do you, Mr. Green, but speaking of 'drains,' I met one last week. I went to see a divorce attorney."

"I hate solicitors. You two should really try to sort things out on your own—otherwise, you are both going to be left penniless."

"Tell me about it! This woman was frothing at the mouth for a fight. I swear, she must have pit bulls and piranhas as pets!"

|| People fall into one of two categories, radiators and drains.

"You have such an imagination," he chuckles. "So, what did this drain, drain you of?"

"Hope mostly. I think she was trying to justify a big fee. She told me what the law said about divorce and my rather unique situation.

"And?"

"It's not good. It's actually so unfair. Not only is Andre entitled to half of the house, but he's also entitled to half of Voicetrax and half of my salary for the rest of his life. Talk about what's insane! I sat there in her office, shaking my head, thinking of a few years before the 'paint the plates blue' incident, when I had the school in the desert."

"You . . . a desert? Where?"

"Palm Springs. Well, Rancho Mirage to be exact. Back then I was commuting 545 miles each way, just to make ends meet. I mean I was always asking Andre to help out, to get some kind of job, but it always fell on deaf ears. He 'retired' from hairdressing with no retirement and promised me he would take his art seriously, but he never did. His 'retirement plan' was me. I told the exact thing to this lawyer, and she said it didn't matter."

"Andre has done quite well for himself as a house husband."

"I think the expression 'house husband' implies that the man is staying home to look after the children. I hardly consider our Yorkie, Ollie, a child."

"The laws in England are tough, but I hear California is far worse. Why does he get alimony for the rest of his life? Isn't it usually just for a few years?"

"Yeah, but because we have been married for twenty years, plus his age, that's what it is."

"I forget—how old is Andre?"

"Seventy-nine. We're twenty-nine years apart."

"Jesus, Samantha, you really are fucking crazy."

I laugh halfheartedly and glance at the clock. "I have to go. It's quite late here, and I have one of my 'Finding Your Voice' lectures tomorrow morning. I have to be up, alert, and charming, ugh."

"You say, 'ugh,' but I think you thrive on them—and by the way, you left out beautiful."

"Thanks, honey. I guess I'll say good night. Oh, and one more thing—I do want you to know that I'm confident Andre and I can work something out. He hates lawyers too. I am determined to have the most loving divorce on this planet."

"I like the sound of that. And if anyone can do it, it's you, Samantha."

"I hope so. Okay, I'm going to bed. Love you loads and thanks for everything. You're the best friend a girl could ever have."

"Get some sleep, Sammy. Talk soon."

I hang up the phone with a click and then there's nothing left but me and the silence.

Part 2

Saturday, 7:10 a.m., February 20, 2010

SAUSALITO, CALIFORNIA

I'm up, exhausted, and depressed. Last night was rough, even with Chris' help. My not being able to sleep is an issue that has been going on for years. Given the present circumstances in my life, it's even worse.

As I pour my coffee, I try not to think about Johnny Truffa. Instead, I turn to thinking about changing my life from "upside-down" to "upside-up."

It's going to be a lot of work, especially because I have to do it alone. I do everything by myself. I always have. I'm sure it stems from the fact that my mother and stepfather were never helpful. They were usually drunk. I remember the early days of my professional career, being totally alone and getting zero support. Before that, there was never any help with the homework or even talk about the world around us. The talk was always about them.

"I got a call today from Bing," my stepdad would boast. He knew that we knew that he meant Bing Crosby. "He's going to come in and record a Christmas show for me next week for Continental Airlines."

"What about Johnny?" my mother would ask.

"Which one? Johnny Mathis or Johnny Truffa?"

"J.T.," as he liked to be called, recorded shows for my 'dad' for TWA.

"Johnny Mathis. He told me when we were having lunch at the Musso & Frank Grill yesterday that he wanted to come over here to the house and look through your album collection for a specific song for a project at Warner Brothers."

I would glance at my big brother and know what he was thinking. Same thing I was. We shared an understanding, knowing that when my parents weren't name dropping, they were name calling.

"Can you believe what that son of a bitch said? I told him to go stick it!" my mother would proudly say after her third cocktail, always referring to my stepfather's boss. "They're even going to Europe. It must be nice to have money like that. Oh! And do you kids know what your real father did? He's taking me to court again to get your child support lowered even further. He's a son of a bitch too!"

The three of us kids would just sit there in silence. So much so that I simply got used to being silent. I never asked my parents for anything. I learned to rely on myself to make things happen.

Now, faced with the possibility of losing my business and everything I have worked so hard for, I keep chanting the words "upside-up" as I drag myself down the hall, knowing it's time to cleanse myself, literally and figuratively.

The shower is where I do most of my thinking about work. My ideas for new classes, catalogue themes—you name it, it happens in there. "Upside-up," I remind myself, focusing on the task at hand. I have about twenty people driving to Voicetrax right now, all of whom are just waiting to be uplifted and inspired by none other than yours truly. These are twenty people whose names I'll have to memorize in the first half hour. Friends often tell me that I put too much pressure on myself to do this, but I disagree. People feel that they matter when you remember them by their names.

The pressure and anxiety in all of this makes me want to crawl back into bed, but instead I slide open my drawer and start applying my makeup.

After two cups of coffee and changing my outfit twice, I pull into the Voicetrax garage and put my car in park. It's dark and quiet. I grab the small stone from my cup holder. A gift from Andre, it reads, "Calm." I rub it between my thumb and forefinger—it feels cool and helps to ground me. I'm always nervous before these lectures. They are always sold-out and most of these people have waited months to attend. What could I possibly have to say that is worth waiting that long for? All I know is that these people have a curiosity about voice-over. Well, most of them do. Some come for other reasons, but at the end of the day, they are all searching for something, and I will help them on their new journey, should they decide to take the ride.

|| People feel that they matter when you remember them by their names.

This is so old to me, but it's new to them. They deserve my best. I will encourage them, inspire them, and love them. Encourage, inspire, love.

I open my eyes and grab my purse and my phone. I see a text that reads, "Knock 'em dead!" It's from Andre.

9:30 a.m.

VOICETRAX

"Good morning, Vicki. You look fantastic." I go behind the counter, kiss the back of her head, then glance at the attendance sheet. "Are they all here?" I can tell that Vicki knows I'm nervous, but, as usual, we don't talk about it. Talking about being nervous just makes it worse for me.

"All but three, but there are still a few minutes to go."

"Well, I'm going to get going anyway. You know I like to start early."

She laughs. "When have you *not* started early?"

As I walk away, I chirp, "N.T.L.T.P!"

"N.T.L., what?" she asks, mystified.

"No time like the present!" And with that I enter the studio.

"Good morning, everyone. I'm Samantha. Welcome, welcome, welcome!"

Here we go.

"Before I 'officially' get started, I always like to go around the room and find out what brought you here. Why you are here tells me a lot about who you are. I was pushed as a fifteen year old, or to be more accurate, I sat in the back seat of my parents' car, pouting that I was being taken to a voice-over lesson rather than a true acting class. That tells you lot about who I was, right?"

A few polite laughs. *This is going to be a tough crowd.*

"When I found out what it was, that I was going to be performing with my *voice* but wasn't going to be seen, I didn't want to do it—I had dreams of being a TV star or a movie star. You guys are here today, I assume, as willing participants. I want to know why. What brings you here?"

No one answers—they look at me like I'm speaking another language. As usual, I'll need to break the ice.

"You, sir. What's your name?"

"Uh, my name is Jon, and I work in sound design for video games here in the Bay Area. We actually hire a lot of your students to voice characters."

"Really! What company are you with?"

"Somatone Interactive."

"Oh, yes, you guys hire a lot of our students. So, you know what we do."

"I do," Jon continues. "I work on the technical side of games, but I'm really envious of how much fun the actors seem to be having."

"We *do* have a lot of fun."

"I doubt that I have the talent it takes for any kind of acting—but I'm curious. You know. So here I am."

"Glad you're here, Jon, and you're going to discover rather quickly that talent can be taught. By the way, where are you from? New Zealand?"

"Really good! Most people guess Australia," he says with a grin.

"Hey, c'mon. I *am* a voice expert," I fire back. The students laugh. "Just in case you're wondering, Jon, your beautiful accent will *not* limit you. We hear all sorts of accents in voice-over, especially in video games."

Jon nods his head. "Cool."

I gesture at another student. "And you are?"

"Leah."

"Hello, Leah. What brings you here?"

"Okay, so I'm the office manager for a European auto-service shop in Greenbrae, and people have been telling me for years that I should get into this line of work because they are impressed with how well I emote with my voice."

Very theatrically, I extend my hand, drop my voice, and say, "And just how do you *emote*?"

Leah giggles and says, "I have to make a lot of announcements over our loudspeakers and people love my voice."

"I love your voice too," I say, "and I'm glad that's what brought you here, but as you will soon learn, voice-over really has nothing to do with your voice." With my hand extended again, I tell Leah that I will *emote* some more about that later and wink at her.

"And you, sweetheart, are?"

"My name is Marley, and I'm in college in Florida."

"Oh, all the way from Florida! Well, you're in good company.

We have students who fly in from all over. I actually just did a private lesson with somebody from Japan. She was interested in video games. What brings you out to California, Marley?"

"I grew up watching cartoons and I loved mimicking the voices. I've always wanted to do cartoons, but my parents are obviously concerned about me earning a living, which is why I'm in my second year of college. Studying business, you know, accounting. I just feel like I'm wasting my time there, because this is what I really want to do."

I smile. "I completely understand. Since I was five years old, all I ever wanted to do was act. I hated school and never even went to college. I feel for kids who are in school with no direction and absolutely no idea about what they want to do when they grow up. The fact that you know is great. I would never say to simply drop out of college, because I think an education is important. That said, if this is what you want to do and you're willing to work hard at it, voice-over is every bit as feasible a career as being an accountant or a dentist. You just have to go to a school like this one to learn."

"Welcome," I say to the next student. "And you are?"

"My name is Iris and I actually *am* an accountant. I specialize in business taxes."

"Ugh, how absolutely brainy!" I glance over at Marley and Iris smiles.

"You're right, Samantha, it is 'brainy,' but that's all. I miss being creative."

"What?" I jump in. "I thought you CPAs were paid boatloads of money to be 'very creative.'" I give a big, exaggerated wink and everybody laughs, even Iris.

"I can't speak to that. However, I recently was asked to do an internal webinar video and I enjoyed it immensely. Many people commented on my voice."

"I'm really glad they did, because that's what brought you

here." I look away from Iris and back at the rest of the class.

"Let me stop right here"—I raise my arms—"and *emote!*" Leah grins, though she's not the only one.

"How many of you here have had people comment on your voice and say that voice-over is something you should check out?"

All but three raise their hands. I walk over and high-five each of those three.

"Welcome to my world!" I say. The three of them look pleased, but the rest of the class looks perplexed.

I return to the front of the room and turn to the group. "In all the years I've been doing this, nobody has ever commented on my voice. I don't have an exceptional voice or a unique voice, and yet I'll contradict that right now and say that, yes, I do, because it's *my voice*. It's the tool that I have to express *me*, and no one is ever going to perform a 'better me' than me. Let me put it to you another way. Let's all imagine a beautiful, farm-fresh, eighteen-year-old girl from Iowa. She was the homecoming queen, she won every local beauty pageant there was, and she never wore a stick of makeup. Don't you hate her?"

The women in the room laugh.

"No, seriously, she's a sweetheart and she's absolutely beautiful. Everyone tells her she should go to New York and become a model, so that's what she does. She walks into one of the biggest modeling agencies in New York for what they call open call auditions, and there in the lobby are fifty other girls who are just as beautiful as she is."

The class begins to nod their heads—they're catching on.

"That sweet beautiful girl is thinking, 'Now what? What do I do?' Well, that 'What do I do?' is why all you people with 'beautiful voices' are here." I let them chew on that for a few seconds.

"Let's move on." I turn to a man wearing perfectly pressed blue jeans and a shirt with so much starch in it that I'm convinced it's holding him up in his chair. I point to him, drop my voice and judge-like ask, "Do you swear to tell the truth, the whole truth, and nothing but the truth?"

He's visibly taken aback. "Uh, are you talking to me?"

"Yeah, you. What's your name and what brings you here?"

"My name is Robert and I'm a lawyer," he says sheepishly. The class roars with laughter.

"Well, he's not a judge, guys, but I was close! What kind of lawyer are you?" I ask.

"I'm a trial lawyer and I want to have more presence in front of a jury," Robert says in a booming baritone. "I know I have this big, deep voice, but I think it somewhat gets in the way, maybe because I don't know how to use it properly."

"Believe me, Robert, with that voice of yours, you have plenty of presence. I think maybe the issue isn't a matter of presence, but of you being convincing. Maybe you lack authentic passion."

"I think you're right," he admits. "Even my wife tells me that."

"Ooh! Well, let's not get too personal now!"

"You're right, Samantha. Anyway, I'm also interested in voice-over as a way to earn some extra money being creative once I retire."

"Well, great, I'm glad you're here."

I point to the next student. "And you, lovely lady in that gorgeous teal blue top, are—?"

"Oh, my God, I am so nervous."

"What's your name?"

"Geriann," she says, bowing her head. "I hate having to talk."

"You hate having to talk and you've come to a voice-over class?" The class is laughing with me. Then I notice her trembling.

She continues. "I know, it's crazy, but that's why I'm here. I'm hoping this will help me get over my being so shy. I'm painfully shy." I can hear the pain in her voice and a lump forms in my throat. I walk over, kneel down beside Geriann, and give her a hug.

Looking into her eyes, I ask, "Why are you so afraid to share your beautiful self with the world?"

"Because I have no voice," she says flatly. "I have been made to feel invisible."

Although painful, the moment is electric for me, as nothing moves me or motivates me more than authenticity. I touch her cheek. "Thank you for being so exquisitely honest."

I stand and address the class. "Okay, guys, we're about a quarter of the way through going around the room with our introductions, and I love all your stories. I really do. We all have a story to tell, right? But what just happened in this room? Do you feel the energy? There is a softness, a sweetness, in the air. It's pure magic. It's called being *vulnerable*. Being honest and open and exposing one's self. We are all so moved right now by what Geriann shared, because she's sitting here feeling vulnerable and we all can relate on some level and want to reach out. Take note, Robert. That's how you connect with a jury. You have to reach out to them and not worry about delivering your closing argument so perfectly. Stop trying to be perfect! Guys, perfect is *boring*. When you can learn that you are so perfect in your imperfection, you've got it made. It is our imperfect selves that we all relate to. It's how we show our humanity, how we move one another—how we touch one another."

I turn to Geriann. "You have touched us. You have touched me for sure. I have had so many people during the past twenty years who have crossed this studio's threshold with your same issue. Don't worry. My job is to make you feel comfortable and feel brave enough to share with the world who you are.

"And you know what?" I say to the class. "You are all incredibly brave and wonderfully to the left for just coming here today. And no, I'm not talking politics. You are a little to the left because you at least feel comfortable enough to attend this lecture—to explore this creative voice inside you that's searching for something. Most people don't do that. They live in the safe little boxes of their lives. They are unhappy, unfulfilled, but they see no other way to live. They probably don't think they deserve to be happy. I bet most of you, if not all of you, shared with a family member or coworker what you were thinking of doing today, and I'm sure some of them looked at you like you were nuts and said something like, 'What? You're going to a voice-over class? That's crazy. You're wasting your money.'" I see heads nodding.

Stop trying to be perfect! Guys, perfect is *boring*. When you can learn that you are so perfect in your imperfection, you've got it made. It is our imperfect selves that we all relate to. It's how we show our humanity, how we move one another—how we touch one another.

"But you guys are different. You are *here*, and from the bottom of my heart, I thank you. And not because you paid fifty dollars." I see smiles. "I thank you for liking yourselves enough to think that you were worthy of taking a risk and exploring something new. And I thank you for me too. For every one of you who is here, there are literally thousands of people who are interested in voice-over, but don't take the time to find out about it properly. They've been led to believe that with a nice voice, you simply take a couple of online courses, then record something and send it off to the powers that be: people in the industry, agents, and casting directors. Those people never hear back because they had no clue what they were doing, no clue what to record. And they walk around after that, living their lives, thinking, 'Well, I tried to get into that business, but it's a closed field. It's all about who you know.' But they are 100 percent wrong. Voice-over is a craft. It's something that can be taught, just not in one, six-week course. I stand firmly behind that claim. Talent can be taught!

"If you want to be a lawyer or a CPA, you work hard and learn how to do it. By taking the time to properly find out what this is all about, you are honoring me and the other instructors here who have devoted their entire lives to this industry. I've been doing voice-over for thirty-five years and teaching for twenty-two years. It's my life. I know of nothing else. I am truly grateful for you being here."

We finish the introductions, and they seem to enjoy hearing one another's stories. I map out the rest of the three hours, explaining that we will first spend some time actually exploring our voices and voice-over techniques, and that I will record some of them. We will then talk about the business, the roles of agents and casting directors, what it takes to be successful, the financial realities, and the acting unions.

"I have to begin by asking you a really important question. How many of you have ever been six years old?" There is no response. "Come on, guys, I'm serious. How many of you have ever been six years old? I want to see a show of hands!" Slowly but surely, hands rise.

"What, you've never been six? Come on, you reluctant ones. That means you, Robert." I go over and physically raise Robert's hand. Voice-over is not about your voice. This is a form of acting. I believe we are all actors, or capable of being actors, because we have all been six years old. It's about having the ability to mentally return to when you were a kid and just *play*. It's about using your imagination.

Talent can be taught!

"When I was little, my favorite TV show was *Bewitched*. My family lived in LA, but Nanna, my grandmother, lived nearby here, in Los Gatos. We spent a lot of our summers here. She had a wonderful orchard of oranges. My cousin, Tracy, lived here, and he and I would spend days playing *Bewitched* in the orchard. I was Samantha and he was Uncle Arthur. Oh, my God, we had the best time. I tried so hard to wiggle my nose but I couldn't, so I used one of Nanna's wooden spoons to help me cast my spells.

As kids, were we *pretending* to be Samantha and Uncle Arthur?"

Several people nod their heads.

"Absolutely not! We believed 100 percent that we *were* those characters. Nor were you pretending when you were running around your yard as an astronaut or superhero. As children, we *believed*, and that's all acting is!

"I assume most of you have children, grandchildren, or nieces and nephews," I continue. "I never had kids, but I've been blessed with a few youngsters in my life. You know when they come home from school and they've painted you a picture, or made some kind of craft . . . is it not absolutely adorable? Is it not perfect in its imperfection? You can see their souls in what they've made for you. If they wanted to paint their tree purple and put yellow polka dots on it with a big white cotton ball on top, they did, and you loved it. And it wasn't perfect. I'm sure that now, you would look at that painting and say, 'Oh, it's so wonderful, so imaginative. I wish I could do that!'

"But you can," I tell them. "You can, because you once did. It's just that now, as adults, we're all so damn worried about being judged. We don't want to make fools out of ourselves. But children aren't afraid. They're so free and they simply *do*."

Everyone's looking a little puzzled. Good.

"I want everybody to stand," I instruct. "Are you ready to be six years old? I'm going to show you how easy it is to create character voices for cartoons and video games. We all do voices because it's simply a matter of placing your voice in different parts of your body. I want you each to visualize the sound of your voice coming out of the top of your head. You are going to keep a feather afloat with your voice. We're just going to use the word 'hello,' and pull it out of our heads."

I raise my arm and place my pinched fingers at the top of my head. In a high, light voice, I say, "hello," and pantomime pulling the word out of my head.

Some of the students smile, while others look uncomfortable. As usual, I'm undeterred. "Come on, let's all do it. Put your hands on the top of your head and do it with me."

"Hello!" some of them say. It sounds like a few old, dying chickens squawking, as about a third of the group halfheartedly attempt it.

"I want everyone in this group to channel being a kid and I want you to blow the ceiling off this place with a beautiful, high-pitched 'hello!'"

They all do it and the clamor is music to my ears.

"See? That's not so bad. Now, those of you who felt a bit dorky doing it, well, that's simply the adult in you that we have to get rid of. A six year old wouldn't feel silly!"

I guide them through the eye placement until they all say "hello" through their eyes. Even the reluctant students are smiling. We come to the Munchkin placement, and I remind them of those characters from my favorite movie, *The Wizard of Oz*.

"It's still rather high, but you have to really open your mouth, and it's also kind of under the ears." I give them the example, except I change "hello" to "Follow the yellow brick road!" They all laugh. "Okay, now you try it."

Everyone jumps right in and shouts, "Follow the yellow brick road!" and it's glorious. I get them all to sing as Munchkins, "We're off to see the wizard, the wonderful wizard of Oz!" They finish and the song dissolves into happy laughter. I have them now. I have their trust, which I don't take lightly. They feel safe, and I know that because they feel safe, I can teach them anything.

In our time together, they create many characters with only their voices. From hummingbirds and spiders to crabby substitute teachers and crusty old pirates, kittens, dogs, rodents, and Southern politicians. From there, we move into the world of commercial voice-over. Now they learn that they have tremendous vocal range simply by being themselves.

"Your voice is going to sound completely different when you act motherly talking to your five year old versus talking to your teenage daughter," I point out. "You naturally sound different when you are being sarcastic or instructional. There are so many emotions living inside us and the vocal tone is different for each one of them!"

We change gears yet again. "When you perform a radio commercial," I explain, "you have to paint a picture for the listener. That's why they call radio 'the theatre of the mind.' You, as the performer, must ask yourself, 'Who am I? Where am I? Who am I talking to? How do I feel? Why am I saying what I'm saying?' You must visualize the situation, just like you visualize when you read a book. You must *see* it as you're saying it."

Some students volunteer to go into the booth and allow me to direct them in recording a radio commercial. They are nervous but excited to perform, and when they finally hear their voices over the big speakers in the studio, their faces light up.

"Television voice-over is completely different. If it's a television commercial, the visuals are already there. You, as the performer, are not painting the pictures with your voice, but merely complementing or commenting on the visuals. Your performance must be more understated. After all, a picture is worth a thousand words, right?" The class nods.

"Speaking of pictures and painting, there is yet another voice-over technique that we voice actors use to create vocal range. We visualize different colors and 'paint' the words in those colors. In other words, you all have a yellow voice, an orange voice, green, blue, violet, brown, black, and any other color you can think of."

I give them an example of a commercial for Hawaiian tourism. I tell them the visuals are of an early morning with the sun coming up and a soft breeze blowing through the palm trees. I visualize a soft yellow color and say, "Come to Hawaii for the vacation of a lifetime." The words sound soft and, well, yellow.

"But what if the visuals are of a beautiful, warm orange sun as it's setting, and we are also seeing the vast blue-violet ocean? I could paint the commercial in an orange voice, or maybe a violet one."

Now, I have to talk about the business side of voice-over, which I do. There are always a few in every class who have been told that after one, six-week class, a demo will be made for them and they will be on their way to financial success. I break the news to them that it usually takes at least three to five years of study, and success does not come overnight. They have to really want this and work hard. I delve a little into the audition process, how people are beginning to audition from home, and what an agent will expect of them.

The lecture is scheduled to end at 1:00 p.m. and it's now 12:57 p.m. I ask if they have any questions.

A hand goes up. "I'm interested in audiobooks, which we didn't cover. Is there a lot of work in this area?"

"Oh, my gosh, yes!" I say. "It's a billion-dollar industry, and I'm sorry we didn't cover that. There are so many areas of voice-over that we didn't cover because there's simply not enough time. There are the worlds of promo, narration, in-house corporate work, talking toys, and even the voices that tell us to 'Press one or press two.' There is so much to talk about. If I had my way, this lecture would last all day, but I have a feeling that before you came here, if you knew this was an all-day thing, you might not have come."

"Yeah, but that's before we met you," Robert says.

I smile demurely.

"Can you talk about your program for a few minutes?" Iris asks.

I take a deep breath and oblige. "I feel so awkward and uncomfortable talking about this, which is why I guess I wait for when we've run out of time. My goal today wasn't about trying to get you to sign up for classes. If this lecture had been some kind of sales spiel, not only could I not live with myself, but I couldn't have endured doing these for so many years. My goal today was to do my best to address that voice inside each one of you that's searching for something more fulfilling—the part of you that possibly even dreams of doing voice-over. I hope I accomplished that."

Their smiles tell me I did. "Now I will spend just a few minutes telling you what we do here at Voicetrax, but at the end of the day, if you are interested, just call us. You're all different with various levels of experience and desire, so your needs will be different. If you choose to do this, then ultimately this is going to be a personal journey that you and I are going to take together. I've devoted my life to guiding my students on their journeys."

I talk briefly about the program and tell them that Vicki is here to answer any questions, but I encourage them to leave and enjoy the beautiful, 70-degree February afternoon. I get them to stand and then ask them to review those vocal placements so they can go home and show their significant others a little bit of what they learned. They want us to sing like Munchkins again, so we do, and then I say goodbye, hugging each one of them. They are no longer the nameless, faceless strangers I worried about while getting ready this morning. Even if I never see them again, they are my Voicetrax family.

As I quickly gather my things and exit the studio, I see several students opting not to take my advice and enjoy the afternoon sun; instead, they're asking Vicki questions and signing up for classes.

I wave appreciatively to Vicki. I fly out of every lecture as fast as humanly possible. I'm escaping, truly, but neither Vicki nor Chuck know why. Nobody knows.

I hop into my car and start the familiar drive down Bridgeway.

The Sausalito afternoon is spectacular and I'd love to savor it, but I have errands to run. I remember Andre's text from earlier. I dial our home number.

"Hey, honey, it's me," I say. "Thank you so much for your text message this morning. It really meant a lot."

"How'd you do? I bet it was a ten."

You've always cheered me on and yet you've sucked me dry.

"You say that every time. I don't think I've ever given myself a ten. Well, maybe once or twice, but today I'd say it was an eight-point-five. I didn't get much sleep last night."

"Well, your eight-point-five is a ten to them. They have nothing to compare it to."

Is that supposed to cheer me up?

"You're right about that," I say lightly. "So, how are you?"

"Pretty good. This morning I puttered around the house, made myself some breakfast, read the paper, and just finished my crossword. I'm thinking of taking Ollie for a walk and then working in my studio."

He's pushing all my buttons. *Puttered around the house that I pay for. Made yourself some breakfast that I pay for. Read the paper that I pay for. "Working" in your studio? Gimme a break! And taking Ollie, whom I miss terribly, for a walk—*

"I have to go grocery shopping," Andre continues. "I must admit, I do miss your cooking."

You miss my cooking, but you don't miss me. My voice goes suddenly flat. "It sounds like you're having a nice Saturday so far." *Why am I torturing myself? Is he never going to see how entitled he acts in this life, while the rest of the world works? Does he not see how alone I feel in this marriage? How I long for a true, equal partner instead of carrying all this weight on my own?*

"So far, so good," he says gaily. "And you?"

"I'm headed off to do some errands," I say, "and then I'm going back to my place—"*(my $1,500 dump of a place that I also have to* *pay for)* "—to work on the new catalogue and do some dotting," I share.

"It's not that time already, is it?" Andre asks.

"Yep, every six months."

"I've never understood why you feel so obligated to write all those letters. Guiding them through what classes to take when there are so many, maybe. The dots I guess are helpful but you—"

I interrupt and decide to fib. "I'm getting another call."

"Okay, then, bye, Sammy."

I exhale noisily and then, surprisingly, my phone actually does ring.

"Hey Samantha, it's Jeff. How you doin'?"

"Hi, honey. I'm good. I just finished my lecture and I'm starting to do some errands."

"Well, don't. This is too beautiful an afternoon to waste. Come on up for a glass of wine. Cathy is just finishing cleaning the house." Jeff's offer is far more tempting than my solo prospects.

"That sounds fantastic. I'll be there in about ten minutes." My frustration with Andre dissipates, as I think about how much I love Jeff and Cathy, my best friends. They are also best friends with Andre, as they knew him long before I was even in the picture, but it doesn't matter. We're a true family and they would never take sides.

Minutes later, like usual, I enter their house without knocking. "Hi, babe. Look at you. You're all pink in the face!"

She playfully flicks a rag at me. "I've been cleaning. You know I love it, it's my exercise routine!"

I smile at her ability to put a positive spin on everything.

"You want a glass of wine? We have a new beautiful Viognier that you'll love, Sammy."

Jeff suddenly appears, kisses me, and leads us to their outdoor patio. I drink in the sweet, fresh air and take in their incredible,

180-degree view of the Richmond-San Rafael Bridge, the expansive East Bay, and the main artery into San Francisco, the East Bay Bridge.

"Cheers!" The three of us clink our glasses together.

"Thanks for inviting me," I say. "I've been feeling a bit depleted. This was perfect timing."

"Jeff told me you were doing one of your lectures today. How'd it go?"

"Okay. The same as usual, I guess."

Jeff puts down his glass with a dramatic thud. "Samantha, you know what a pain in the ass you are, but I gotta say, you're a brilliant teacher. You're a genius at what you do, and I hope you know it." He throws his arm around my shoulders and gives me a squeeze.

"Your teaching seems like it's totally unconscious," he says, softening his voice. "Like you don't really know what's going to come out of your mouth. I've watched you so many times, and it still never fails to blow me away."

I laugh. "I don't really know how to respond to that, Jeff. You're being so nice! Actually, Andre says the exact same thing."

"Well, he's right," says Cathy. "You make it seem so natural and spontaneous. Do you even know what you're going to say?"

"Not really," I admit. "I'm just in the moment and whatever comes out, does."

"Speaking of Andre, how is he doing?"

"Jeff, you're his best friend. How do you *think* he's doing? He's totally fine. He told me how he spent his morning puttering around, reading his papers, walking Ollie, and now he's in his studio working. Sort of."

Jeff shakes his head in sympathy and understanding.

"I mean, what is there for Andre to be upset about?" I ask. "He has an incredible life." I give Jeff a pointed look. "I know, and you know, that he will never change."

Jeff nods. "You're right."

"I know I'm right. He actually innocently said that he missed my cooking. He didn't say he missed *me*. He doesn't. He just misses what I do for him. Anyway, let's not talk about him." I turn to Cathy and see the cute little sad face she is giving me. "So, what are you guys doing for the rest of this weekend?"

"Well, tonight we're just going to hang out, and tomorrow I have to go into the city, because one of my ballet companies is performing."

Jeff jumps in and interrupts.

"Hey, Samantha, why don't you just hang here and have dinner with us tonight?"

"I really shouldn't." I hesitate. "Really. Because it's dotting season, and I'm getting a bit behind."

"The dreaded dots," Cathy says.

"Fuck the dots," Jeff adds. "You're staying here."

"Tell you what," I say. "I'll stay under one condition: You guys let me go to the store and cook dinner for you. You know how I love to cook, and I don't get to do it anymore. Cathy, I'll even make you your favorite, lamb chops!"

"We certainly can't refuse an offer like that," Cathy chirps, as Jeff claps his hands.

And with that, I grab my purse and head out the door to the store.

I've eaten just a quarter of the meal I had such fun preparing. "Jesus! Why do I always eat so slowly?"

"Maybe you like relaxing a little?" Cathy offers.

"She eats slowly because she's always fucking talking," Jeff quips.

"Perhaps you shouldn't ask me so many questions," I counter, stifling a laugh, knowing he's right. "Here, have another lamb chop, Jeff, and be quiet."

"Samantha, I know what's going on with Voicetrax, but what's happening with your own voice-over work?" Cathy asks. "Max told me that your rock star cartoon *Jem and the Holograms* is back on the air. Did you know that?"

"Yeah, it's been on the Cartoon Network for quite a while, which is crazy. Maybe I didn't tell you, but last year, I was asked to speak at a *Jem* convention in LA. There were hundreds of people there from all over the world. It felt so strange signing autographs for a character I played twenty-five years ago."

"Are your other shows airing on the Cartoon Network?"

"Yeah, and it sucks, because none of us actors are getting residuals anymore. We really should, and we're trying to get SAG to do something about it."

"You still going to LA a lot?" Jeff asks with his mouth full.

"Nah." I shake my head. "It's kind of sad. I just don't have the time. I barely audition here either."

Cathy raises her eyebrows in concern. "Why?"

"I was actually supposed to go to LA on Monday for an audition that I was a client request for," I reply. "It's a new cartoon series, and they wanted me to read for three roles. I turned it down."

"Samantha," Cathy says, aghast, "that's terrible! You can't do that. It's your career!"

"Unfortunately, Voicetrax has become my career. There just aren't enough hours in the day. I stare at voice-over copy all day teaching, and then when I get home there are usually three to five auditions to record, and the last thing I want to do when I get home at ten o'clock at night is stare at more copy and perform. I'm so burnt out by then. I've decided it's best to do just enough to keep my toe in it, to remain current. You know, so I don't become some loser teacher who teaches because she sucks and no one will hire her."

"But your career has always meant everything to you." Cathy continues. "Are you sure there isn't a deeper issue here? Is it because of what you're going through with Andre?"

"God, no, or at least I don't think so," I sigh. "I think I'm just losing the will to perform. I have been performing professionally since I was seventeen. That's, what, thirty-three years?"

"Samantha, that's utter bullshit." Jeff pours another glass of wine. "I bet if you didn't have Voicetrax, you would still want to perform. It's in your blood."

I look over at Cathy, and I can see she's silently agreeing with Jeff.

"Okay, so you guys are right! I've been performing since I was five years old. It's the only thing I have ever wanted to do, but you know what, Jeff? *Life* happened! Voicetrax, with all its responsibilities, exhausts me! Andre exhausts me! And then trying to keep up an *acting career*? You gotta be fucking joking!"

I look down at my plate embarrassed by my outburst. The room is silent.

"I'm sorry, guys. I know you mean well." As I meet their gaze, once again I see not only sympathy, but memories. Memories like that Bastille Day in 1989, when the four of us snuck into the Luxembourg Gardens in Paris, France. It was 7:00 a.m. Cathy thought it was a brilliant idea for me to become Mrs. Paris in Paris, so Jeff was going to spiritually marry Andre and me then and there. At the time, Cathy was seven months pregnant with their son, Max.

"You want to watch a movie?" Jeff asks, diffusing the moment.

"You know, I think I'm going to pass." I let out a "forgive me" giggle. "I love you dearly, but I just want to go home and get some rest." I circle the table to give him a kiss on the top of his head. "This has been fantastic. I'm sorry I just got crabby. Thank you so much."

"You okay to drive home?" Cathy asks, taking the dishes to the kitchen.

"Oh, God, yes! And besides, I'm not going home to Petaluma, remember? I'm in Sausalito in the rental."

"Oh, right," Cathy says, frowning. "You know, Samantha, I'm sure Andre misses you in his own way. Maybe he just doesn't show it. I know he loves you."

"I know he loves me too, in his own way, but his way just isn't good enough. I deserve better than that. I know I should have done this years ago, but I just didn't have the courage. I was afraid of being alone. Anyway, you know all this, we've talked about it."

"I know," she says, her voice trembling.

"Don't *you* be sad." I squeeze her cheeks between my hands. "I'll get through this. Please, don't worry about me."

On the drive home, I think about how no one can go through this painful process for me. Turning my life upside-up is up to me. It's like when you have to rip a Band-Aid off your arm. You can have friends standing around you and encouraging you, but you still have to be the one to tear it away. No one, but you, is going to feel the pain of those hairs being pulled from your skin.

Having people around who love you helps. Jeff and Cathy are a huge help. Gabrielle, my childhood girlfriend, has been a huge help, as has Chris. But still I have to go it alone.

I turn the key to the apartment and step inside. It is cold and damp. I head for the bed, crawl between the sheets, and pray I sleep.

Sunday, February 21, 2010

SAUSALITO, CALIFORNIA

I wake to the sound of pouring rain and the glorious sight of 7:30 a.m. on the clock, a sign I slept through the night. Friends, Viognier, and lamb chops must be the elixirs of life.

I dance around the room before I realize that I'm also absolutely freezing and in desperate need of a pee. Once I take care of business, I throw a sweatshirt on over my pajamas and head into the kitchen to get my coffee going. I'm also in need of something for my bare feet. I open the closet and see the monster in it—three massive Voicetrax binders holding 327 student history reports.

I told Jeff and Cathy that I was behind on my dotting, but the truth is that I've barely started.

N.T.L.T.P.

First, I need my coffee. I go into the living room and turn on the fireplace. I feel relaxed and content. For more than twenty years I've been like a hamster on a wheel, juggling my voice-over career and going back and forth to LA, my wifely duties of grocery shopping, cooking, laundry, and ironing, on top of the mountains of work that come along with Voicetrax.

How would I ever have done all this, if I'd had a child?

That would have been spinning yet another plate in the air all by myself. I shake those thoughts from my head and turn my attention to the notebooks lying in wait in my closet. I sigh. I have such a love-hate relationship with this dotting process. I have to read each student report thoroughly so I can "dot" with a green highlighter which classes they should take for the new term. There are always about seventy different classes to choose from, so how could the students possibly pick the right ones themselves? Whether it's my Type A personality showing through, or if I just understand how overwhelming having to choose from seventy classes can be, is not exactly clear.

Then I write each student a handwritten note explaining what I want them to work on and telling them that I love them. I give them a pep talk and maybe tease them about some dorky thing they recently did in class. I actually have fun with these notes, and it's the least I can do. I'm their mentor, their guide, and I made a promise to take them by the hand on this journey.

However, the reality is that I can only do four or five an hour, and there are more than 300 of them. And I have to go through the whole process twice a year. That last point is what I hate about dotting. What I also love about dotting is how excited the students are to receive them in the mail. I'm told they love them, cherish them even, and some have kept all my notes for years. So, I *know* this work matters.

I pour another cup of coffee and begin.

Let's see. Colin should definitely take "Creating Characters" with Chuck and me and take "Colors of your Voice" with Tommy. And "VO 411" is super important for him, because he needs to hear firsthand from Nate what a top talent agent expects. If you're going to reach true excellence you have to know where the bar is . . .

Talent's Name: *Colin Brogan*

COURSE	RECOMMENDED*
FOR BEGINNERS	
Beginning Seminar	
Beginning Workshop	
Creating Characters	
Introduction to Narration	
Simply Acting	
To Paris And Back	
FOR INTERMEDIATE STUDENTS	
Colors of Your Voice	
Founder's Seminar	
Improv for Voice Actors	
The Taming of the Mic	
Voice-Over 411	
What A Character	
FOR EVERYONE	
Inside the Voice Actor's Studio	
Intro To Home Recording	
FOR INTERMEDIATE / ADVANCED STUDENTS	
3... 2... 1... Blast Off! with Brian Sommer	
Animation 101	
!Animania!	
Audio Tour Narration	
Comedic Radio Ads	
Copy 911: Turning Disastrous Into Fabulous	
Direct Thyself II	
Got Game?	
Imagination Revisited	
Making It Sound Easy	
Scene Study with Jeannie Elias	
Script Analysis	
Simply Acting II	
Taking On The Prototypes	
Think Visually, Act Vocally	
Timing Is Everything	
Tours, Tutorials & Tales: The Story Within	
Voice-Over Angel	

YELLOW HIGHLIGHTS indicate CLASSES YOU'VE TAKEN
GREEN DOTS are SAM'S RECOMMENDATIONS

COURSE	RECOMMENDED*
FOR ADVANCED STUDENTS AND WORKING PROFESSIONALS	
3... 2... 1... O M F G!	
Be A Bad MotherChucker	
Comedic Radio Ads II: The Writer's Code	
Dialect Intervention	
Get In The Acting Game	
How To Walk, Talk & Chew Gum	
Inv. A Gathering Of Actors	
Inv. All The World's A Stage	
Inv. Holy Cow! I Get It Now!	
Inv. Lunch With Punch	
Inv. Place Your Order!	
Inv. Say NO To The Go-To	
Inv. Stand Up And Act	
Inv. Voicetrax TOP Voice: San Francisco Edition	
Inv. Women Only	
Pinto's Playbook For Professionals	
Power Up!	
Remotely Speaking	
The Color Of Acting	
The Fast & The Furious	
The Good, The Bad & The Weird	
Three In A Row	
Three Script Monte: SF Edition	

*Marked with "Samantha's Dots" *21 February 2010*
Classes highlighted in red are either new, or revised enough that you should review their descriptions

Handwritten notes:

I'm sending you a huge hug & xo Love, Samantha

You were hilarious as that smarmy guy in the Purina script.

Holy Cow! you knocked it out of the park in our Founders class & your script Analysis has improved so much And you took direction like a champ! Colin, it's so hard to believe you've only been at this for 9 months... I couldn't be more excited for you or About you. And listen. Don't shy Away from Character work —

Um . . . L.C. should definitely take "Animania" with Natanya. She will love working with a LA animation agent. And "Lunch with Punch" for sure. She will totally geek out taking class with the actual "Tick" and "Pinky" of Pinky and the Brain, *so she will need Townsend Coleman's class and Rob Paulsen's . . . and for sure, Laraine Newman. Who wouldn't love to learn about comedic voice-over from none other than an original* Saturday Night Live *conehead?*

Talent's Name: *L. C. Buxton*

COURSE	RECOMMENDED*
FOR BEGINNERS	
Beginning Seminar	
Beginning Workshop	
Creating Characters	
Introduction to Narration	
Simply Acting	
To Paris And Back	
FOR INTERMEDIATE STUDENTS	
Colors of Your Voice	
Founder's Seminar	
Improv for Voice Actors	
The Taming of the Mic	
Voice-Over 411	
What A Character	
FOR EVERYONE	
Inside the Voice Actor's Studio	
Intro To Home Recording	
FOR INTERMEDIATE / ADVANCED STUDENTS	
3... 2... 1... Blast Off! with Brian Sommer	
Animation 101	
!Animania!	
Audio Tour Narration	
Comedic Radio Ads	
Copy 911: Turning Disastrous Into Fabulous	
Direct Thyself II	
Got Game?	
Imagination Revisited	
Making It Sound Easy	
Scene Study with Jeannie Elias	
Script Analysis	
Simply Acting II	
Taking On The Prototypes	
Think Visually, Act Vocally	
Timing Is Everything	
Tours, Tutorials & Tales: The Story Within	
Voice-Over Angel	

YELLOW HIGHLIGHTS indicate CLASSES YOU'VE TAKEN
GREEN DOTS are SAM'S RECOMMENDATIONS

COURSE	RECOMMENDED*
FOR ADVANCED STUDENTS AND WORKING PROFESSIONALS	
3... 2... 1... O M F G!	
Be A Bad MotherChucker	
Comedic Radio Ads II: The Writer's Code	
Dialect Intervention	
Get In The Acting Game	
How To Walk, Talk & Chew Gum	
Inv. A Gathering Of Actors	
Inv. All The World's A Stage	
Inv. Holy Cow! I Get It Now!	
Inv. Lunch With Punch	
Inv. Place Your Order!	
Inv. Say NO To The Go-To	
Inv. Stand Up And Act	
Inv. Voicetrax TOP Voices: San Francisco Edition	
Inv. Women Only	
Pinto's Playbook For Professionals	
Power Up!	
Remotely Speaking	
The Color Of Acting	
The Fast & The Furious	
The Good, The Bad & The Weird	
Three In A Row	
Three Script Monte: SF Edition	

*Marked with "Samantha's Dots" Classes highlighted in red are either new, or revised enough that you should review their descriptions

handwritten: '21 Feb 2010

handwritten left margin: I love you so much it's not funny!

handwritten right margin: We need to work on your out direction !!! good

handwritten note below table: Hey L.L.! you know... when you get out of your head and just let go you make my owl shine... As a matter of fact it's shining right now as I write to you! Thank you for sticking with this. You are blossoming as a person and most certainly a voice actor. We're not quite ready to make a demo as I told you last week, but if you keep this up by years end you might be ☺☺☺

"Ugh," I groan aloud. "How many have I done? *One, two, three.* I can't believe I'm even asking myself after only three of them. I look at the clock. It's still early—8:30 a.m. I charge on.

"Okay, how many have I done *now*?" I ask aloud again. "At least eight more, for sure!" *One, two, three, four, five.* I bury my head in my hands.

Holy cow. I sigh and do another one.

I stand from the table to stretch. It's been two hours.

I hear Andre's voice again: *Take time for yourself, Sam. Show yourself the love you give to others. Just fucking relax!*

He's inhabiting my head and my house. *"Fucking relax?"* That's one luxury I don't have. I've never had.

Life's a one-way journey, Sam. Enjoy the ride. You know what comes at the end of it is uncertain. The journey is all we have . . .

His words, when coming from a caring place, have always been welcome. When you marry somebody twenty-nine years older than you, they ought to teach you some things. Andre softened me. That might seem funny, based on my tough-love teaching style, but he really did. I am much more open-minded about the world and how people choose to live their lives. There is no right or wrong way, we are all just simply who we are. And we are perfect in our imperfections.

|| There is no right or wrong way, we are all just simply who we are.

Andre brought art and culture into my life. And, most important, he believed in me in a way nobody did in my youth, except my grandmother. He actually had more faith in me than I did in myself. God knows, I'm still a work in progress, but he did open my eyes about an awful lot . . . if only I could have gotten some of this when I was younger. But then again, how could I?

Bobbi Block, 1972

BURBANK, CALIFORNIA

It's my usual break time between tap dancing and modern jazz class. I take my usual walk down Ventura Boulevard in Studio City to sit at my usual counter seat at Little Sambo's coffee shop, eat my grilled cheese sandwich, drink my Tab, and dream. I'm a little plump for twelve and I know it. I mean, I don't exactly look like Lana Turner. But that doesn't stop me. Only one thing matters in the whole wide world: I must become a famous actress.

1975

BURBANK, CALIFORNIA

As my mom is about to drop me off at school, she says that she and my father have something to discuss with me at dinner.

I hate it when she calls my stepfather—who she makes me call "Dad"—my father. I shoot her a worried look.

"Oh, Bobbi!" she says, all exasperated. "Don't look at me like that. Must you always wear that frown? You look just like your father. And why must you *always* worry? I have no idea where you get that from."

Really, Mom? The last time you told me that you and my father had something to discuss, I was ten, and it was actually my real dad and you guys told me you were getting a divorce!

I worry every single night because you get so drunk and you refuse to close and lock the front door. It's so damn hot in the house, and we have to attempt sleeping with only that crummy screen door, which means nothing to you because you're passed out, but I'm scared to death that someone is going to sneak in and murder me. I don't know how not to worry.

"Please, Bobbi," she says, waving me out of the car with her cigarette. "Just go to school, and we'll talk tonight. Everything's fine. It's actually good news. You'll like it."

Says who?

The school day drags by. I hate school. Why go to school, unless it's acting school? That's all I want to do anyway. Act. Live in that other world, behind the screen, where things make sense and people are nice. Where fathers are fathers and mothers are—

The bell rings, I'm out the door. I take my time walking home. It's not dance class day, and I have no rehearsal for the musical I'm in. It's just a day to go home and do homework, which I absolutely dread. Plus, I've got the ridiculous discussion with my mom and stepfather.

"It's called *what*? Voice-over?" My stepfather has just explained it to me.

Now, my mother will try. "Bobbi," she says, her voice edged with her usual impatience, "it's when you hear commercials when you are listening to the radio. Those *voices* on the radio. Or when commercials on television have voices talking, but you don't *see* the person. It's just their *voice*. Or when you watch cartoons. The drawings don't talk. People *add* the voices."

Really? I always thought Fred Flintstone was Fred Flintstone!

I look at both of them, shocked. "I don't want to go to that class on Saturday," I say. "I don't want to do voice-whatever. Dad, you were a disc jockey on the radio. So was Grandpa Martin. I don't want to be on the radio. You both know the only thing I want on this entire planet is to be an actress!"

I storm down the hall, slam the door to the bedroom I am forced to share with my sister since my parents got divorced, and promptly burst into tears.

My little sister is watching some kid show on TV. I bury my head in my pillow. *Why can't I be on TV like other kids?* Some commercials come on. I watch. All those lucky people on TV. Then I hear it. There's someone talking who I'm not seeing. I've never paid attention to this before—I'm always watching without listening. My sister's show comes back on.

I sit there like a zombie until the commercials return. There are voices again, even a young voice for Mattel. It's not *being* on TV, but it's still cool. I march back down the hall to the kitchen, where my parents are sitting having their usual after-dinner vodka tonics and cigarettes.

"What's it called again?" I ask. "Voice-what?"

Three days later, Saturday arrives, and I'm with my stepfather in the Blue Boat, a huge, four-door Mercury Marquis that they bought new, but now has dents in it everywhere, probably from their drunk driving. From our home in Burbank, it's a short drive to Hollywood. Wally Heider's recording studio is at the corner of Cahuenga Boulevard and Selma Avenue, conveniently located across the street from one of my parents' favorite Italian restaurants, Martoni's. My stepfather can always park in their lot.

My stomach twists itself into knots as we cross the street. I have no idea what to expect. The voice-over teacher happens to be someone who occasionally works for my stepfather. My "dad" supplies many of the major airlines with the music that passengers can get on their headphones, like radio stations with preprogrammed music and DJs.

As we enter the lobby, there are adults drinking coffee and eating donuts. The door to the actual studio is open, and I can hear somebody recording a commercial.

My stepfather and I pop our heads in. The room is dark, but there are lots of buttons and knobs and little blinking lights. It looks like the inside of an airplane cockpit, only bigger! Besides the teacher, who is later introduced to me as Johnny Truffatore (Truffa for short), there are probably twenty other people, all standing around or sitting on sofas.

Then I see another, smaller room with a glass front. A woman is standing in there, reading a commercial into a microphone. Everyone listens.

When she finishes, Johnny speaks. "Baby, it's just not real, man, it's just not real. It's too contrived."

Contrived? What the heck does that mean?

"You've got to really talk to me, baby. I know you can do it. And this is take four."

I close my eyes to listen, but all I hear is my heart pounding. The woman finishes the take and comes out of the box, looking down. Johnny tells her that the fourth take was better, but that she is never going to make it in this business if she can't be real.

How hard is it to be real? A couple then walks into the little room. As they start to do a husband-and-wife commercial, something comes over me.

I've heard these two before. I've heard them on the radio. A lot!

They are the famous Joan Gerber and Lennie Weinrib, the goddess and god of the voice-over world. Of course, I don't know this at the time. They are at the class as special guests for all the other students. Also, I later discover that Casey Kasem, Sean Morton Downey, and Joan Caulfield are also guests of the class.

"Bobbi, would you like to give it a try?" Johnny asks.

You mean, do I want to throw up? "Sure," I say.

He hands me a script for Little Friskies cat food and tells me that I am supposed to play a kitten. I am escorted into the "booth," as I hear someone call it, and my heart is pounding.

What does a kitten sound like? I don't like kittens. I don't like cats! When Mom married Bill, he had two cats that I now have to live with, and they make me sneeze.

I stand behind the microphone and take a minute to read over the script. The man who controls all the buttons out in the other room, the engineer, closes the booth door. Silence surrounds me—silence like I have never heard before. Johnny Truffa's voice comes through the speakers, "Ready, Bobbi?"

"Sure." But I'm not. The silence in this booth is so freaky that I can hear my heartbeat pounding in my ears. My mouth is dry and my hands are dripping with sweat.

I can do this. I can do this and I will be brilliant because I have to be. This is my first chance at becoming a famous actress, and this is now the most important moment in my life.

"Bobbi Block, take one," the engineer says.

In an instant, I decide that a kitten must sound like a six-year-old girl, so I become little and change my voice. I perform the script and when I reach the end, I don't realize it's the end. It's just that there are no more words left on the paper. I went somewhere else while reading it. I was just *being* that damn kitten.

With a smile slipping into his voice over the speaker, Johnny asks me to come out of the booth. As I open the door, the applause begins, and it doesn't stop.

Why are they applauding? They haven't done that for anyone else.

I'm shaking, desperately trying not to burst into tears. I see my stepfather in the corner of the room. He's not clapping, but he is smiling. Johnny stands and motions me over. He takes both my hands, which are still wet and shaking, looks me straight in the eyes, and then turns to the entire class.

"Ladies and gentlemen, we have just had the pleasure of listening to a true star in the making. Young lady, you are going to be a star!"

Now my heart has stopped. This man just said the words I had dreamt of hearing my whole life. *I am going to be a star!* My real dad used to say it to me all the time, but he left and I've never heard it since.

I feel my stepfather suddenly behind me.

"Hey J.T., thanks for giving Bobbi a shot." They shake hands.

"Are you kidding, man? Bill, your kid here is the real deal. I hope she will join us next Saturday." I immediately give the two of them an uncomfortable glance. I hated hearing the words "your kid."

"Hey, you *do* want to come, don't you?" Johnny asks.

I snap back to reality. "Are you kidding? I want to come back more than anything in the whole wide world. I can't wait for next Saturday!"

I hear some laughter from a few of the adults, and the next thing I know, we are back in the car.

"Gosh, that was amazing! Thank you so much for bringing me here. I really loved being that kitten. And it was so easy!"

"Well you certainly got what you wanted. Attention and applause," my stepdad says, half-laughing, as he looks straight ahead at the road.

I roll my eyes and try to push the hurt away. My real dad would never have said that. If my real dad had been with me today, he would have been on his feet clapping louder than anyone.

"I miss you, Daddy," I silently mouth, looking out my passenger window. "I miss you so much." I find myself silently singing, "*I feel pretty, Oh, so pretty, I feel pretty and witty and gay!*" My daddy used to stand me on the bathroom counter and sing that to me when I was about four or five years old. Now, I remember being six and I see myself coming out of the dressing room at Saks Fifth Avenue in Beverly Hills. "Oh, Daddy, I like this dress the best. I like the alligator they put on it. I point to it at my chest. Can I wear it to lunch?"

"Of course, you can, sweetheart. And you'll be the prettiest girl there at the Polo Lounge."

"It's my birthday, and I'm going to this fancy hotel where there will be lots of movie stars!" I squeal to the lady cutting off the dress tags. I remember my Daddy laughing.

We did the same thing when I turned seven, eight, and nine. After shopping and lunch, we would drive all around Beverly Hills admiring the big fancy houses. I think that was my favorite part. I would concentrate so hard on which house I would have someday. "I think this Spanish one is the best, and I'm going to buy it when I become famous. You are going to be so proud of me!"

"You're awfully quiet."

I jump. My stepdad's voice shakes me. "Wake up, kid, we're almost home."

"Oh, sorry. I haven't been sleeping. I've just been thinking about a paper I have to do for school. We have to write about someone famous, so I decided to write about Judy Garland. I'm just thinking about what to write."

I turn back to my window, longing for my father. I really want to call him and tell him about today, but I know I can't. My mom will get mad. I can hear her say, "What do you want to call your deadbeat father for? He hasn't paid his child support for years. If he loved you, he'd pay for you."

I cringe, hearing her voice so full of hatred, and I can feel the sting of her slap when she struck me hard across my face. Yep. Simply for protection, loving my father was going to have to become a thing of the past, or maybe just my secret.

I go back to "dotting" until almost dark, taking the occasional break to relax and to reflect on my life and Voicetrax. I step outside to watch the sky paint itself red. Then I make myself a cup of tea, flop down on the couch, and smile, imagining my students' delight when they read their reports.

I did forty reports today. Only 287 to go.

1988

MILL VALLEY, CALIFORNIA

I have achieved my greatest dream. To get out of LA and some-day live near the Golden Gate Bridge. I am twenty-eight years old, and I have just moved to Mill Valley, California. My recent divorce from Tommy prodded me to make this decision, and my acting and voice-over career has made it possible. My new home is wonderful, so different from the hustle and bustle that I'm used to. It's in a wooded area, secluded and quiet. The phone rings.

"Hi, my name is Tom Appelbaum, and I got your phone number from Thom Pinto in LA. I'm interested in taking voice-over lessons."

"Thom is a wonderful teacher," I say. "Do you want a recommendation? You can't go wrong with him."

"So I've heard," Tom says. "That's why I called him. Problem is, I live here in the East Bay. Mr. Pinto said you're a wonderful teacher too. I'm interested in taking lessons from you."

I am struggling to think quickly on my feet because of the simple fact that I don't teach. I don't want to embarrass my ex-husband, but I also don't know why Tommy said that. "Uh—yeah, I teach. I'm still kind of busy, though, getting settled into my home . . ." I hedge.

"How much do you charge?" he asks.

Shit! Charge? I don't charge. I don't teach! "Fifty-five for fif-ty-five." *Where in the hell did that come from?*

"Fifty-five dollars for an hour? That's cool. When can we get together? I'm free on Fridays."

I've come too far to back down now. I tell him 2:00 p.m. on Friday will work, and I give him my address. We hang up and I immediately call Tommy.

"Thom Pinto speaking," he answers.

"And this is me speaking. Your ever-loving ex-wife. I just finished talking to Tom Appelbaum."

"Oh, great, he called you."

"Yes, he called me! Why did you say that I teach? You're the brilliant teacher!"

Tommy laughs. I think he is amused by the panic in my voice. "I told him you taught, because I know you would make a great teacher. Besides, you barely know anyone up there, so this way you can meet people. It'll be good for you."

I'm not mad, really, as much as I am completely panicked. "I don't have any of your teaching materials, obviously. No attitude sheet, situational variables, or your vocal color chart. May I use them?"

"Of course. I'll put them in the mail tomorrow."

"He's coming in two days. I just got a fax machine. I know you don't have a fax machine yet, but can you go to SBV Talent Agency and use theirs? I'm sure they won't mind, since both of us are clients."

"I'm actually headed there for an audition right now," he says. "No problem."

And so, it begins. Tom Appelbaum is my first student, and then Michael Tsitovich. And then there are three, and then four. News spreads. In the meantime, I'm now dating this wonderful older, debonair British man named Andre Paris. He lives in Mill Valley too, and he doesn't like the fact that all these strangers keep coming to my house for lessons.

"You're too secluded up there," he warns me. "Anything could happen."

"I think I'm okay," I tell him, "but if you'd feel better, you can come over during lessons and sit in my downstairs living room."

"Great! I'll do the crossword while you teach."

1989

MILL VALLEY, CALIFORNIA

Andre and I are married. A few months before the wedding, I sold my house and moved in with him. He built me a sweet little studio above his art studio. It was formerly his attic and overlooked a creek.

It was idyllic until it wasn't.

This teaching thing is taking off. I have at least forty to fifty students now, and I'm trying to do my own voice-over work in San Francisco, while continuing to fly to LA to do my voice-over work there. Keeping up with the demands of all these students, who each want an hour of my time every week, is getting to be too much, so I start doing workshops a couple of nights a week plus weekends. I also have to rent a recording studio in Sausalito, because my place is too small to fit eight to ten people in it.

Then I start receiving beautiful letters from my students, heartfelt thank-you notes that say how these lessons and classes are transforming them. I'm helping them to find their voices and discover their true passion. Some thank me for the fact that they are now booking more voice-over jobs than ever, and that's great. But is this what I'm supposed to be doing: teaching voice-over? It is becoming harder and harder to do my own voice-over work.

It was effortless until it wasn't.

"Andre, what do you think?" I ask. "I keep getting all these letters."

"I know, and I hope you're saving them. You should put them in a box, so when you're eighty, you can enjoy them all over again."

"I know, honey, you already told me that, and I will. But I mean . . . well, I'm wondering if maybe I should be in the newspaper or something. Maybe there's a story here. How do people get in the paper anyway?"

"A publicist," he says.

"A publicist? I'm not a movie star! Only famous people have publicists."

"How do you think business stories get in the paper?"

And so, I get a publicist.

It's Monday, and I'm about to appear on a local television show called *People Are Talking*. I'm nervous because it's live. I'm used to doing TV, but acting in commercials and episodic television is completely different from live TV. Not to mention the fact that I'm not playing a character—I'm me!

Andre and I drive to the station. I don't know who's more nervous, him or me. But I do the show and it goes great. It is a total blur actually.

"Andre, I can't even remember what I said. I hope it wasn't geeky. Did I even mention that I teach? They were asking me so many questions about my career.

"Yes, I think you did. Don't worry about it, you were great. One thing, though: you have to stop saying 'um' so much before you answer questions."

I glare at him. "*Um*, okay. I didn't know I was doing that. I'll try."

When we get home, I have at least fifty messages on my answering machine. I guess I did mention that I taught, and my publicist, Leza, must have given the TV station my phone number to display on the screen. My phone rings while I'm rushing to take down the names and numbers of all the people.

"Hi, Samantha, it's Leza. I have great news! Both the *San Francisco Chronicle* and the *Examiner* want to do articles on you."

"Are you kidding?"

"No, I'm not, and Ronn Owens of KGO radio wants to have you on his show this Friday morning from 11:00 to 12:00. You know he has about a million listeners."

"A *million* listeners? And it's live?"

"It's live," she says. "But you were great today and you can do it!"

I hang up the phone and tell Andre. He beams from one ear to the other.

The newspaper journalists interview me and the articles come out the following Friday morning. That same morning, I go on Ronn Owens' program. I do his show and it not only goes well, but I have so much fun. I am so much more comfortable on the radio than I am on television. I'm told by Ronn's producer immediately after the show that while I was on, the phones at the station were ringing off the hook! So many people were trying to call in to ask me questions.

Andre and I go to lunch to celebrate. When we come home, the red light is blinking on my answering machine. There must be 300 messages on it—the cassette is full. Meanwhile, my phone won't stop ringing. I'm scared, and there's a horrible feeling growing in the pit of my stomach. I quickly put in another cassette. I cannot answer the phone, and it doesn't stop all weekend. By Monday at noon, I have received more than 1,000 phone calls. Andre is so proud of me. I am stunned.

It was all so simple . . . until it wasn't.

Monday, March 15, 2010

SAUSALITO, CALIFORNIA

I drag my ass into the kitchen and fire up the coffeepot before heading to the shower. The howling wind and rain obscure the view of the bay, which is fitting for my mood. I have a full day of teaching nothing but private lessons and I dread it.

I step into the shower and turn on the water as hot as I can stand. It's my last private time of the day, before I turn myself over to others and their needs.

Private lessons can be really rough on me, as they're laden with expectations, both on my part and from my students' perspectives. While classes can also be intense, there's always an uplifting lightness about them. I joke with the students, and laughter makes any day better. But privates are so different.

First, they are expensive. Long gone are the days of "Fifty-five for fifty-five," so there is a pressure I put on myself to make sure the hour is worth their hard-earned dollars.

Second, they have had to wait at least two months to even get a private with me, and that's a fact I feel even guiltier about. Then I know most of them are driving to Voicetrax emotionally charged, so the stakes are quite high. Some are extremely nervous because maybe we haven't worked together in a while. They might have had several classes with other instructors at Voicetrax, and now they've come to show "Mom" how much they've improved.

Some have even more at stake, because they are hoping that after our lesson, I will say they are ready for me to make a demo for them to submit to agents in hopes of getting representation. Actually, these students know that if I make them their demo, they almost certainly *will* get an agent, which makes my "green light" even more important. So, when I have to deliver the news that the light is still "red" or "yellow," I feel bad charging them when I have delivered a heart-sinking blow—even though it's honest and in their best interests.

I constantly hear, "Why do I always suck with you, Samantha, but I do so well with the other instructors?"

My response is almost always, "Because you know I'm way harder than they are. It's my job to constantly remind you of where the true bar of excellence is to be competitive, and you desperately want to please me."

Then, after that, it's my job to pick up the pieces and make them feel good before they walk out the door. "Come on, Suzy/ Fred/Mary, why do you put so much pressure on yourself? You know I love you no matter what," I say, which is true. "You know that as long as you are trying, I am totally proud of you," I say, which I am. "And you know that together, we are going to do this! Just maybe not as quickly as you would like."

Yep, I extinguish emotional fires that I help create all day long. And some that I don't. Some issues go beyond their pending voice-over careers, reaching back into their private lives. They share such personal pain with me, that at times I feel like an untrained therapist rather than an actress or voice-over coach. It can all be overwhelming.

Meanwhile this shower is my therapist. I drag it out as long as I can. I let out a scream and start to cry, my tears disappearing down the shower drain. My ears ring. I scream again until I lose my breath.

This is exactly what I used to do driving down the 101 on my way to work from Petaluma. For years, I had conversations every morning with Andre, because he could sense my mood as soon as I set foot out of the bed.

"I hate my life," I would tell him. "I miss acting and I cannot keep teaching like this."

But he never listened. He didn't care that I was unhappy. My working myself to the bone meant *he* didn't have to. He could simply live his life, free as a bird. That's why he would dismiss my feelings.

"Sammy," he would say, "you know you *love* teaching. You're brilliant at it. Besides, you're young!"

I always used to wonder what he meant by that. Because I was twenty-nine years younger than him, was I supposed to be a willing slave to a career I didn't want?

So, on more mornings than I care to admit, I screamed in my car all the way to Voicetrax. Now I'm doing it in my fucking shower in Sausalito.

Enough, Sam. Get it together.

As I dry off, I decide this is most definitely a jeans, sweatshirt, no-makeup kind of day. I open my closet and smell something sour. Then I see it. It's a huge leak and nearly half my clothes are soaked. I fall to my knees and start crying again. I am so alone and simply want to die.

A few minutes pass. Dying is not an option, so I pick myself up off the floor and pile my wet clothes on the bathroom floor, for later. Then I remember my coffee. As I pour, steam rises, and I force myself to snap out of my awful mood.

I get dressed and look in the mirror. My puffy eyes tell me that this cannot be a no-makeup day. I put on my minimal face paint, down the rest of the coffee, and head for my car.

I think about the conversation I need to have with Vicki and Chuck. Neither of them know about me and Andre. I've gotta tell them. I dread that too.

Beginning my drive down Bridgeway, I wonder why I never asked Andre what he meant when he said, "But you're young." I wipe the thought from my mind, just like my windshield wiper does with the pouring rain. It really doesn't matter anymore.

Show time.

9:30 a.m.

VOICETRAX

"Good morning, guys. Man, it's wet out there." I give my umbrella a few good shakes just outside the door, so as to not carry rainwater into the office.

"Don't bother, Samantha," Vicki says with a grimace. "We have a leak right over my desk and the one usual spot in the studio. Chuck's gone to get the bowls."

"I guess it's pointless to ask if you called the landlord?"

"Yeah, Victor knows, but you know he never fixes anything."

Chuck arrives with the bowls. "He said when the storm is over, he'll see to it." The three of us just look at one another. I enter the studio to hang up my coat, still trying to shake off my morning, and I realize that I did not call my own landlord about my wardrobe leak at home. There's no time, so I walk back out into the office to see what's on my desk.

"Hey, I know your day is starting soon," Vicki says, looking up from her desk, "but do you have a sec for me and Chuck to talk to you about our Facebook page?"

"What's happening with it?" I ask. "We got anything interesting?"

"Oh, my God, Samantha, it's not do we *have* anything, but what do we post first?" Vicki is cheerier than anyone has a right to be on such a dreary Monday morning.

"Okay, fill me in, but quickly." I glance at the clock and turn to Chuck, because he's in charge of social media.

"I just finished typing three of them for your approval," he says. "I'll print them out for you."

"How many stories are there?" I ask.

"Seven, which is too many for posting twice a week. I know

you don't like to come across like we're bragging all the time. Even though—"

Chuck's grinning. "Even though what?" I ask.

"Tell you what, darlin'," Chuck offers, "I'll print them out but also e-mail them to you at home. You can look at them tonight. The braggin' part is that six of the eight roles that were recently auditioned for a new video game were booked by Voicetrax students."

"And Chuck was one of them." Vicki chimes in. "And Roni Gallimore just booked her fifth audiobook."

"But wait a minute, let's go back. What's the name of the video game project?" I ask.

"Unfortunately, it can't be disclosed yet. Not until it's released. If I told you, I'd have to kill you," Chuck says. Their enthusiasm is contagious, and I can't keep from smiling.

"Oh, and also," he continues, "yesterday when Vicki was walking out of the studio at One Union Recording for her Cisco session, our resident soccer mom, Vilija, was walking in to record a national commercial for Clorox."

"And I got a really great picture of the two of us to post!" Vicki shows me the photo on her phone.

"Ah, that picture is so wonderfully dorky! I love it. And congratulations to both of you, my shining former students. Who says talent can't be taught? With you guys now having such successful voice-over careers, why the hell are you working for me?"

Chuck and Vicki grin at each other, and Chuck wiggles his fingers in front of his mouth. His diabolical voice emerges. "We love the pain . . ."

"Hi, everyone." The three of us turn and say our hellos to Brenda, while she does her own umbrella shaking. She has been studying here for about a year and is my first private of the day.

Vicki crosses over to the counter and hands Brenda her scripts. I look at the clock. I've got fifteen minutes before my mile-long day of privates begins.

"Brenda, we're just finishing up a quick meeting," I say. "Why don't you go on into the studio, dry off, and start rehearsing? I'll be with you in a few minutes."

"No problem!" With that, she gathers her scripts and goes in. I turn back to my team.

"Guys, I've been putting off telling you this for ages, but the circumstances are such that I have to share this with you now. For more than two months, Andre and I have been separated. We're getting divorced. He's home, and I've been living in an apartment here in Sausalito."

Vicki's jaw drops, and without looking at Chuck—I can't—I know I have absolutely devastated him, not because of what he just learned, but because I didn't come to him sooner. He has been my lovable, 280-pound, little brother protector since the days when I had the additional school in the desert, and he was my first student at that location. He bows his head, and I can tell he's doing that, because he has seen this coming for years.

"I try so hard not to bring my personal stuff into the office, and I refuse to bring it into the classroom. I just felt that if I told you guys, you'd be forced to live with a secret, which I don't think is right. Anyway, you're forced to secrecy now. It's been rough," I admit, my voice cracking, "and I'm not sleeping too well."

Vicki jumps up to offer a hug. "Samantha, I'm so sorry. Is there anything I can do? Anything we can do?" She glances at Chuck.

"Thanks, honey. I didn't mean to start crying. I can't. I have to go in and teach. I don't want you guys to feel sorry for me, because it's my own shit and I'll get through it. I know I'm suffering from depression, but I'd like to think of it as situational depression."

"Are you on medication?" Vicki asks.

I shoot her a you-must-be-fucking-crazy look. "God, no! My doctor suggested it, and I gave him the same look I just gave you."

I manage a small giggle through my tears. "Chuck knows I'm way too stubborn for that."

Chuck gets up and crosses over to me. He simply engulfs me in his arms. "Oh darlin', I'm so sorry." He strokes my head, and his gentle breathing and the silent tenderness of the moment calm me immensely. I look up at him and he gives me his adorable puppy face that he knows makes me smile.

"Guys, your love means the world to me, thanks. There is a work-related reason why I decided to share this with you, but I must admit, keeping this from you has not been easy, and I do feel like a burden has been lifted. I need to take some time off. The dotting is done and the catalogues are going out—"

"Tomorrow afternoon and two days ahead of schedule," Vicki proudly interrupts.

"Fantastic. So, I'm hoping that taking some time off will help. My 'sister' Karen—you know, Chuck, the one who works for Sparkling Ocean—called me a few days ago and said there was a last-minute opening for a guest speaker onboard one of their ships. It's a twelve-day cruise from Miami to Barcelona. I will be expected to do four, forty-five-minute presentations and my trip will be completely paid for."

Vicki looks a bit confused. "I didn't know you had two sisters. I thought you had just one."

"Technically that's correct, and I haven't spoken to my real sister in years. I don't think I even have a phone number for her. However, I have a whole wonderful adopted family, thanks to Andre. Chuck knows about them, as Karen's sister, Lynda, lives in the desert. She was in classes a few years ago with Chuck."

Vicki turns to Chuck, who chuckles and scratches his head.

"I know what you're thinking, Chuck, and we both agree," I say. "Lynda is balls-out nuts, but I love her. She's my family. I'm sorry, Vicki, we don't mean to leave you out of this. I'll fill you in later. So anyway, I took Karen up on her offer. I leave in two weeks, and I'll be gone fifteen days."

They both nod their heads in approval.

"Chuckie, I'm going to need you to use the Voicetrax credit card and buy me whatever I'm going to need to be able to record on the ship. Vic, I obviously don't have time today, but I'll come in early tomorrow and figure out how to reschedule everything."

Vicki grabs my hand and gives it a reassuring squeeze. "It's no problem at all, Samantha. Whatever you need." Chuck just looks at me, bends his hands up by his face and barks like a 280-pound puppy.

I smile and walk over to the studio entrance and throw open the door.

10:00 a.m.

"Beautiful morning to you, Brenda! Are you ready to be brilliant? It's been a while."

"Well, I finished a class with Thom Pinto about a month ago," she says, "and I have one coming up with—"

"Rob Paulsen," she and I say in unison.

"Does anything get past you, Samantha?" she asks.

"Um, not too much. At least not when it comes to you guys. Tommy told me you felt a bit timid in class, because you aren't familiar with a lot of celebrities, so doing the 'Celebrity Prototype' class was difficult."

"Yeah, I don't watch enough TV, and I don't remember the last time I watched a movie. My work is really nuts."

As we walk into the booth and I adjust Brenda's microphone, I remind her that all work and no play makes for a lousy voice actor. I close the booth door and take my seat in front of the controls.

"Which script would you like to start with?"

"This McDonald's one looks fun," she says, leafing through the stack. "I'll start with that."

"Great! There's no reason to slate, as it's just us, so on my cue, go. You're rolling."

She begins. "I'm not big on chocolate. I never touch the stuff. Ever. Nope, not me. Not a chocolate-craving bone in my body. Not even on my worst days do I even so much as think about indulging in such a thing."

"Sweetheart—" I stop her. "Not to be rude, but I'm not believing you for one second. You actually sound like you're reading. Put somebody specific in your head to talk to and let's try it again. You're rolling."

Unfortunately, I get the same unconvincing performance, so I stop her again. "Let's start at the beginning. Who are you talking to?"

"A girlfriend of mine. We're at the beach sunbathing, and I see someone eating chocolate ice cream."

"Okay, that's not a bad choice, but do you see that by the end of the script, you say that if you can't get a McDonald's Hot Fudge Brownie Sundae in the next five minutes, you're going to hurt someone?"

"Yes."

"Well, how are you going to get to a McDonald's in five minutes, if you are sunbathing on the beach? It would take you at least that long to get to your car!" I exclaim, laughing.

"Good point, Sam," she acknowledges. "Shall I try it again?"

"You need to be at McDonald's with your girlfriend, eating some kind of boring fruit salad. What you *really* want is a Big Mac, but you're trying to be sensible. Remember, you have to get into your little black cocktail dress Saturday night."

"I do?" She looks up from her script, puzzled.

"No, not you, silly, but your character does."

"Oh, right. Duh, of course." She seems distracted.

"So, you're sitting there, watching everybody else in the restaurant eating what they want, and at the table right next to you, this kid is thoroughly enjoying his chocolate sundae. You're *dying* for dessert, because your lunch was so lousy. You're crazy about chocolate, but you're saying these first few lines in denial, trying to talk yourself out of your love affair with chocolate. Now, as you begin this piece, you'll have more fire in your belly and a lot more energy. Let's give it a go. You're rolling."

Brenda's third performance is only marginally better. I know she's better than this, and it's strange. Not only is she lacking passion, but I'm also not really hearing her full voice. It's like her voice is trapped. Or like her words are stopping in front of the mic rather than traveling through it. I let her finish the whole piece, so as to not be too harsh by stopping her again.

"Okay, it's a little better, but like Thom said to me, you sound a bit timid." I demonstrate to her how the words need to extend beyond the microphone. "Bring your hand up and hold it just on the other side of the mic. Now this is just an exercise, so don't worry about your acting. I want you to say these words and as you speak them, think about the words literally coming out of your mouth and dancing beyond the mic. I want you to feel them hitting your fingers."

Just then, Vicki walks in, crooking her finger at me.

"Sorry to interrupt, but your next private just cancelled. It's Stephanie and she lives in Stinson Beach. Because of the storm, Highway One is closed. Mudslides, I guess."

"Oh, well, tell her not to worry about it and to stay safe. Actually, Vicki, that's great, because now you and I can use that hour to sort out the rescheduling nightmare my cruise has created."

"Oh, that's perfect!" Vicki exclaims, backing out the door. "Okay, sorry to interrupt."

I turn back to Brenda.

"Sorry, honey, my next private had to cancel because of the

storm. So, are your *words* dancing up a storm? Let me hear."

She begins again, "I'm not big on chocolate. I never touch the stuff. Nope. Not me."

I have to interrupt her again. "Honey, you're still only giving me half your voice. Hang on. I'm coming in the booth with you. I hate talking on this talkback mic." As I enter the booth, Brenda is staring straight ahead at her copy. "You know Bren', it's like you're afraid to let go and perform."

"I don't know why, Sam. I'm really trying."

"Of course, you are! I know that." I affectionately tickle her and suddenly see tears streaming down her cheeks.

"Oh, my God, Brenda, come here. Let me hold you."

She takes me up on my offer and then just cries in my arms. And cries.

"Come on, let's get out of this booth and sit. I'll get you some water."

She sits and I go to the bar to get a glass and a box of Kleenex.

"Talk to me, Brenda," I urge her. "What the hell is going on?"

"Oh, Samantha, my life is a mess. I'm a forty-seven-year-old mess. I can't believe you said I sound trapped, because that's exactly what I am. I'm in such a bad relationship and I want out of it."

I take a deep breath and in that split second, my own situation flashes in front of me. I snap back into the moment.

"Are you married?" I ask.

"No, but we've been together a long time—nearly twenty years."

"Please don't tell me he beats you."

"No, not physically, but definitely emotionally. He is really abusive."

"Well then, why don't you leave?"

"Because it's not that simple. My son still has two more years of high school, and I don't know how I would support him."

"Well, you have a job, right?"

"Yeah, I'm in research and I hate it. I'm not good at it either, and my supervisor might fire me."

"Well, that wouldn't be the end of the world. Why waste your life doing something that you hate?" My familiar chant plays in my head.

I cannot keep doing this anymore.

"Why waste your life being with someone who's horrible to you?" I ask, focusing my attention back on Brenda.

"Samantha, I keep asking myself those two questions all the time, but I just feel like I don't have a choice."

She's crying again.

"Oh, sweetheart, I know just how you feel. I really do. But you do have choices. Look at what you're doing right now—you made a choice to do something for yourself and study voice-over."

"Yes, and I love it, but if I decide to leave Jack, I'll have to give it up. I won't be able to afford it."

"But that will be temporary and, believe me, if you are really as miserable as you say you are, the moment you make the decision to leave, you will feel *so* much better."

"I'm just frozen in fear and insecurity," she admits.

"The Brenda I know is beautiful, daring, creative—Shit, look at you! Look at how, in this year we have been working together, you lost all that weight. Look at how cute you are." I admire her arms with my fingertips. "You are one determined woman."

She meekly looks up at me. Our eyes meet and she manages a small smile. As she begins to look down again, I raise her chin to meet my eyes once more.

"Honey, the power to change things is there within you. I've seen it. And it all starts with the true and simple belief that *you deserve better.*"

She takes a deep breath. "Thank you, Samantha, for being here for me today. I feel like a big weight has been lifted."

Isn't that just what I told Vicki and Chuck?

"I guess I just have to make a plan," Brenda says.

"Exactly! Let me ask you: How long have you been miserable with Jack? Three years? Five years?"

"More like fifteen."

I feel you, sister.

I push thoughts of Andre out of my head. "Well, that is crazy, but it will make what I'm about to suggest even easier for you than I thought. Look, start carving out *now* the life that you know you want to live once your son graduates. If you hate your job, start looking for one that you would love. Stop taking these voice-over lessons and start saving your money. I bet you will find that Jack doesn't do your head in nearly as much, once you know that you have your escape date set. If you've been miserable for fifteen years, you can tolerate two more for the sake of your son. And keep going to the gym! You are going to love that hot body of yours once you're single." Now I get a big, shy smile from her.

> The power to change things is there within you. I've seen it. And it all starts with the true and simple belief that you deserve better.

"But I love this," she says sadly, as she gestures around the room.

"I know you do, but for now, you've got to get your life in order. This place will still be here in two years. Hell, I've been here twenty-two years. You think I'm going anywhere?"

Brenda giggles, beginning to put her misery out of her mind. I take both of her hands in mine.

"Honey, we are only putting your voice-over dream on hold. I want you to hear my voice in your head every day, saying that someday you *will* be a successful voice actor, because you will. You have the capacity to be every single thing you dream of becoming."

"Thank you for that, Samantha. I will carry your voice with

me. It's like you're the mother or the sister I always wished I could have had."

My internal voice plays on. *What about my own horrific mother and my nonexistent relationship with my sister?*

"You are so incredibly intuitive, so insightful, it's scary," Brenda says, bringing me back in the moment.

I laugh. "It scares me sometimes too. I have no idea where it comes from. But believe me, it means the world to me that you felt safe enough to let go." Our eyes meet and in that split moment I feel a true sisterhood with her. "Now, do you feel a little better? You wanna get back in the booth and continue our lesson? We have fifteen minutes."

"Oh, I don't think so. This has been enough of a lesson for one day. Probably been the most important lesson of my life!"

"Well, please, don't give me that much credit." I laugh uncomfortably. "I'll tell you what. I'll ask Vicki to put you on my priority list so if someone cancels in the next couple of weeks you can come back."

And with that, I throw open the studio door. As Brenda and I walk over to the counter, I give the "don't charge for today" glance that both Chuck and Vicki are so familiar with—when they see that look, they know another student of mine has just had a meltdown and that I feel far too guilty to charge. I just have to look at times like this as a part of my day. You would think by now I would have stopped assuming that people sign up for these classes simply because they want to explore something new, or maybe start a new career. It's obviously way more than that. They are seeking guidance, support, and love. They are putting their full trust in me to help them find their way. To find their voice.

I wish to hell I could find my own.

Nearly every day at work, I feel like Dorothy in *The Wizard of Oz*. The scene I have in mind takes place toward the end of the movie when the Wizard of Oz reaches into his bag and pulls out the diploma for the Scarecrow, the heart for the Tin Woodman and the medal of courage for the Cowardly Lion. All three of them get what they were seeking, and Dorothy is standing there, happy for them. But then she turns to the Wizard and says sadly, "I don't think there's anything in that black bag for me."

Yep, that's how I feel every damn day.

I turn to Brenda, give her one last hug and then, smiling, point my finger right at her nose. "Remember what I said, young lady!" And with that, I walk back into the studio.

10:50 a.m.

I take a couple of deep breaths and walk behind the bar to get a yogurt out of the fridge. All I can think about is the fact that Brenda thought I was intuitive. It's crazy. I'm just teaching voice-over. I do think, however, that after my escapade in the shower this morning, I'm fucking psychic and should go buy a lottery ticket immediately. I bury my head on the counter and close my eyes.

I empathize with Brenda because I know what it feels like to feel trapped. I feel for all my students struggling or hurting, and I want to be able to erase the pain from their lives. I really do try, which is why I know what I do matters. What puzzles me is, why isn't that enough?

Vicki pops her head in. "Do you want to work on the schedule in here, or do you want to come out into the office?"

"Oh! You caught me taking a catnap. Let's do it in here. I can think better." As she leaves to get the scheduling book, I wonder why I even have a desk out in the office. I never use it. As beautiful as the office is, with the view of the bay and all the boats, I've always felt like I'm working in a fishbowl out there. I prefer to work deep within the cavern of the studio so I can hide. I look around the room, trying to calculate just how much time I've spent within these four walls.

I do the math, thinking out loud, "Let's see, fifty-two weeks in a year. So, let's say that I'm actually here for forty-eight of those weeks. I probably teach fifty hours a week, so fifty times forty-eight equals . . . 2,400 hours a year. Then I have to multiply that by twenty-two years and that's . . . 52,800 hours."

Holy cow.

I've spent 52,800 hours in here. I feel like these walls know me better than I know myself. I close my eyes and pray to the walls to give me answers.

Why do I feel so trapped? What exactly is it in the Wizard's bag that I want? Is it in the bag or over the rainbow?

Vicki returns, bringing me back to reality. "Okay, Sam, I've got the book, and your student private lesson request book." She plops them down on the console. "Also, just FYI, Brenda really wanted to pay for her private, but we told her you wouldn't accept anything. She was really touched. She'll probably bake you some of those cookies you don't like."

I look at Vicki and plead, "Oh, God, no! Say it isn't so!" I offer up a weak laugh.

"Are you okay? You seem tired."

"I had a rough morning at my apartment, and I also think I'm feeling a bit relieved about you and Chuck knowing what's going on," I say, "so it's been a tiring day already. Anyway, I believe we have some monster rescheduling to do."

"True," Vicki says, as she opens the book. "So, let's get it done."

And so, we do.

Thirty minutes later, I stand and stretch. Anything else?" I ask, hoping against hope that the answer is "no."

"Yes," Vicki says. "Nancy called when you were with Brenda. You're booked to do a TV appearance with entertainment reporter Jan Wahl while you're away."

"Okay, I'll talk to Nancy about the 'Hat Lady' (referring to Wahl's habit of wearing a hat). Anything else?"

"One more thing," Vicki says. "I just want to say that I love you and if you ever want to talk, I'm here."

"Thank you, honey."

Vicki looks at the clock. "One last thing, because we still have some time," she says. "What was all that business about your other family? You did promise to fill me in."

"Oh, right. Well, it isn't a big deal to me, but when I share this with people, they are kind of amazed. So, Lynda Paris is Andre's ex-wife—the one Chuck was giggling about. My surrogate family is actually Lynda's family. There's Lynda and Karen—"

"The one who works for Sparkling Ocean cruises," Vicki interjects.

"Right. And she has two other sisters, a brother, and her mother and father, Janet and Eddy."

"Wait a minute. Your surrogate family is Andre's former in-laws?"

"Every single crazy one of them, and I love them dearly. We go to Janet and Eddy's house in Dallas every Thanksgiving. One time, I went on a two-week Sparkling Ocean cruise with the whole family and bunked with Karen. Andre didn't even go."

Vicki looks stunned, just like everyone else I share this with. I can't help but laugh.

"I consider Janet my true mother. She has been for twenty years now."

"Your ex's ex's mother."

"Yep. I cannot tell you how loving and supportive she has been. She's always so damn proud of my accomplishments. Every time I send her the new Voicetrax catalogue or an article written about me in a newspaper, she gushes like I just won an Academy Award or became president of the United States. Sadly, I *never* got any of that from my mother or my stepfather. An article would come out and my mom would indifferently glance at it in the office, criticize the photo of me, put it down, and, in front of my employees, say she'd read it later.

1985

BURBANK, CALIFORNIA

"I'll be there in a minute," my mother calls from the kitchen. "I'm just finishing up the dishes."

My friends, Tommy, and I have all gathered around the television in my parents' living room to watch the first of my two episodes starring opposite Michael Landon in *Highway to Heaven*.

"Look, there you are!" says Gabrielle, excitedly.

My stepfather is snoring away, passed out drunk on the couch. I am actually relieved. Three days ago, I had stopped by with some dry cleaning I had picked up for my mother. As I walked in the door, a television commercial I had just done as the voice of Lucy from the Charlie Brown cartoon series was playing.

"Well, would you look at that. What a brat you are!" my stepfather says laughing. "What perfect casting."

Now I turn up the television extra loud to drown him out. God only knows what kind of comments he would make this time.

At the half-hour commercial break of the show, I get up to go to the kitchen. There at the kitchen table my mother sits, staring vacantly out the window, nursing a vodka tonic, and taking a drag of her cigarette.

I open my mouth to speak, think better of it, and return to the living room . . .

11:39 a.m.

The memory mercifully fades away, and I am in the Voicetrax studio, where Vicki is listening sympathetically, puzzled by my long silence, waiting for me to continue.

"I had only one source of true support growing up, Vicki, and that was my grandmother, Nanna. In my adult life, it would be Andre and Janet, but Janet is special. She never had any ulterior motives. I guess that's why it's never bothered me that I was not close with my own mother. Somehow, the universe knew I got a raw deal in the mother department, so it gave me Janet."

Vicki's mouth is still hanging open when I am done. "There," I say, "does that explain everything or what?"

Just then, Chuck pops his head in. "Vicki, Nate's on the phone about a booking for you tomorrow."

"Cool! Tell him to hang on." Vicki turns back to me expectantly but I give her a nudge in Chuck's direction.

"Go get 'em, tiger—duty calls."

As she gets up and grabs all of the scheduling stuff, she cheerfully reminds me, "You mean my *other* duty calls," and we both smile.

"And Samantha," Chuck adds, "your next private is here." I glance at the clock—it's 11:45 a.m.

"Great. Vicki, can you tell Paula to use these fifteen minutes to rehearse outside? And Chuckie, can I see you for a moment?"

I motion for Chuck to close the door behind him. He comes in and sits down, and he too is looking at me expectantly, but for another reason. I feel really bad about not telling him about Andre sooner, and I know he knows.

"I'm sorry, honey," I say. "I didn't want to say anything to you this time, because I felt like it was a little bit like the boy who cried wolf. You knew I left him two years ago and stupidly went back."

"That's why you couldn't come to me this time?" he asks, shaking his head. "Sam, you're crazy." He says it softly and I can see the hurt in his eyes.

"I guess I feel ashamed about all of this," I admit, trying to hold back tears, and not succeeding.

"Ashamed? Samantha, why? You've done everything possible to make your marriage work. That's what's always pissed me off. You spoil him and have done way too much." He hands me a Kleenex and then continues.

"Look, I like Andre. Who doesn't? He has so much talent as an artist, and I really admired how well-read he was, so knowledgeable on all sorts of topics. I loved talking cars with him. But I also saw firsthand what nobody else ever saw, or just refused to see. He totally took advantage of you. When we first met in the desert and I was taking classes, I couldn't believe you were driving back and forth from Rancho Mirage to Sausalito, running two schools. That's why I offered to help out."

"I know. And you were wonderful."

"Come on! I did have a bit of an ulterior motive. I wanted to make sure you had enough energy to keep the school down there going, so I could have a voice-over career." Chuck grinned. "But when I saw what was really going on, that you worked and he did nothing but his *art*, that pissed me off."

I dry my eyes and steer our discussion down memory lane. "Do you remember the time I was up here teaching for like two or three weeks? You were down there in Rancho Mirage every night to open up and be the engineer. And when I got back—"

Chuck chuckles to himself. He knows I love to tell this story.

"You had cleaned the studio, the bathrooms were immaculate, and you had put a chocolate on every student chair and folded the toilet paper all fancy, just like in a hotel."

Chuck tries looking stern. "Yeah, and what thanks did I get?"

"I know, I know. I told you that you'd forgotten to clean the coffeepot!" We're both doubled over laughing. "Look, Chuckie, I'm really sorry. Can you forgive me?" As soon as the 280-pound, puppy-dog face appears, I know that all is well.

"Darlin', of course it's okay," Chuck says. "There's nothing to forgive. Hell, I owe my whole life to you. My amazing career, my wonderful life, it's all because of you."

"I think we make an amazing team," I tell him. "Those years I spent in the desert were rough, but it was worth it because I met you. Given the choice, I would endure it all over again."

As my eyes now fill up with tears, Chuck grabs my chin. "And you know I will walk to the ends of the earth for you, Paris."

"I know, honey. That, I really do know."

We both glance at the clock. It's 12:04.

"Okay, I gotta get Paula." I jump off the stool, wipe my eyes, and give Chuck a hug.

"No more secrets," he says, wagging his finger.

"Okay, okay I get it. Now I've really gotta go."

Chuck opens the studio door and steps aside as Paula walks in. He turns back and gives me a smile.

"Remember, Paris, to the ends of the earth," he says. "Even though you're fucking crazy."

12:05 p.m.

"Hi, Paula. Wow! Don't you look beautiful today!"

"Why, thank you, Samantha. I'm feeling good today. You heard I got my first booking, right?"

"No, I didn't. I'm usually the last to know around here."

"I only told Vicki on Friday. It's for a travel app. They wanted someone with a British accent, but I figured most Americans can't tell the difference between someone British and me being

South African, so I said, 'Why not?' and gave it a go and I booked it. I am *so* excited!"

"Oh, Paula, I'm absolutely thrilled for you! I will always remember my first job like it was yesterday."

"I would not have had the nerve to audition for this even six months ago, but you all have made me feel so much more confident and comfortable in my own skin. I threw all caution to the wind and just did it! I feel totally reborn at fifty."

"Well, then, I'm going to wish you a happy birthday today. Your new birthday is March fifteenth," I say with wink. "Now skip into the booth and let's get going!"

1:05 p.m.

"Hey, Clifford. Ready for your private?"

"Ready as I'll ever be, I guess," he says, sheepishly, standing up from the lobby couch.

"What kind of attitude is that? Where's my forever-upbeat Clifford?"

All I get is a silent shrug.

As he enters the booth and I adjust his mic, I punch him on the shoulder. "Okay, give. Why all the doom and gloom?"

"It's nothing, really. I had a class with Thom last night and didn't do so well."

"So what? It's your first narration class. Narration is hard. It's a lot more technical and you are more of an instinctual person. I have all the confidence in the world that you will get it. And lucky for you, there is no narration copy in your packet today, so let's get going!"

2:05 p.m.

I give a final shout-out to Clifford as he exits the studio: "Bye, Clifford, I love you. You did great!"

"Hey darlin', I took it upon myself to bring you your favorite salad," Chuck says, walking in. "I know you're short on time. I thought maybe we could go over the postproduction on Tim's demo."

"Oh, you are such a dear." I see that his other hand is empty. "But where the fuck is my water? You buy me a big bottle every morning and today you forgot!" We both laugh.

"I think we're having another 'you forgot to clean the coffee-pot' moment, Paris, but you are absolutely right."

"Would you mind going and getting me one? I meant to ask for it an hour ago."

"I live only to please you, Miss Paris," he says as he bows.

"Well, if you really want to please me after we work on Tim's demo, you'll finish clearing out the storage room. You still have those boxes of old recording cables and shit to go through."

"I know, I know, it's been taking me a while. I can probably finish it late this afternoon."

"Good, because I can hardly move in there, and it's driving me nuts."

"Didn't we agree that you are already nuts? But I'll take care of it. Promise."

"Do you know that I actually found two boxes of fresh, Ampex 456, quarter-inch tape and six, 10-inch reels?" I laugh. "Jesus, I remember back in the day, how expensive audiotape was to buy. I went through reels and reels like running water."

"Speaking of which, let me run out and get yours. I'll be right back."

While he's gone, I go behind the bar to grab a fork and some pepper, wondering if we could sell the tape on eBay. I've been told you can sell anything over the Internet.

I shake my head. The days of audiotape are long gone, but the memories from my youth sadly remain. I see myself in the back room of Johnny's house that was his makeshift studio when he was away from Wally Heider's in Hollywood. Sitting there alone, while he floated on a raft in his pool, my job was to sort through stacks of reels, listening to hours of audiotape that my fellow classmates had made in class.

In addition to bringing Johnny his coffee and donuts, keeping the take log, and shamefully having sex with him, I had to decide which commercials they performed best and which takes were the best. Then I would splice these onto a smaller reel that Johnny would listen to before making the final edits. That's how he would make someone's demo. He would spend ten minutes on it and charge a king's ransom. Little did his students know that it was actually a seventeen-year-old girl in a back room deciding their voice-over fates. The memory makes me sick to my stomach.

Chuck spares me, returning quickly. He plops my water down on the console and assumes the position behind all the controls.

"Okay, so, Tim's demo. Let's have a listen."

"I already listened over the weekend," I tell him.

"Fantastic! That saves us some time. What'd you think?"

"I'm fairly happy with it, although I do have a couple of issues. On the Safeway spot, I think the music is a little sleepy. If you remember, on the day we recorded Tim, he was struggling with this."

"I know, we had to cut the crap out of it. It was a real Frankenstein job."

"Exactly. And by the way, your edits were brilliant. Anyway, if Uncle Joel could put a music bed under him that's a little more upbeat, but not corny, retail upbeat, more hip upbeat, I think that will do the trick."

"Okay, I'll tell him."

"And then, when Tim's doing that piece where he is the contractor, the sound effects are a little too complicated. There's a jackhammer in the background that I don't think we need. It's annoying. I like that, uh, what's it called? A Skil saw?"

Chuck nods.

"Yeah, I like that buzzing in the background, and maybe Joel could just add a few guys hammering as well. Do you agree?"

"I absolutely do," Chuck says. "What about Tim's animation piece? Did you like what Joel did? I'm thinking we could still go a bit more traditional Looney Tunes-style with the music."

"You know, I didn't think of that. You're absolutely right, because not only will it lift that piece, but also the contrast as we move to his Pacific Health spot will be great. Let's have Joel change that too."

"I'm on it, darlin'."

I stick out my hand formally, and drop my voice a couple of octaves. "It's been a pleasure doing business with you, sir."

Chuck points at the clock to show me that we've finished right on time.

"Yeah, yeah, I know, no rest for the wicked." I laugh somewhat exhausted.

"Jensen is here for his 2:30 private," Vicki says, popping her head in. "And don't forget you have to call Nancy."

"Oh, shoot! That's right."

Lucky for me, I just get her voicemail. "It's me. Sorry I'm just calling now—it's the usual crazy. Vicki told me about Jan Wahl, but I can't do it. I'm going to be out of town. We should talk. How about our usual 8:30 a.m. phone chat tomorrow morning? Hope you're having a great day. Bye."

I hang up the phone just as Jensen enters, all full of energy with a big smile on his face. I can match the smile, but I have to dig deep to find the enthusiasm that he deserves.

2:30 p.m.

"Hi, honey bunny. You ready to get going? Did you bring in some of your home auditions for me to listen to?"

"I did," Jensen says, "and I have the scripts for you so that you can see what they were looking for. I'm actually feeling better about my auditions, even though I haven't booked anything yet."

"Jensen, that is such a fantastic attitude to have. I am so proud of you. You keep your head screwed on like that and you will eventually start booking like crazy!" I pop his memory stick into the computer and his voice comes through the speakers. We listen.

3:30 p.m.

I'm walking Jensen out. "Okay, so tell me what you're going to write on that Post-it note and stick right on your copy stand?"

He chuckles and smiles mischievously. "I'm going to write, 'I'm a genius voice actor.'"

"Well, you are, but that's not what we talked about."

"I know. I'm going to write 'Heart not Head,' to remind myself to work from the inside out, not the outside in."

"Very good! And I'll see you next week in class."

I give him a hug and a push out the door—then turn to Bret—who is, finally, my last private of the day.

"Ah, my last little ray of sunshine. Hello, beautiful Bret! How's life over in the East Bay? What's that tiny little place you work for? Pixar?"

She giggles. "Yeah, they've got me really busy with a couple of new projects, but it's okay. I love my job."

"I know you do, and you're brilliant at it. Oh, and thanks for arranging that incredible Pixar field trip for all of us. The students loved it, I loved it, and the casting lecture that Kevin did was informative, interesting, and fun. That was one great evening."

"Yeah, it worked out really well. I was pleased to do it."

"Okay, well, let's now focus on what's soon to be your other job—voice-over! Let's set you up in the booth."

4:35 p.m.

"All right, love, we're done for today. I want you to walk out of here floating on air, because you have certainly reached a new level in your acting." As I walk over to open the booth door and Bret collects her things, I sense that our hour is not over.

"Samantha, do you think I'm ready to make my demo yet? I really want to get an agent and start auditioning."

I pause, relieved by the fact that I don't have to give her a "red light" but rather a "yellow" one.

"I think we're getting close," I say cautiously. "But remember, when your agent sends you auditions to record from home, I'm not going to be there telling you what to do. We still need to strengthen your self-direction skills, because you obviously don't want to send auditions that suck to your agent, let alone producers. For your next private, I want you to record the scripts we didn't do today and bring them in, so we can listen to them together. Does that sound good?"

"Yeah, I know you're right. I'm just getting a little anxious."

"Have faith! You've gotten this far. Remember the tears you used to shed in the booth because you couldn't really act? Now look at you. It will happen. Trust me! Remember this date, because a year from now, you will have a commercial demo, a character demo, and an agent, and you will be booking jobs. So, the process between now and then is just part of this wonderful journey that you're on."

Bret smiles and gives me a kiss. "I love you, Samantha Paris."

I take her sweet face in my hands. "I love you too, honey. It's all going to happen. You know I won't let you down."

It's 4:45 p.m., and I'm done for the day. As I collect my things, I'm so relieved that I don't have to teach a three-hour class tonight. I go out into the office and see that the rain has finally stopped and the sun is shining. I turn to Chuck. "When did Vicki leave?"

"I think it was 2:30-ish. She had a session down in Sunnyvale."

"Mind if I leave? I'm knackered."

He looks up and smiles at me. "I don't know what the hell 'knackered' means, but you're the boss."

I cross over to him and give him a kiss on the head. "I take that as a 'yes,'" I say, "and by the way, 'knackered' is British for 'exhausted.' I'll see you tomorrow." I open the front door.

"Oh, my gosh, Chuck, you have to come see this."

He joins me. We're looking at a rainbow, big, bright, and colorful, arching over the bay. We gaze at it for a long moment, together in silence, and then Chuck takes my hand.

"Well, would you looky there," he says in an Irish brogue (one of his specialties). "Make a wish, Paris."

"I'm on it, darlin'," I reply. He puts his arm around my shoulder and gives me a squeeze.

"You know everything is going to be okay, Sam. You haven't a thing to worry about. I really believe that."

I gaze up at him. "I kinda believe that too. Thanks, Chuckie, for everything."

5:00 p.m.

SAUSALITO, CALIFORNIA

The rainbow follows me along Bridgeway, Sausalito's bayside main street. I start singing softly,

> "Someday I'll wish upon a star
> And wake up where the clouds are far behind me . . .
> Birds fly over the rainbow
> Why then, oh why can't I?"

I sigh. Sadly, the hopeful mood I shared with Chuck moments ago, has immediately dissipated. I identify with that song so much. I have always felt troubled, empty, and alone. As I turn the key and enter my apartment, those feelings are solidified once again. I'm greeted by a damp smell, which tells me my first order of business is to call the landlord and the second is to start the laundry. The thought of rewashing and ironing what were already perfectly clean clothes depresses me. I turn on the heat and open my laptop to check my e-mails. I'm happy to see that there are only two things to handle: the Facebook posts that Chuck e-mailed for my review and a contract to be signed from Sparkling Ocean.

First, I print, sign, and fax. Then I look at the posts. One is about a student winning an audiobook award, another is about a student signing with Stars Talent Agency and booking her first audition; both with cute pics. The third is all text and all about us:

"Voicetrax has long been chuffed about the students who train with us, become wildly successful here in the Bay Area, and then decide to make the move south to LA. And why wouldn't we be? The list includes talents like Roger Jackson (the villain in

Scream and animation/video game extraordinaire), Dionne Quan (*Rugrats*), Chopper Bernet (NBC and MSNBC promos, and the voice of *The Ellen Show*) and Dave Fennoy (narrating for National Geographic programs, the Discovery Channel, and voicing characters for video games, such as *Star Wars* and *Lara Croft Tomb Raider*). And to this list, we add our recent T.O.P. Voice winner, who will be tearing up the airwaves in LA."

I stop reading, seeing that I'm only halfway through it, and make a mental note to tell Chuck this one is too long, and we are bragging way too much. I mean, I am proud of these guys. No question about it. Their success fuels me to work even harder. But there are other meaningful forms of success that aren't just found in booking gigs. Philip has found voice-over to be his drug of choice, giving up cigarettes after twenty years of smoking. And, after a lifetime of paralyzing shyness, Amy aced her job interview last week. Yeah, we gotta rethink these posts. I do want people to think of voice-over through a wider lens.

I go into the bedroom to inspect the damage to my clothes. As I begin to sort through what needs to be washed and what will go to the dry cleaners, my thoughts suddenly turn to Johnny Truffa again.

Maybe it's the musty damp smell. This is now the third time in less than a month that he has unwelcomingly invaded my psyche. For years, I've done everything in my power to *not* think of him, but, unfortunately, he took up permanent residence in my subconsciousness long ago. I should charge the asshole rent. I would give anything to be able to evict him.

I decide it's time for a glass of wine, the fake fireplace, and a little bit of tennis. It's the big BNP Paribas Open tournament down in the desert. I used to go to it every year when I had my second school down there.

I turn on the TV, hoping it's Rafa playing or my second favorite, Roger Federer. I know they both got through their second rounds, but I missed watching the third.

"Oh, man," I whine. It's Novak Djokovic versus Marcos Baghdatis. I cannot stand Djokovic. He's really full of himself and a poor sport, not at all a sportsman, like Rafa, Roger, or my other true favorite, Andre Agassi.

"Come on, Baghdatis. Put it away!" I yell.

Shit. Right in the net.

"It's okay, buddy," I say to the screen. "It's your serve now, you can do it. Throw an ace."

Bam! Shit. Right in the net. I always feel like Djokovic is so damn lucky.

"Okay, you can do it. Second serve. Come on! Give me a second-serve ace."

Pow! An ace! "You heard me. Thank you!" Hoping the neighbors won't hear, I let out a cheer. I get way too carried away watching tennis. But hey, getting carried away is what I need tonight.

Match over, I grab my blanket and my wineglass, and move out to my little patio, still happy with Baghdatis' success. The rainbow of this afternoon has been replaced with a sea of light, sparkling pinpoints of millions of stars, putting the lights of Sausalito to shame.

There's nothing like success to erase depression. I have first-hand knowledge about that. In the past, no matter what my woe in life, every time my agents phoned me about a new booking, my heart soared, and my troubles would magically disappear. Or so they would momentarily. When I got my *first* booking, I thought I had died and gone to heaven. I sip my wine, which is heavenly too, remembering that day.

1977

I can see the building on Melrose, the interior of the lobby and the studio. It was all wood paneling. So 1970s. I can't remember for the life of me what I was wearing, but maybe that's a good thing. It was most likely bell-bottoms.

When I got the news, it was honestly the happiest day of my life. I was to record a commercial for Burger Chef, and I hadn't even auditioned for it. The producer, Shannon Silverman, had attended Johnny's voice-over class, and I guess was impressed enough to give me my big break.

The session was at Buzzy's Recording studio at the corner of Melrose Avenue and Orange Drive. My voice-over classmate, Ken, offered to be my parental guardian for the afternoon. I think he was twenty-three. I was only seventeen at the time, and until you turned eighteen, you had to have a parent or guardian—someone over the age of twenty-one—with you on set at all times. The rule applied whether you were doing a movie, a TV show, or a simple voice-over commercial that would probably only take half an hour.

My parents refused to go with me. They said, "If you want to have this career, you're going to have to do it on your own."

"I refuse to be a stage mother," my mother added. She actually refused to be a mother at all. Or at least a loving one.

So off Ken and I went.

I wasn't nervous, just really excited. When we walked into the studio and I saw my fellow actors, I couldn't believe my eyes. It was Joan Gerber and Lennie Weinrib, the two voice-over gods I had heard on the day of my first class. They were playing the "mom and dad" to my "kid." With a slight acknowledgment from both of them, I took the copy Ms. Silverman handed me and headed into the booth. *Now* I was nervous.

I skimmed the copy to find my lines, quickly discovering that I only had to say four words, thank God. The session began, and all I cared about was not blowing it. I was too nervous to let go and surrender to the scene, to actually *listen* to my fellow actors. I was following the script with my eyes, wondering how I was going to say my one line. When the moment of truth finally came, I blurted out, "I like two pickles!" with such conviction, such profound love and joy for Burger Chef's finest two pickles on the planet.

Before I knew it, the take was over and we were asked to do another one "just for fun." At least, that was the direction for Lennie and Joan.

"Bobbi, can you back off just a little from your love for the pickles?"

I was so embarrassed and praying my face didn't look as red as it felt. "You got it," I said, vowing to listen to my "mom and dad" this time.

"This is Burger Chef, take two," said the engineer. I had never even heard him slate take one, so I knew I was doing better already. This time I nailed "I like two pickles" and everyone was pleased. The take finished, and we were done. My first job was over in all of fifteen minutes. Since I was five, I had dreamed of that magical moment. My first fifteen minutes of fame.

I was seventeen. What a lifetime ago! What nobody knew was that I already had a history with pickles. As a kid, pickles tormented me. After my first dance recital at age five, my father put me on diet pills. I was too chubby in my "Pink Poodle" costume, or at least that's what he told my mom.

"She's never going to make it in Hollywood if she's chubby," he said to her.

While all the other kids got to snack on Twinkies and my personal favorite, the pink Sno Balls, my mother would just wrap a napkin around a big dill pickle for me. I made that pickle last for hours. I had to. I was always hungry. Those diet pills didn't seem to curb my appetite. They just made me anxious, and I often had a hard time sleeping.

Now sadly, forty-five years later, nothing has changed.

Will I ever feel safe and at peace enough to breathe and to actually sleep?

10:00 p.m.

SAUSALITO, CALIFORNIA

The fog has moved in and the stars are gone. It's cold. I've been transfixed by the thought that if success erases depression, then why have I been in a constant state of sadness for all these years? Not having the answer to that, I scoop up my stuff and head inside.

The voices are back. *"What did you have for lunch today?"* Johnny's voice haunts me again. *"You know you gotta stay skinny, Bobbi. You'll never work and become a famous actress if you don't."*

Then Andre's voice criticizing me about my thighs. At 122 pounds, my size two blue jeans weren't good enough. *"I know you go to the gym, but you're not working your legs hard enough."*

Ah, yes, the men in my life. I make my way to the kitchen to quiet my growling stomach. Sadly, my only choices are soup or cereal. Bare cupboards can make me feel so lonely. I am definitely single and now living my worst nightmare: being alone.

What have I fucking done? My internal voice screams, as I put my soup pot in the dishwasher. *It was all so simple years ago.*

A lump starts to form in my throat as I crawl into bed. Nanna's voice tucks me in. *Sugar, just close your eyes. There's no need to worry. Close your eyes and sleep.*

I try, but my chant as a little girl begins. *When you die, you sleep forever.* I cringe at the thought. I take in a deep, relaxing breath and think about that little girl who used to be me. And Nanna, of course, who loved that little girl in a way that no one else ever has. It's been twenty-five years since her death, and I have yet to find anyone who comes even close to what she meant to me.

I miss you, Nanna. Where are you? I miss you so much.

I wrap my arms around my pillow and try to remember not feeling so alone. When I was little, I used to be afraid she would die and leave me alone with the world.

"Sugar, don't worry like that," she always used to say. "Nanna loves you and she's not going anywhere. I will never leave you."

"But you did," I whisper, as I cry myself to sleep. "Nanna, you did."

Bobbi Block, 1977

VAN NUYS, CALIFORNIA

"Hey, I know your parents don't have much money, so if you become my assistant, you can take all my classes for free, rather than just the one on Saturdays. His offer is music to my ears, because I desperately want to begin my career as a professional actress with an agent and everything. Unfortunately, I will later learn that his lessons are anything *but* free.

The first thing I discover is that I am no longer thinking for myself. It's weird because with my parents never "present," I was always thinking independently.

"You'll never make it in this business without me telling you what to do every step of the way," Johnny would say. Did Johnny actually *really care?* He seemed so much more passionate than my parents about my well-being and about helping me realize my dream. It felt good believing him, even though I didn't exactly like what he was always saying. Soon I discover that he has a terrible temper.

"You're nothing without me, Bobbi," he says tightening his grip on my arm. He shakes me violently, reminding me of my mother. "If you leave, you will have no career."

Before long, I am believing him. I'm trapped between what I'm hoping to be true, and the familiar feeling of being beaten down. One day he's holding me up in front of the class as the best, a rare talent. The next, he screams at me in front of the other students when I flub a line.

I have now become his "protégé." Sadly, he lures me into having sex with him. He convinces me that he will be much gentler than a young boy my age. He says when a girl loses her virginity, it's painful. My mother neglected to talk to me about sex and boys, so I had no way of knowing. He also has me totally brainwashed that he loves me and will always take care of me. I do feel safer and much happier with him than when I am at home.

So, I give in. And it's awful. I feel absolutely horrible, and I know it is wrong, but somehow, I want to believe everything he tells me. That he loves me, he will care for me and, yes, that someday I will become a famous actress. I go to school each day secretly feeling dirty. I don't have a "boyfriend" and I know people are wondering why, but there is no way I can tell a single soul.

I long to turn to Nanna, the one person who I know really loves me with all her heart. But she lives far away, and if I tell her what is going on, she won't understand. She will be disappointed in me, and I can't risk losing the one person I trust who taught me to believe in myself, work hard, and always do the right thing. That's what kills me. I know that what I am doing is wrong.

Am I his student? His assistant? His protégé? His girlfriend? I'm so confused.

1978

HOLLYWOOD, CALIFORNIA

I'm a little smarter now, but still trapped. Getting jobs, finishing high school, and still working for Johnny Truffa.

And he's still keeping tabs on everything I do.

"How'd that TV shoot go?" he asks. I'd gotten a small reoccurring role on a TV series, *James at 15*. "Did you play it like I taught you?"

"Sure, Johnny," I fib. The only thing he'd taught me was not to blink too much on TV. "I noticed one thing, though. Lance Kerwin had his personal acting coach on the set."

"Who the hell is Lance Kerwin?"

"He's the star. He's James. Anyway, it got me thinking that maybe I should have an acting coach. I mean, you're the only teacher I've ever had. Don't you think it would be a good idea for me to go to acting school?"

"Look, you're already working," Johnny says. "You're on this James-whatever series, you've shot what? four national on-camera commercials? And how many commercial voice-over jobs have you done?"

"I don't know. Fifteen? Maybe twenty?

"Right. And I also got you that gig on the Heartbeat Theater radio drama. What makes you think you need an acting coach?"

I mull it over, choosing my words carefully. "Look, I know you have always said I was a natural, but there's stuff I definitely don't know how to do. Like last week, when we were shooting a school scene, there were certain movements I made on certain lines in the master shot. Then, when it came time for my close-up, I didn't make those same moves, and the continuity lady called me on it."

"That doesn't have anything to do with acting. Those are just technical things you'll pick up along the way."

"Everyone else seems to know that stuff already. I was embarrassed. I really want to go to acting school and I can afford it. I just don't know who to go to."

Johnny glares at me, then shrugs. "Boy, you just don't quit, do you? Nothing is ever enough! All right Bobbi, if you want an acting coach, the finest one in all of Hollywood is Nina Foch. You'll have to audition for her to get in. I'll set it up."

And after several weeks and several reminders, he does. The school bell sounds, and I show up at her studio just in time. I've been rehearsing my audition monologue for a week. I am ready.

Nina Foch is an old lady with cold eyes. "You're next," she says.

"Hi, my name is Bobbi Block, and I'm going to do Mary from *The Children's Hour* by Lillian Hellman."

Nina nods, flips my black-and-white headshot over to look at my résumé, but doesn't say anything, so I take a deep breath and begin the monologue, exactly as I have rehearsed it.

"Young lady," Nina says, raising her hand and motioning me to stop just ten seconds in, "that's quite enough, thank you. You don't have it. I can't help you. You have not only wasted my time, but you are wasting your own time. You have absolutely no talent, and I suggest you do yourself and the world a favor and find another profession."

She calls in the next auditionee, and I retreat to the bathroom, hot tears running down my cheeks. She is just one more person from an already long list of people beating me down. I throw cold water on my face, and pray my eyes will look less red and puffy when I emerge.

I look at my reflection in the mirror. "You are wrong, Nina Foch. You don't know who you are dealing with or what you are talking about. I am going to prove you wrong. Just you watch."

I punch the mirror so hard, my knuckles start to bleed. I hide them on my way out.

Johnny asks me how it went, and like a fool I tell him. "Told you so," he says. "I'm the teacher you need."

I'm beginning to realize he's not.

As I live out the finale of my teenage years under Johnny's influence, he personifies everything I swear to myself I will never become: someone whose life is one big lie, who masquerades as a winner but is nothing but a loser.

Johnny had been a child actor. In class, he is always talking about this ONE movie he did, which of course I never heard of, considering he is twenty-five years older than me.

In the early 1960s, Johnny had made it big in Tampa, Florida, on the radio waves as a disc jockey. He was known as the Purple Banana Basher. "Mr. Weasley" was a character voice he did that became his alter ego. Johnny loves to tell me how both Johnny Truffa and Mr. Weasley were superstars.

"Do you know who I am?" he yells, when I don't follow his instructions to the letter.

*You mean, do I know who you **were**?* Of course, I always keep my mouth shut.

"I was one of the biggest DJs of all time," he crows. "As big as your grandfather."

On the inside, I laugh hard at that one. My grandfather, Martin Block, happened to be the first disc jockey in US history. His show, *Make Believe Ballroom*, on WNEW in New York City (not in Tampa, Johnny, I'm careful not to say), launched the careers of countless singers, including legends like Frank Sinatra and Dinah Shore.

I'm the only one who knows Johnny's deepest, darkest secret.

That he's a has-been. He's constantly making up stories to tell his students about his voice-over career.

"I just came from this booking . . ." he'd say. I would roll my eyes, knowing it was all bullshit. He actually had spent all day on his boat fishing in Catalina.

The only voice-over jobs he booked had been several years ago, long before I was even in the picture. He was the voice of some animated character for some macaroni brand, but I always forgot which one. The residuals from those commercials bought him his boat—and, with the aid of an investor, the new studio he's building, so he can hustle more students and overcharge them with his "sign up here and get rich quick" false promises.

Yes, Johnny has taught me a lot—about what true phoniness is.

I have gotten somewhat more successful at avoiding him when I can. My days are filled with school, auditions, and bookings. I rarely work for him during his two weekly evening classes, but I still help out with his Saturday workshops.

One day, however, after school, the Purple Banana Basher is hunched over the wheel of his big, blue convertible Cadillac, waiting for me. Johnny wants to show me the progress on his new studio. I figure I might as well go along. My eighteenth birthday is in two days and high school graduation is in three. Freedom is so close I can taste it.

"I'm gonna call the new school, J.T.'s Voice-over Emporium," he boasts proudly, as I slide into the front seat. "Glad to see you all smiles today."

"I'm looking forward to being on my own," I say. "I'm going apartment hunting this weekend."

"Don't you think you're a little young to be living by yourself?"

"Since when have you become my parents?" I shoot back, laced with both sarcasm and mild disgust for all three of them.

"It's expensive. You'll have to furnish the place, and it's a lot of responsibility."

"I'm just going to see what's out there. You know I hate living at home." I say. Then, to change the subject, "How's the new studio looking?"

"You'll see," he says, lighting a cigarette. "But we won't be staying long, because I want to get the spots done that you'll be recording over at Wally Heider's before the workshop starts."

"What spots?" I ask, confused.

"Oh, maybe I didn't tell you. You're recording a 30- and a 60-second spot for the school. To advertise J.T.'s Voice-over Emporium."

"Oh." No longer all smiles, I sink lower in my seat and stare out the window.

The new place is massive. There are workmen everywhere. Johnny leaves me to speak with an electrician. I turn around slowly, hardly able to believe it. It was once a screening room at Sunset Gower Studios, but now the stage has been torn down to the ground and the recording booth is being built in its place.

Why does Johnny need something so big? Just how many students does he think he can get? Does he think he's going to teach fifty people at a time?

Behind all the theater seats, still wrapped in plastic, is a long row of tiny boxy rooms.

"What do you think?" Johnny asks, swaggering toward me with a grin.

"I think this is really huge and this all looks really expensive," I say with my eyes bulging. "And what are these for?" I ask, pointing to the boxy little rooms.

"Those are for the closers."

"Closers?" I ask.

"We're going to flood the airwaves with your spots, and then I'm going to have people set up in these rooms, answering phones, closing deals, signing 'em up, and hauling 'em in. We're going to pack this room three nights a week and Saturdays too."

"With students?" I ask. "So many? How are they all going to get enough practice time behind the mic? How will they learn?"

Johnny gives me a funny smirk and walks away.

I get it. The students won't learn, and he doesn't care, so long as he gets their money. That's all he cares about. I feel sick to my stomach.

As the construction carries on in front of me, and Johnny is a healthy distance away, I make a vow just loud enough to keep it to myself: **"I swear on my life that I will never lower myself to teaching. I will always be a working actress. I will never become some loser, former actress who has to teach. I will never ever become a loser like you."**

Tuesday, 6:30 a.m., March 16, 2010
SAUSALITO, CALIFORNIA

Ugh.

I wake up with a horrible neckache. I stare at the ceiling, as I cannot turn my head. I know I slept wrong, because I dreamt of Johnny again. I remember it was the last time I saw him, and I was barely twenty. It was so vivid, like it was happening in real time.

I saw myself in my first real acting class, finishing my monologue. My teacher was faceless, and I can't remember his name, but I remember finishing my scene. After thunderous applause from my fellow classmates, the teacher rendered himself speechless. Actually, I was too, it was that good, and the best part was that I had it on tape. I was on such a big high and so excited that I had to show it to Johnny before going home to my apartment.

Having a key, I let myself in when I found the back door locked. I heard the TV on in the living room and Johnny was talking, but to who? Then I heard his new thirty-year-old assistant's voice. It was Kelli. I stood frozen in the kitchen. I wanted to run, but something told me to enter the room, so I did.

There they were, naked, lying on the same bean bag chairs Johnny and I always laid on, draped with the same blanket, and watching Johnny's favorite movie, *The Umbrellas of Cherbourg.* My heart was racing, but I managed to control myself and simply cleared my throat to get his attention. He was startled, jumped to his feet, and I immediately saw in his eyes the pathetic lie he was going to try to whip up. Just like the ones he would whip up to his students. I saved him the trouble.

"I just came from my acting class, and I was so excited I wanted to show you this video." I said it with such calm, as I knew I was in shock.

Then Kelli got up, as I started to make my way back to the kitchen and out the back door. I heard her yelling, "It's not what you think, Bobbi. We're just friends. You don't understand."

But I did understand. I felt sick at my stomach and relieved at the same time. I rushed out the door, hopped in my car and drove off. I thought of nothing except trying to stay focused through my tears, keeping my eyes on the road.

I turned the key to my apartment, closed the door behind me, and sank to the ground. Another rejection. I couldn't believe how gullible and naïve I had been. Believing that he cared. That he loved me. I felt dirtier than ever. I couldn't get undressed fast enough and entered the shower. I kept scrubbing myself and scrubbing until I started to bleed. And then I woke up.

I close my eyes and drink in a deep cleansing breath, knowing fully why I dreamt that. I felt so lost and alone then. Much like now. But the worst part, back then, was that I was so incredibly ashamed and couldn't tell anybody. I had to work through that horrible pain alone. It wasn't just my neglectful parents who sent me on a path of keeping everything to myself. I had my one and only "mentor" to also thank.

Now, at age fifty, I'm slightly better. I do share things, but only to a point. I remember Andre once telling me that all of us really are all alone. We come into the world alone, and we go out the same way. *ALONE.* So, our individual journeys are just that. I chew on that thought for a while, and then struggle to look at the clock.

It's 7:15. I try to ease the pain in my heart and my neck, as I gingerly roll out of bed. "Deal with it, Sammy" I say out loud, and then begin moving like a robot tottering down the hall.

"Shower, coffee, makeup, hair." I am in full robot mode and repeat. Grinding the coffee beans, I ponder what Andre might chant this morning. "Ollie pee, coffee, paper, crossword, sunshine, sculpting, and pot." I roll my eyes. No need to aggravate myself so early in the day.

"Coffee on!" My "about face" has me heading toward the shower contemplating the day ahead of me. I have six private lessons, followed by class tonight—nine hours of teaching, plus whatever else the day brings when one owns a business. Then I remember my 8:30 a.m. phone call with Nancy.

8:30 a.m.

Andre always used to say, "I've shit, showered, and shaved, and I'm ready to go." It must be a guy thing. I look in the mirror, and think, the good news is, my hair looks great. The bad news is that

I'm beginning to look like my mother.

Fuck. That's scary. I turn away from the mirror. I grab some more coffee and sit on the sofa to face my new best friend, the fake fireplace. I dial Nancy.

"Hey, Sammy. How are you?" comes Nancy's familiar voice through the phone.

"'Troubled,' I believe, is the word that comes to mind."

"I'm sorry, honey. Do you need to talk? How about we meet for coffee?"

"I would love to," I tell her, even though it's not the truth. What I'm feeling is not anything I would want to share with anybody. "But my day is too tight. It's nothing new. Long days, long nights. Hearing your voice is making me happy, though." That last sentence, spoken in the vocal color of "sunny yellow," was 100 percent bullshit, and Nancy knows it.

"That's my Sammy. Always wanting to put on a brave face. Well, I have some good news as a reward."

"If you mean Jan Wahl, then I have some bad news. "I'm going out of town, so I can't do the show. I'm not even sure I *want* to do it."

"Where are you going? Is it a vacation, I hope?"

"I'm actually not sure what it is. Karen arranged for me to be a guest speaker on a Sparkling Ocean cruise."

"Oh, Sammy, that's marvelous! They will love you, and this is such a great opportunity. Just think, you'll be sharing your message with people from all over the world."

I let out a tired laugh. "I love how positive you are about this, but I have my reservations. It's going to be mostly a bunch of old, retired people onboard. Why would they want to learn about voice-over?"

"Samantha, you know as well as I do that it's not all old people onboard. Think of the age span of your students. You've got twelve year olds in your classes, in addition to people who are nearly ninety."

"Okay, fair enough. But why would some Canadian, British, or Chinese person want to learn about voice-over?"

"Voice-over affects every single living soul on this planet. Everyone hears commercials, watches cartoons, listens to audiobooks—"

"Not pygmies, I bet." I just had to throw that in.

"Sammy . . ." Nancy continues patiently. "Everybody is affected by voice-over and besides, you teach so much more than voice-over."

I groan, as usual.

"You still don't get it, do you? When are you going to realize that what you teach—your message—goes way beyond voice acting? You don't think Karen knows that? She's watched you teach."

"I know, I know," I say, repeating what she and the rest of my staff always say, "I'm the only person who refuses to drink my own Kool-Aid."

"You've created one heck of a mixture. You should try it sometime," she teases me.

"I told you I woke up on the wrong side of the bed. I'm sorry, Nancy." I glance at my watch, knowing I have to wrap up this conversation and get to work. "Can we talk about Jan Wahl?"

"Of course. You're thinking you don't want to do it?"

"I guess I'll do it, because you went to a lot of trouble to get me on. It's just that when I go on TV, I'm always asked the same dumb questions." I change up my voice to imitate a dorky reporter, squeaking, "So, do you have to have a deep voice to get into voice-over? Can anyone make money at it? Do a funny voice for us, Samantha!"

"If you like, when I call to reschedule you, I will really drive home the point that you want to talk about what we pitched."

"It *is* a super-sexy angle, and it's so true. With everyone texting, tweeting, and e-mailing, nobody talks to one another anymore. Can you imagine the five year olds of today's world? What are they going to do when they have to go to a job interview and actually sit and talk face-to-face with someone? Real, interpersonal communication is becoming a thing of the past!"

"I totally agree, and I will make sure that's what you talk about."

"Thanks. And please don't think I don't appreciate everything you do for me. Meanwhile, I gotta scoot to work. I love you and we'll talk soon."

"I love you too, honey. Have a super day."

We hang up and I shake my head.

Nancy has always been one big bundle of love and positivity. She is always so damn positive that I wonder if it's real. I mean, I know it is—that's *her*. But how does she fucking *do* that?

I ponder that briefly, *very* briefly, then grab my keys and head for work.

4:45 p.m.
VOICETRAX

My last private. "James, all you need to do now is smooth out your delivery and pick up the pace, which actually go hand in hand. If you pick up the pace, your delivery will have no choice but to be smoother. It's a thirty-second spot, and you're coming in at thirty-three. You're rolling."

As James starts reading once again, I know within the first three seconds that he's got it. When he finishes, he immediately does a fist pump before my voice comes over the talkback. I hear a "yeah, baby" and immediately I concur.

"'Yeah, baby' is right. That was absolute perfection and I'm so proud of you. What's even better is that you knew it was good without me telling you or having to hear it back. Great job! Now let's look at the promo script."

"Actually, Samantha, I know we only have about ten minutes left, and I'd like to spend this time talking, if it's okay with you." He gathers up his stuff and comes out of the booth. "Man, that felt so good! I am so pumped for the T.O.P Voice competition. I want to win that thing! I want to talk to you about Los Angeles. I want to move there, and I'm hoping you could make me my demo and then help me get an agent."

"Wow," I say, taken aback. "What's with this wanting to *win* T.O.P Voice? You know this is, first and foremost, a class, and your goal should be to grow from the experience."

"Yeah, yeah, I know all that. But there is going to be a winner, and I want that winner to be me!"

"And if it isn't you, then what?" I ask, knowing he won't have an answer. "Yes, somebody is going to be selected to go to LA and audition at DPN for a week. But there are so many valuable lessons to be learned during the experience, and if you're only thinking about winning, you're going to miss out."

"How so?" he asks, even though he's not really interested in the answer.

"You'll miss out on really learning what you are most marketable for, instead of thinking you can do it all. And you will learn to compete graciously."

"Compete graciously?" He looks at me like I'm nuts and continues. "Athletes don't compete graciously. If they did, they would never win."

Internally I smile, knowing that Roger Federer and Rafa Nadal are two iconic athletes who have learned the very thing I am trying to teach James.

"Honey, you are about to enter a profession where you will be competing nearly every day of your professional career. I am training you now to ultimately be respected by your peers."

I can see the disappointment written on his face.

"James, this is an opportunity to hear from two of the biggest agents in the industry where you stack up at this point, and what steps they feel you need to take to become truly professional. This is also supposed to be a class where you learn to perform under pressure and perhaps deal with some intense nerves. Some of my most brilliant students have choked in this class."

James slowly shakes his head. "Do you think I'm going to choke? Is that why you're telling me this?"

I gaze at him and recall my own grit and determination in the early days of my career. Nothing, and I mean *nothing*, mattered more to me than winning every audition. Because of it, I choked more times than I care to admit.

The fact is, I don't *think* he's going to choke, I *know* he is; but I dodge that bullet. I also know a couple of other things. He made it to the finals not because of his true skill level, but because he was fortunate enough to be born with an amazing voice. When you combine mediocre skills with a great voice, sometimes you reap rewards. Yet the rewards are never long term. If one wants a successful full-time career, which I know James wants, he's got a lot more work ahead of him.

There are other students in the T.O.P Voice class that will eat him just for an appetizer, people who have worked harder and far longer than he. I have students who have taken the class before, choked, been devastated, got back on the horse, and competed the next year. I've also had some who have competed year after year after year. Those are the students I really admire. The ones who recognize that there is always a lesson to be learned. They are not afraid of "failing," because they understand that they are not failing, but learning and growing, truly opening up to the journey that is their life. They don't fight it, they go with it.

"I don't know whether you will choke or not, but it won't matter to me. I'm already proud of you, no matter what, and I know you will ultimately achieve your dream. Have patience, James, and drink in the amazing experience you are about to have. Enjoy the love and support you're going to get from your classmates and perhaps consider giving a little of that back to them as well. If you're open to the lessons the universe is going to provide that day, you will have won, whether or not you're actually selected."

Those are the students I really admire. The ones who recognize that there is always a lesson to be learned. They are not afraid of "failing," because they understand that they are not failing, but learning and growing, truly opening up to the journey that is their life. They don't fight it, they go with it.

James is gathering his stuff to leave.

"Hey, are you okay?" I ask, hoping he knows I really do care.

"Yeah." He smiles ruefully. "I'm okay. Thanks for bringing me back down to this planet. You're actually telling me what my parents have been telling me, except you seem to say it in a way I can hear it."

"Maybe it's because you and I are so much alike, James. I was exactly like you at your age. Sometimes us old farts know a thing or two."

He laughs.

"Oh! You mentioned LA?" I bring up that last bit, knowing he no longer needs to talk about it, but I want him to know I was listening.

"Yeah, I'm thinking about moving there, but just from this conversation, I know it's kind of silly."

I smile, cross over to hug him, and take his face in my hands. "It's not silly, James, not at all. It's just a bit premature. Now scoot! I've got to get ready for my class. See you at T.O.P Voice."

Chuck, rushing by, stops. "Hey, darlin'," he says. "I'm going to get a coffee. You want anything?"

"Nah," I say, waving my hand. "I'm going to stick with my water, but if you get a cookie, you know I'll pinch a quarter of it."

"Well, then, just what kind of cookie do I want?"

"You want either a peanut butter or chocolate chip cookie today," I say with a wink.

"Done." He tips his hat, even though he's not wearing one. "I'm so glad I don't have to think. I'll be right back."

On my desk, I see that Vicki has left me a stack of checks to sign with my favorite green pen. One guest instructor check after another—the amounts are staggering. I hear Chris' voice in my head. *Samantha, numbers are fascinating. They tell a story.*

If the numbers tell a story, this one is epic. The newly born CEO in me vows to address this issue when I return from the cruise. Surely, we can cut back expenses without allowing the quality of the instruction to go down.

I quickly turn on my computer to check my e-mails, and I'm relieved to see there are only two. The first is from my business lawyer, Roger, a former Voicetrax student who now juggles voice-over and law. I had sent Roger my thoughts on what I felt my divorce settlement should be and asked him to write up something simple.

"Please don't include a lot of legal wah, wah, wah. I want it to read as loving as possible." I had even written in my rough agreement that I would make lamb chops for Andre once a month, should he want them. I decide to read Roger's message in greater detail once I'm home.

The second e-mail is a student thank-you note forwarded to me from Voicetrax, because my personal e-mail address is private. I see it's from Louisa and place it in my electronic "Thank You" folder because I'm out of time.

I grab all of the day's private lesson copy to file away and pinch a quarter of Chuck's cookie. "Peanut butter, yum." I kiss his head. "I'll be across the way prepping for tonight's class if you need me."

As I lock up studio C and cross back through the courtyard, Nick Stratton has his nose buried in his phone and nearly crashes into me.

"Funny bumping into you, Nick. Literally! You remind me of a teenage girl, glued to her phone."

"Actually, I was just texting my teenage daughter," he admits.

"Chuck told me you did a darn good job in 'Creating Characters' last weekend."

"I kind of surprised myself, because I didn't think I could do different voices. When I got home, my son was playing a video game, and I started goofing around with him, changing up my voice. I was becoming the characters in his game."

"How'd that go over? Is he a teenager too?"

"He's twelve. He kind of dug it. It had been quite a while since we just hung out together, so it was great."

"Oh, I'm glad! Well, remember, you have to put that phone away in a few minutes, as I'm about to start class."

"Don't we still have ten minutes?"

"Technically speaking, yes, but I always start early if students are here. You know, N.T.L.T.P.!"

Looking a little puzzled, he puts away his phone and follows. Class folder in hand, I enter the lobby of the studio. Five of the twelve students have arrived. I plop the first script down on the coffee table.

"Empty"

Radio :60

CROWD: Powers presents, "The Worst Monday Ever."

SPX: Elevator chiming, doors opening.

MAN: Good morning, everyone. (voice echoing)

MAN: (echo) Hello? Helloooo? Paula?

PAULA: Morning, Mr. Peterson.

MAN: Where is everybody?

PAULA: Cheryl's in labor, Michael and Diane eloped to Italy, and the IT department left this morning headed to Alaska.

MAN: Why?

PAULA: Reality show.

AVO: When you're short-handed, Powers staffing solutions is here for you.

MAN: Is big Mike here?

PAULA: Liposuction.

MAN: What about Billows?

PAULA: He quit.

MAN: Quit?

PAULA: Yeah, he set your desk on fire before he left. I was putting it out when you came in. I don't think he liked you.

AVO: We have well-trained, highly skilled temporary staff in all disciplines.

MAN: Well, Paula, guess it's just you and me.

PAULA: No sir, it's just you. I'm here because I left my sunglasses in my desk. (walking away) I'm on vacation this week.

AVO: Powers serviced more than 27,000 companies nationwide in 2003, and our local offices are eager to start working with you. Call x-xxx-xxx-xxxx to experience the Powers difference today.

CROWD: Powers. Good to know you.

"Guys, we're going to start with an audition exercise, which means I will be taking you into the studio three at a time. I look around the room and begin casting. "Nick, you're going to be Man; Tina, you are going to be Paula; and Dan, you'll be the AVO. Go on into the booth and start rehearsing. I'll be there to mic you in a minute."

I turn to the other two. "Guys, I'm not sure what part you'll be playing just yet. Just be ready to play any role. When the others arrive, tell them the same."

I am rewarded with one salute and one nod.

I enter the studio. My first threesome is rehearsing. As I mic them, I remind them that pacing is going to be their friend, as it's sounding slow and very much my-line and then your-line. I close the booth door and sit at the controls. After another couple of minutes of them rehearsing without me listening, I bring up the mics and talkback volume on the board.

"You guys ready to go?" I ask, knowing that whether I give them three minutes or thirty, it's not going to make any difference. They are mere beginners. "Voicelings," as I call them.

"Yeah, sure!" Nick offers.

"You guys are rolling."

They finish the take, and it's both too long and too flat. They're reading the words and not visualizing the scene and placing themselves in the scene. Basic stuff.

"Nick, who are you in this?"

"Well, I'm the boss and nobody's around."

It's not a great answer, but I don't want to feed him all the answers just yet.

"And you, Tina?"

"I'm his assistant. Or, wait! I'm probably the manager, because I seem to know what's happening with everyone. Perhaps I could play her sounding more efficient? That will give my character more energy."

"Very good, sweetheart. I'm impressed! Dan, let's talk about the AVO. Who are you talking to?"

"I assume the audience, because I'm the announcer."

"WRONG!" I say in my "you lose" voice. "Dan, if you do it like that, it's going to sound 'announcery,' which producers *never* want. I suggest you talk to Nick, because you have the solution for him."

"Got it," he says, and I can see he's already thinking about how different his delivery will be.

"Okay, let's give it another go! You're rolling."

The following take is better for Tina and Dan, but there's no real change in Nick. "Tina, that was so much better. I want to add one other thing that will help with your performance. It's Monday morning, and you say you came back for your sunglasses. Do you think you wanted to go to the office in the first place?"

"No way," she says.

"So, you would want to get in and out of there quickly—definitely before your boss comes in, right?"

"Absolutely!"

"And then, when you got there, you had to put out a fire, literally. So how would you feel in this situation, when your boss arrives?"

"Flustered. Wanting to get out of there before he begs me to stay. Gosh, Samantha, how do you see all that?"

I chuckle. "Tina, how long have you been studying this?"

"Four months," she shares proudly.

"Do you know how long I've been staring at copy? Thirty-five years!" I point to her and then to myself and chant, "Four months, thirty-five years." I repeat it again.

Tina giggles. "Thanks for reminding me, Sam."

"No problem. Okay, Dan, that take was much better but you threw away 'the Powers difference today' at the end. Your eyes were done with the words, but your mouth wasn't. Remember,

Powers is who's paying you, and the performance is not over until the last syllable of the last word. You must stay committed. The microphone will pick up on the fact that you shut down."

"Got it, Sam."

"Now, Nick, I don't really think you have a handle on this character. You said you walked into the office and nobody but Tina was there. While that is true, all you have done is explain the situation but not who you are as the character."

"No, I did explain. I said I was the boss."

"Yes, but what kind of boss?" I prod.

He thinks for a moment. "I don't know, I'm the boss. Do you want a voice or something?"

"No, I need you to understand and play the scene. What happens with your voice will just naturally happen."

"I'm a busy boss," he adds.

Holy cow. He doesn't see the bunny and it's right under his nose.

*This character is the Nick I met nearly a month ago when we had our first private lesson, all full of himself and clearly unliked by his peers. He doesn't see that the bunny is **him**!"*

"Nick, your desk has been set on fire, another employee quit, others have abandoned you, for one reason or another, and your trusty right arm, Tina, is trying to escape. So, I'll ask you again. What *kind* of a boss are you?" I see Nick shaking his head, and I sense I might have hit a nerve.

"I guess I'm not well-liked. Maybe I live in my own world a bit," he offers.

"There you go, now we're beginning to create a character. You can't just do a silly voice. That will make for a shallow character. Remember Mr. Slate from the *Flintstones* cartoon? I see this character like that. He's this big bombastic boss who doesn't realize what an asshole he is. After all, isn't that what makes an ass an ass? They don't know they are!"

They all laugh.

"Oh, I totally remember him. I can do that."

"Then let's give this another go. Okay, guys, you're rolling."

As they begin this third take, Nick is doing better. It's going to require a fourth take, however, which is not something I normally do, given that this is an audition exercise. In a real audition, one is usually in and out of the booth in one or two takes. I decide to bend the rules. After all, down the road, Nick might remember this as a life lesson and as an acting lesson.

"Okay, guys, one last time. Tina and Dan, you're on it. It's great. Your job is to now remain consistent. You know, at an actual commercial session you might be asked to do it twenty to thirty times, so you have to always know how to stay in control of the performance.

"Now Nick, it was much better. You might think that I'm picking on you, but I'm not. We have to make one more, simple tweak. You're definitely an asshole now, but we have to pull it back a bit. You need to be a *likable* asshole. We need to infuse some vulnerability. After all, we all loved Mr. Slate, right? At times, we felt sorry for him. So, be your big bombastic self at the beginning, but by the time you discover Billows quit, start to infuse some vulnerability there when you say 'Quit?' and then when you deliver your last line to Paula, make it a little more like a question. Like you're hoping she's not going to abandon you too; which of course, Tina, is exactly what your character's big concern was. Getting out of there before he could ask you to stay. See how it all fits together, guys?"

"I do see it," says Nick. "I just hope I can act it."

"I know you can. You all can. Okay, last take, here we go. You're rolling."

The take is completed and Nick is much better. Not perfect, but better. "Okay, guys, great job. You can come out of the booth." The three of them file out, talking and smiling. I stop them for a brief moment. "Although it wasn't perfect, it was one hundred times better than where you were when you first started with it."

And that's what matters.

"Dan and Tina," I continue, "it was good, but not as good as your third take. You weren't quite as connected on this one. Nick, what can I say? It was a huge improvement. You have the character now, but you were acting a little singularly. You needed to surrender to Tina more, to let go and really listen to her, so you could react to her. I'm being picky. Your improvement was tremendous, and that's all that should matter to you at this point. True brilliance will come later, I promise."

I get up to walk them out to the lobby so I can bring the next group in. The whole rest of the class is assembled there reading over the script. "Alrighty, next up. Iris, you are Paula; Jay, you're the boss; and Tom, you're the announcer. In you go!

And so it goes on all evening. Life lessons, voice-over lessons. Life lessons, voice-over lessons. I leave my wonderful engineer the task of closing up and make my familiar, twenty-two–year walk down the stairs, into the garage, and then to my car. I enjoy the simple silence before turning the key in the ignition. I don't listen to music in the car. Uninterrupted silence is my music of choice.

As I make my drive down Bridgeway, my thoughts immediately turn to Nick. It's nice to see him enjoying himself. Since our private lesson, he's had two different weekend classes, plus he's in his third week of "Beginning Narration," and now my audition class. He's determined, which I respect and admire, but I know he doesn't have a clue just how long his journey will be. Like an onion, there are many layers that must be peeled to get to the core. A lot of other industry professionals would judge Nick and think it will be impossible to get him where he would ultimately need to be, to be successful.

Of course, I think differently. First, I have years of teaching experience on my side and believe that *talent can be taught*. But there's an even more important factor in this equation. Without knowing it, Nick is discovering his inner six year old. He is beginning to let go.

He told me how he sat down with his son after class to play a video game with him, and I am quite certain that it had either been ages since he had done that, or he had never done it at all. But he took the time to stop and *play a game.* To have fun and connect on a truly authentic level. That's really all acting is. Connecting and being authentic, which is why I'm certain that if Nick sticks with this, he will become a successful voice actor.

As I put my car in park and walk toward my apartment, I smile at the notion of Nick *playing.* It warms me. I remember when I hugged him and looked into his eyes after our first lesson. I saw a beautiful soul that was locked tight.

"Nick," I whisper, as I stick my key in the door, "you can try to run from yourself, but you will not be able to hide. We will get to the core of who you really are and you will learn to speak the truth, your truth. And then you will be paid handsomely to do it." Smiling, as I enter my place, I take comfort in knowing that my buddy Nick is going to be just fine.

Part 3

3:00 p.m., March 30, 2010

THE *SPARKLING EMERALD*, DAY ONE

9046 . . . 9048 . . . 9050. *Aha*!

I enter my stateroom to find that my bags have already arrived. I close the door and survey the room. From outside, the *Sparkling Emerald* looks a bit like a wedding cake. From inside, it looks like a five-star hotel. I take a deep breath. I've stayed in a lot of hotels throughout the years—countless business trips, trips abroad, and a couple of trips just to London to visit Chris, and even though a lot of the time I was alone, I didn't feel alone because I was married to Andre.

This is hard. I try to remember the last time I felt this insecure. *Put on your grown-up pants, Sammy.*

I begin to unpack my bags and create my nest, beginning with my carry-on, which holds lecture material, recording equipment, and my framed photographs. No matter where I travel, I always bring them. There's the photo of Andre and me on our porch with our two Yorkies, Sophie and Ollie. I have another one of just Ollie with two bones sticking out of his mouth, and another one of my "mother," Janet.

As I survey the room to figure out where to place them, I notice a bottle of wine, chocolates, and a card. It's from Karen and it reads, "Bon voyage, Sammy. Have a great time. I know you'll do great! Love, K." I glance at a separate envelope on my desk as the phone rings.

"Hello?" I answer.

"Am I speaking with Samantha Paris? I'm Bonnie, the assistant cruise director."

"Hi, Bonnie. I just got here and I'm unpacking."

"Great, well, I'm just calling to remind you that the meet and greet with passengers is in one hour in the Creative Learning Center."

"Meet and greet? I'm not sure what you're talking about. Nobody told me anything about it. Actually, I haven't talked with anyone about anything yet."

"Oh! I sent you an e-mail about a week ago with the schedule. Did you not get it?"

Well, obviously, I didn't get it. Duh!

"Um, no, I didn't."

"Okay, well, everyone who is going to be a speaker or instructor has to do this meet and greet. We have a table set up for you. If you want to bring any handouts, or perhaps if you've written a book you can bring that, and passengers will pass by all the tables and talk with you about what you're going to be presenting. Did you receive your name badge?"

"Name badge?" I ask. I cast a sidelong glance at the desk and see it by the unopened envelope.

So dorky.

"Oh, yes, I see it," I muster.

"Make sure you have it on when you come to the meet and greet. We actually require that you wear your badge at all times when walking around the ship."

I take a deep breath. There is a reason I've always been self-employed. I don't conform well. "Will do, and I'll see you in an hour," I say in my phony, smiley voice.

What the hell have I done?

I continue unpacking, trying to think of what I can possibly take to put on my stupid meet-and-greet table. I don't have any-thing. If I put out the packets of scripts and pictures of cartoon characters that I brought, then I won't have them for my actual presentations. I'm sure Bonnie knows about the video about Voicetrax that Nancy sent, which is supposed to play in all the staterooms via the closed-circuit televisions the day before my first lecture, as agreed to by the Sparkling Ocean management.

"Yikes! I only have twenty minutes," I say aloud. I quickly change my clothes, freshen my makeup, and charge out the door, only realizing halfway down the corridor that I forgot my badge. Begrudgingly, I go back and get it.

The Creative Learning Center is on level six, and I've vowed to myself that I'll never take the elevator during the entire time I'm onboard. I figure that if I go to the gym each day and take the stairs, I won't gain any weight.

As I enter the room, I see people milling about, chatting. It's immediately clear that a lot of the speakers already know one another, and I'm the new kid on the block.

"Hi, Samantha, welcome." A cute, perky, blonde woman in a white uniform extends her hand. Looking at her, I can't get the image of Julie from *The Love Boat* out of my mind.

"You must be Bonnie," I say, zeroing in on the "Bonnie Wilson" on her name badge. We shake hands, and she leads me to my table at the end of the room with a small sign that reads, "Samantha Paris. Voicetrax. *Discover the world of voice-over.*"

"We're so excited you could join us, Samantha. In a few min-utes, Kent, our cruise director, will be here to speak with every-body to review company policies and answer any questions before the guests arrive. Is there anything you need in the meantime? Did you bring anything for the passengers?"

"I don't have anything for here, because I brought a video that—"

"Oh, that's right!" Bonnie exclaims. "Kent told me about it, but I haven't watched it. Don't worry. I'm sure you'll have a great time just explaining what you do with the passengers."

"Do you know when I'm doing my first presentation? I never received that e-mail you spoke of."

"I think you're scheduled the day after tomorrow, but I'll find your schedule and have it sent to your stateroom."

I circle the room, nodding and smiling at the other presenters, taking in all of their specialties. There's the "Computer University at Sea," art instruction, knitting, Tai Chi, bridge lessons, ballroom dance, and even foreign language studies. The *Sparkling Emerald* wine sommeliers have a table to talk about wine tasting, which would be desperately needed after all these activities. And for those seeking "enlightenment," they're offering lectures on wellness.

Passengers will stuff their faces, drink themselves silly, and attend wellness seminars. I laugh to myself at the mental image. I read the materials on a presenter who has published ten books on world affairs, with a concentration on all things nuclear and terrorism, and another specialist who is lecturing on DNA and forensics. I wonder how my voice-over program will play up against this array of other programs.

Kent strides into the room, authoritative in his starched, white uniform. He looks like a man who's been told he's a little handsomer than he actually is. And believes it.

"Hello, everyone. It's nice to see so many of you back, and to our new presenters, a special Sparkling Ocean welcome to you all." Everyone applauds politely. "We only have a few minutes, so I would like to take this time to remind you of some important policies and what will be expected of you while you are a temporary Sparkling Ocean employee. We would like you to show up at your venue at least ten minutes ahead of time. Please keep your presentation to the allotted time. There can be no . . ."

Wah, wah, wah.

"And if problems occur with . . ."

Wah, wah, wah.

"Your schedules can change due to . . ."

Wah, wah, wah.

"Please wear your . . ."

Wah, wah, wah.

"And remember our strict no-profanity and two-feet policies."

No profanity? I'm fucked.

"Thank you very much, ladies and gentlemen, and enjoy your cruise."

What the hell is the two-feet policy? I never go anywhere without both of mine.

I make a mental note to have Vicki check the rules and regulations booklet that arrived in Sausalito two weeks ago and is still on my desk at Voicetrax, unread. Yikes. Passengers filter in and mingle with the presenters. Everyone acts like old friends catching up since the last time.

There must be thirty to forty passengers in the room, and not one of them is at my table. As each minute passes, I feel myself dying a little death. Ten people leave, but twenty more take their place. I'm feeling very unpopular.

Is it because I'm at the end?

My table neighbor promising bridge lessons is getting a lot of action.

"Whaddya think, Alan? Do I smell funny? No one has come to my table," I say.

He glances at my sign. "Perhaps people don't understand what it is you do. I don't. What's voice-over?" I get that a lot at home. I constantly have to explain what I do and what voice-over is. I often think it would be easier to be a brain surgeon, except for, well, the actual performing brain surgery part.

"Well, you know when you hear commercials or watch a cartoon, maybe listen to an audiobook?" But Alan has already turned away to greet a couple approaching his table.

Time continues to tick by at a snail's pace. Then I make eye contact with a woman who apparently cruised the whole room before approaching my spot.

"Hello, ma'am. I'm Samantha Paris." I extend my hand.

"I'm Mrs. Waterman. You're new on the *Sparkling Emerald*, aren't you?"

"Why, yes, and I'm going to be giving voice-over lessons."

"And what is that, exactly?" she asks, smiling but clearly puzzled.

I begin my explanation, but in less than fifteen seconds I can tell she's not interested, so I cut it off quickly.

"How charming," she offers. "I wish you the best of luck, dear." She turns and walks away. I look at my watch and then see Alan had just taken in my exchange with Mrs. Waterman. I give him a sheepish shrug, utterly humiliated.

One of my favorite cartoon characters growing up, Snagglepuss voiced by Daws Butler, pops into my head. "Exit, stage right," he'd say, whenever he felt uncomfortable or in the wrong place . . .

Only five minutes left in the meet and greet, and no one will miss me, that's for sure. So exit, stage right, I follow his cue.

The side door leads to an outer deck. Alone, I lean against the rail. The ship is still at the pier but to the north I see the famous Miami Beach studded with colorful umbrellas. Against my will, I find myself looking for one in particular . . .

1968
MALIBU, CALIFORNIA

Our beach umbrella has big red and white stripes, so you can't miss it. Mom always sits under it in her floppy hat and gigantic sunglasses.

As soon as I drop my stuff on the blanket, I run to the surf as fast as I can, because I love the water so much and also my feet get hot from the sand. I love to body surf, and I'm really, really good at it. Once in a while this thing called a riptide is really strong and tries to pull you under, and you end up eating a mouthful of saltwater and scraping your knees on the sand carpet of the ocean floor, which hurts.

Sometimes I get so busy surfing that I lose track of Mom on the beach. And when the sun is really bright, some of the beach umbrellas look exactly the same. But I've always been able to find her.

The last wave that came in was bigger than I thought and gave me a good smack. I came up sputtering, and I'm probably getting sunburned because the ocean water is stinging my eyes, and when I scrunch my face, my cheeks hurt. I'm also hungry and ready for a snack. I look for the red and white umbrella, but I can't find it. I run down to the next lifeguard station, but I can't find it there, either. Tears well up in my eyes.

"Little girl, did you lose your mommy?" a man in a blue swimsuit asks me.

I nod mutely.

"Maybe we can find her together? Can you tell me what she looks like?"

Mom is hard, but the umbrella is easy. We comb the beach for what seems like hours, first in one direction, then in the other. He even holds my hand.

"There, that's her!" I shout. I spot the red and white umbrella with my mother under it and run toward her, tripping in the hot sand. The man in the blue swimsuit follows right behind.

"Your daughter was having so much fun in the water, she lost track of you," the man in the blue swimsuit says with a smile.

My mom peers over the top of her book at us, not even lowering her sunglasses, seemingly annoyed that we have interrupted her reading. I can't see her eyes, but I know she's glaring at me.

"I'm so glad we found your mommy," the stranger says to me. "You guys have a great rest of the day, and be careful not to stray too far when you're swimming."

"You should pay more attention when you're out there playing in the water. Where's your brother?" My little sister, Lori, is sitting on her towel trying to pick the sand out of her deviled egg sandwich. I plop down next to her. I have no idea where Larry is and I don't really care. My face is stinging and I'm hungry. I look back at the nice stranger, ashamed and embarrassed, wanting to thank him, but he's already down at the water's edge, headed back where we came from, and isn't looking at me anymore.

Nobody is looking at me.

9050. How did I get here? I've climbed the stairs all the way to my stateroom, lost in a memory. Trapped in a memory.

I put my key card in, open the door, and as it closes behind me, I sink to the floor. Old, awful feelings of being rejected have now come alive in the pit of my stomach. I bury my head in my arms. Growing up, that's the emotion I felt the most on all fronts: my family life and in school—I actually ran for class president and lost, every single semester of junior high school.

And then, of course, my early years as an actress. I shake my head, and then groan as I realize that, in comparison, today was nothing. I'm sitting here acting like a fucking baby. Thankfully, I've gotten a bit out of shape with always taking it on the chin, taking another hit.

Truth be told, I'm just mad that I didn't listen to my instincts.

Isn't that what I tell my students? Listen to your inner voice? I should have called Karen the moment I had second thoughts and cancelled the whole trip.

I get up and wash my face.

Time to get it together, Sammy.

"Good afternoon, ladies and gentlemen," comes the blaring voice of Kent, the cruise director, through the stateroom speaker. "We set sail for Barcelona in approximately ten minutes. Please join us out on the pool deck for a champagne toast, as we set out on this magnificent voyage."

I ponder the invitation and decide "getting it together" does not mean torturing myself by having to be charming and mingling. The ship's horn blows and we're on our way. My stateroom has a verandah, though, so I step out to watch the pier slip away.

As we slowly sail away from the Port of Miami, Louis Armstrong replaces Kent on the loudspeaker.

"I see trees of green, red roses too
I see them bloom for me and you
And I think to myself what a wonderful world . . ."

His song, his presence, is a welcome gift, and I receive it gladly. I'm about to travel clear across the Atlantic to another part of this wonderful world. I see people from the dock waving at us. I wave back, catching the eye of one man, and we begin to have our own private wave fest.

I blow him a kiss, and he hops back on one leg to show me he got it and that it was a doozy. I smile and blow another one. He smiles and blows still another back. I bring my hand to my cheek in acknowledgment and offer one final wave. I have calmed down and feel happy. Yes, the kindness from a stranger did the trick. It's *giving love* that is the elixir of life. It is my elixir for sure.

I go back inside and finish unpacking. Everything must be put away in the perfect place and in perfect order, just like my spice shelves at home. My friends tease me because I alphabetize them, but I can't help it. I must have order. I've often wondered where that comes from, as no one in my family is that way, but I must always be in control. Being in control means safety, I suppose.

|| It's *giving love* that is the elixir of life.

I zip up the last case, slide it under the bed, and survey my progress, taking notice of the unopened envelope that had been in my room when I arrived. It's a fax from Andre.

"Knock 'em dead," it reads. "Love, A." He's drawn a picture of Ollie with a bubble that reads, "I love you, Mummy!" It's so cute; it reminds me what a shame it is that Andre could never discipline himself or believe in himself enough to take his great art seriously.

I position the fax by the other photos, put my key in my purse, and check my appearance in the mirror. A little makeup is in order but nothing major, which is good, because I'm hungry and ready for a cocktail. I look at my badge on the desk.

I'm not wearing you tonight.

It's not like anyone knows me onboard. God knows none of the passengers stopped by to talk with me today. I'm going to dine incognito.

I make my way toward the door and stop.

Where are you going, Samantha? You're acting like you're going to meet Andre at the bar, but you're not. You are alone. Alone, as in you're going to have to be social, talk to people, and do all the stuff you don't like to do outside the classroom.

I sit on the bed and think about it. It's true. I'm so content with my few close friends. I detest big parties and weddings. I could never do a convention, and I secretly don't like Easter, Halloween, and Christmas. I never go to plays my students invite me to, or any kind of function where I'm going to have to be with people I don't know. I find it exhausting.

Shit. I've been so worried about whether what I do is going to translate on this ship, that I forgot how I was going to survive for the twelve days when I'm not teaching. "Why did I say yes to this?" Groaning, I reluctantly stand and begin to drag my feet to the door like I'm walking the plank.

Sammy, why do you constantly torture yourself?

The first bar by the sun deck pool is nearly deserted, and I can't believe my ears or my eyes. There's a Filipino trio playing. The same three who played thirteen years ago on the other Sparkling Ocean ship I was on when I cruised with my "adopted" family. These guys were old and bad then, and they're older and even worse now, playing Madonna's, "Like a Virgin" so off-key.

Exit, stage right.

I make my way to The Rodeo Club and, not surprisingly, find that it's packed. I'm relieved to see a seat at the bar. "Excuse me, is this seat taken?" I ask.

"Oh! Please, excuse me. No, not at all. Please join us," says the woman, whose bag and scarf had been occupying the empty bar stool.

"What can I get you, young lady?" the bartender asks, smiling.

"I think I'd like a Grey Goose up, really chilled with an olive."

"You got it!"

I survey the room and see a good mix of forty-somethings and beyond, and everybody seems to speak English. I take a sip of my cocktail.

"Hello, I'm Carolyn," says the owner of the bag and scarf, "and this is my husband, John. Are you by yourself?"

"Yes, I am," I smile. The question shouldn't sting, but it does.

"My name is Samantha Paris. It's nice to meet you."

"Oh, Samantha Paris. What a beautiful name," her blue eyes flash at me warmly. "You must get told that a lot." Her British accent is musical.

"I have been told that once or twice before, but there is a downside to having Paris as a last name. "

"And what is that?" asks John, smiling.

"Throughout the years, I have received Eiffel Tower coasters, Eiffel Tower topiaries, Eiffel Tower serving dishes, hand towels, and T-shirts as gifts." They start laughing. "That's just the half of it. Let's talk about the things that say 'Paris' on them—I've got hats, backpacks, and picture frames."

"And where are you from, Samantha Paris?" Carolyn asks, laughing.

"San Francisco." Sausalito is too complicated.

"Oh, we love San Francisco," Carolyn says, looking lovingly at her husband. "It's such a romantic city."

"Well, I certainly hear that you two are English. Where are you from?"

"We're from Essex, dear. Are you at all familiar with England?"

I could simply say, "yes" and leave it at that, but holding back when the answer is truly so much more feels dishonest. "I am quite familiar. You live in a beautiful area. My soon-to-be ex-husband is originally from London. I have one dear friend who lives in London and another who lives down south in Devon. I visit there a lot."

Just then I notice that John has his nose buried in his phone. "Federer lost today," he tells Carolyn.

"Oh dear, what a shame," Carolyn says.

They're tennis fans! My soul is now soaring. John must have been checking on the Miami Open. "You like tennis," I say, perhaps too excitedly.

"Oh, yes, we're huge fans." Carolyn says. "I especially love

Roger Federer."

"I love him too," I say, "but I can't help myself. I am over the top, absolutely goo-goo for Rafa Nadal."

We chat for at least another thirty minutes, and I begin to feel like I had known them for ages. We agree to meet at the paddle tennis courts at 11:00 a.m. tomorrow.

"It's been lovely, dear, but we must scoot for dinner. We have reservations at Cala Maro." John stands and pulls out the chair for his wife. I stand and give them each a hug.

"You are such a lovely girl," Carolyn says.

I smile. "And you two are so wonderful. Enjoy your dinner tonight." I linger longer to listen to the music, until my stomach reminds me about my own dinner. I know both specialty restaurants will be full, so my only option is the dining room. I make my way to the fifth floor. The 8:30 second seating has only been underway for about ten minutes. I introduce myself to the maître d' and ask if there is a table reserved for presenters.

He peers down his nose and looks at me with utter disgust. "Madam," he says with disdain, "we are completely full. There is no table for you."

"Do you mean there is no table tonight, or no table period?" I ask.

"There is no table for you. I'm sure you understand." I am completely taken aback. Not only am I not blind, but I'm a voice expert. This prick of a maître d' Zolton's tone of voice was saying, "I am far superior to you. Get the fuck out of my restaurant." I serve him back a disgusting smirk to match his own, then turn and exit, stage right.

It's the second time today that old feelings of rejection have reared their ugly head. But this time, I remind myself that I am the CEO of my own company, a special guest on this ship, and a tough cookie besides. No one gives me that look and gets away with it.

You haven't seen the last of me, Zolton.

THE *SPARKLING EMERALD*, DAY TWO

I hop on the elliptical machine and set it for an hour. Between the TV built into this piece of machinery and the wide-open ocean view in front of me, I have plenty to distract me. The water is calm and it's going to be a beautiful day, perfect for paddle tennis. I'm not quite sure what I'm going to do with myself the rest of the day, as the day's activities are really nerdy, and my first lecture isn't until tomorrow.

I know all this because when I got back to my room last night and ordered room service, my dinner companion was the *Sparkling Emerald* daily program, the ship's chatty newsletter with the next day's activities, profiles on speakers, and stories about upcoming ports.

I could go to the movie that is showing later, but I've never heard of *Take the Lead* with Antonio Banderas. I could also go to "Napkin Folding Part One" or the "Tara Pearls Talk," which is "Everything You Wanted to Know about Pearls but Were Afraid to Ask." Jesus. I'm not used to not having anything to do, and based on what's being offered, I'm grateful for the life I lead at home.

I turn on my machine's TV and there is *Sparkling Emerald*'s version of *The Today Show*, which stars Kent and Bonnie bantering about all of today's happenings onboard. They could definitely use some of my coaching. I switch channels. Now some guy is talking about Spanish architecture, Antoni Gaudi to be exact, and sites around Barcelona where we will eventually end up. I change the channel again.

Holy cow, there I am! They're running my video. I quickly change the channel again, as I would not want someone to discover me watching myself. I decide to watch CNN. Twenty minutes pass. What was the news anchor talking about? I realize I've been distracted by the ocean. The sunlight is dancing on the water, and the seagulls are putting on a show. The thought of being able to fly and also able to dive into the ocean thrills me.

Another twenty minutes pass, my mind a blank. I look around the gym, hoping no one saw my video with me watching. I start to think about Nancy and all her encouragement. I pray she is right about my lectures and that they will be well-received . . .

Done. Sixty minutes and I've burned 580 calories. I get off the elliptical and decide to join the stretch class in progress.

11:00 a.m.

I believe in dressing for success, and success in this case means not blowing it with my doubles partner. I've got my paddle, and I'm wearing a cute tennis outfit sans badge. I haven't played this game for a few years, and I know firsthand just how seriously some folks take their paddle tennis. As I approach the courts, I see John playing and I can tell he is of the *serious* player caliber.

Carolyn motions to me from the bench. "You are a cheeky girl!" she whispers, smiling. "I caught your video this morning. You didn't tell us last night that you're a presenter."

"I'm sorry," I sigh. "I wasn't hiding anything. It just never came up, and I didn't wear my badge because I find having to wear it so—so dorky."

"I see you're not wearing it today, either."

"It would ruin my outfit," I say, looking down at my chest. "Don't you think?"

"You and I are going to get along just fine," she laughs and pats my hand. "We'll talk about what you do at lunch."

"Okay," John says, approaching from the court. "Who's up next? Oh, hello, Samantha. We saw your video. Carolyn," he continues, "why don't you play with Samantha and Tricie and Ding? Why don't you two have a go?"

"Do you like forehand or backhand?" Carolyn asks me, as we enter the court.

"Look, I can tell you and John cruise a lot and play this a lot. You pick what you're best at, and I'll fill in the blanks."

She motions me to the advantage court and secretly, I'm glad. My backhand has always been better. As we begin to warm up, I know I'm in over my head. Our opponents are fantastic, clearly at home on the court and the ship. We begin the match and I can't help it, my competitive streak rises to the surface. I'm whacking the shit out of the ball. I can't remember the last time I felt this free and happy.

We give Tricie and Ding a run for their money, but they take the match. I move on to play with John, a gentleman named Richard, who cruises a lot, and a Sparkling Ocean employee in charge of all the beverages onboard. I hold my own with a record of two for two.

John pulls out my chair for lunch poolside. "Well," he says, laughing, "we now know you do voices and play a mean game of paddle tennis."

"I'm not nearly as good as you guys, and my serve sucks," I say. "I'm going to have to practice it."

"Samantha, tell us about your school," Carolyn pleads. "Don't be so mysterious."

"I didn't mean to hide anything last night. It's just that I'm better at doing what I do than talking about what I do."

"I get that," says John. "But your video does it very well. And to think you're in Sausalito. Carolyn and I loved it there."

"You should be proud of what you do," says Carolyn. "We were impressed."

A soft smile forms on my face. "Thanks."

"How long have you been doing this?" John asks.

"Well, I've been doing voice-over work for thirty-five years now and—"

"Thirty-five years?" John exclaims. "You must have started doing voices just out of your mother's womb."

"Not exactly," I giggle. "I started when I was fifteen. I've had my academy now for twenty-two years."

"How large is your school?"

I hear Andre's voice in my head. *Sammy, you are humble to a fault. You give other people way too much credit and never take any credit for yourself.*

I hear my mother shouting down the hall at my father. *Gene, stop telling Bobbi she is special. She is NOT special. You keep putting thoughts like that in her head and she will grow a big one.*

Then I hear my Voicetrax students talking to my mother, when she was the office manager. *Wow, you must be so proud of your daughter.*

Her reply was always the same. *I'm proud of all three of my children.* And then she would change the subject, abruptly.

I take a deep breath. "I actually have the largest voice-over academy in America. It's really big."

"In all of America?" John echoes incredulously.

"Yeah. It keeps me quite busy."

The waiter comes over, and we order three iced teas. I'm saved. John then looks at the two of us. "Lunch, ladies?" We agree that a nice salad from the buffet is in order and we all get up. I'm relieved that, for now, there are no more questions.

The hour whizzes by in a blur of conversation about their children, my lack of children, tennis, travel, and how I'm recently separated after twenty years of marriage.

"What are your lectures going to be about?" Carolyn asks.

"To be honest, I know what I'm going to do for the first one, but after that, I haven't got a clue. I've come prepared with recording equipment, scripts, all sorts of things, but I'm afraid very few people are going to show up. No one visited me yesterday at the meet and greet."

"I don't think you have a thing to worry about. They're going to keep playing your video, and I think you'll have loads of interested passengers. John and I are going to come."

"Really?" I look at both of them, grinning. "That's fantastic. Well, at least I know I'll have two."

After lunch, we part ways, John for paddle tennis with the captain, Carolyn to the computer room to e-mail her daughter, and me—well, I have no clue. I decide to stroll around all of the outdoor decks. John mentioned there is a storm headed our way, so for the next couple of days we can expect rain and some rough seas.

The sun is warm and healing. I lean against the teak rail, closing my eyes to drink it in. I take several slow, deep breaths. When I open my eyes again, I have to squint, the sun is glinting so brilliantly on the water, like millions of diamonds.

"You look at things but you don't really see them," Andre used to tell me. One time he plucked a simple flower from his garden and made me really *look* at it. He was right. I was twenty-eight years old and actually looking at a flower for the first time.

I'm always in such a hurry, afraid to slow down. As I gaze out to sea, I think of Nancy's always positive "Go, Sammy, go" expression. Albeit encouraging, I'm thinking that maybe, "slow, Sammy, slow" might be a better mantra. *Slow down.* I'm never going to find what the Wizard has in his bag for me, if I'm always rummaging so quickly through it.

Boy, Bobbi, you're so dumb. You've been staring at that cover forever! I hear my brother Larry's voice in my head.

I can't believe you don't see the bunny. It's right in front of your fat face! Now I hear myself back at Voicetrax in the classroom.

"Guys, you will never find the bunny, if you're rushing. Don't be in such a hurry to perform. You must first understand your script. Search for the bunny! It will reveal itself, but not if you're rushing."

I stare out at the vast expanse of ocean and take in another deep breath. Maybe my bunny revealed itself years ago, but, like

Andre said to me in the flower garden, I'm looking but I'm not seeing.

"Excuse me, aren't you Samantha Paris?"

"Yes?" I turn to face an older woman.

"I'm sorry if I'm interrupting," she continues, "you seem so deep in thought, but I noticed you at lunch, and I was sure you were the woman I saw on the video this morning."

Another English-accented voice—and this one is familiar. She grabs my hand with both of hers. "I always hoped I would run into you again someday. It's Lilian. Lilian Jones. I used to study with you years ago, when you first started. You were Bobbi then. You didn't have the place I saw in the video. I was one of your students at your home in Mill Valley."

"Ah, yes, Lily," I remember. I absolutely adored her. "Oh, my goodness, it's so wonderful to see you!" I give her a hug and a kiss and notice how frail she is. She has to be in her eighties.

"You are Samantha now. I think that's lovely. Is Andre here with you?"

"Sadly, no. We recently separated."

"Oh, that's such a shame. I always remember your lovely home and how it was situated on that creek. And your studio was above Andre's art studio. You know, he made me a lovely cup of tea once while I was waiting to have my lesson with you. You were running a bit behind. You were such a busy young girl."

I smile, thinking how nothing has changed, except that now I have wrinkles.

"How are you, Lilian? It has to be at least twenty years. Come, let's get out of this sun and find some shade." I grab her by the arm and slowly help her down one flight of stairs to the pool area where we can sit at a table under an umbrella. "It's amazing running into you. It really is a small world, isn't it?"

"Yes, it is, Samantha. And you know, I wrote to you years ago, and my letter was returned. I guess you had moved."

"Andre and I moved to Petaluma."

"Frank and I moved back to England. His health was failing, and we thought it best to move back home."

"Is he here with you now?" I ask nervously, worried that perhaps he had passed away.

"Why, yes, he is. We're here on the ship celebrating our sixtieth wedding anniversary."

"Oh, that's beautiful. Really wonderful."

"Well, listen, dear. I want to share with you what I wrote in my letter. Am I taking you away from anything? Perhaps we could have a cup of tea."

I think about today's lecture that's being offered: "China's Agenda, America's Challenge: The Future of Transpacific" something or other.

"No, Lily," I say, "you are not taking me away from a thing." We order tea from a passing waiter and settle in for a chat.

"So," I say. "Your letter. What did you write?"

"You probably don't remember, but I came to you rather late in life," she begins, smiling. "I had recently turned sixty-five, and one of the things I had yet to address on my to-do list was to return to performing. I had loved it when I was a young girl in England—and then, of course, life happened."

"Yeah, life has a funny way of doing that, doesn't it?"

"Exactly. I got married, had four beautiful children, moved to America, and worked alongside my Frank for many years. But I always had this, as you put it, this voice inside telling me to follow my heart and perform. So that's what I did. I came to you. Samantha, you were marvelous. You awakened so many things inside me, and I was devastated when we had to move back to England."

"I remember you had to drop all your classes. I didn't know why."

"It was sudden. Frank was ill."

"That thing called life getting in the way again," I said.

"Yes, except with one very large difference. You had given me the strength and courage I needed to follow my dream, to not put it on the back burner again. You taught me to love myself and that I mattered, that my own happiness mattered."

"So, what happened?" I asked, as the waiter brought our tea.

"We moved just outside London, and I started doing plays in our village. I had never been so happy. I knew I had found my purpose in life."

She found her bunny.

"Then a friend of mine came one night to the theatre with a lady friend of hers who represented actors in London. For adverts, you know."

"You've been doing commercials."

"Yes! I got my first on-camera commercial at seventy-two. Imagine starting my performing career at that age, and I have you to thank for it. As a matter of fact, I just retired from acting last year at the ripe old age of eighty-six. So anyway, I wrote to you after I was cast in my first advert, and you can imagine my disappointment when my thank-you note was returned."

My eyes fill with tears, I'm so happy for Lily. But there was a bigger revelation occurring. I knew in my heart of hearts that if I had received that letter at Voicetrax, it would be sitting in a box, and I would have, at best, just skimmed it. Instead, here I am out in the middle of the Atlantic Ocean receiving the most beautiful gift of Lilian's heartfelt gratitude.

Jesus, I'm so fucked up. I'm such a shit.

Vicki's right. I always toss those notes aside. Then I remember Louisa's e-mail note, sadly still unread on my computer. I will myself to not lose it in front of Lily.

I take both of Lily's frail hands in mine and bring them to my lips. I gently kiss them and whisper, "Thank you. You are so kind, Lily. Your words mean an awful lot. What a gift to run into each other after—"

"Cheers, Samantha!"

I jump and turn to see John. "Hi, John. How was your game with the captain?"

"He got me today, but I won't let that happen next time."

"I'm sure you won't. John, I'd like you to meet Lilian. She was a student of mine years ago, and we just ran into each other on this ship."

"Isn't that brilliant?" He extends his hand. "It's very nice to meet you, Lilian. Will you be attending Samantha's lecture tomorrow?"

"Believe me, John, I know firsthand that it's not to be missed. I can assure you, my husband and I will be sitting front and center."

"Well, my wife and I will be there too." John turns to me. "Samantha, dear, you now have four." He smiles and walks away.

"Is he a friend of yours?" Lily asks.

"No, I only met him and his wife, Carolyn, last night at The Rodeo Club. They are a lovely couple. It's funny, I was worried about how I was going to get on all by myself, and, in just twenty-four hours, I've encountered three beautiful souls."

"Well, you never met my husband, Frank. I do hope you'll join us for dinner one night. Frank always wanted to meet the woman who gave me my new lease on life."

I smile uncomfortably. My knee-jerk reaction wants to say, "I'm busy," "I've made other plans," or "I'm teaching, but thank you for the offer," but I can't do that here. The thing about a ship is that you're trapped on it. I know that knee-jerk reaction is just my muscle memory, my "go to" reaction, and that it's wrong.

What is the matter with me?

"Lily, I would love that. Just let me know which night works best for you, and we'll do it."

"Why wait? Unfortunately, we've already booked the Italian restaurant for tonight, but let's have dinner together tomorrow after your lecture. Would the dining room be okay?"

I think of Zolton and smile, eager for our next encounter. "That will be absolutely perfect."

We finish our tea, and I stand to help Lily from her chair. "Thank you so much for finding me today," I say, hugging her. "Where are you off to now? Can I walk you where you need to go?"

Lily lets out a tiny laugh. "Oh, no, Samantha. I'm fine. Frank is listening to the lecture, and I'm off to needlepoint. We'll be there front and center at the lecture tomorrow."

Between paddle tennis, lunch with John and Carolyn, and tea with Lily, I can't remember the last time I had such a great day. I feel incredibly blessed. Now what? I'm so used to always having something to do, that I don't know how to relax. I don't want to go back to my stateroom yet, because the sun feels glorious and I will most likely be cooped up there all evening. The paddle tennis court is vacant.

My serve sucks and I need to practice.

As I hike up the stairs to the courts, I hear myself telling my students to embrace their "sucky-ness." Love being really lousy at something and love slowly getting better. Ultimately, you feel such a great sense of accomplishment. What's sexy about already being really good at something and then getting better? Being horrible and then truly brilliant, now that's sexy.

I lift the gate latch and enter the court. I toss the ball and hit my first serve. It misses the service box. I do it again. Toss, hit, miss. Toss, hit, miss. I smile.

If sucking is sexy, I just became a Victoria's Secret supermodel and snagged the cover of *Sports Illustrated.*

I hear myself telling my students to embrace their "sucky-ness." Love being really lousy at something and love slowly getting better. Ultimately, you feel such a great sense of accomplishment. What's sexy about already being really good at something and then getting better? Being horrible and then truly brilliant, now that's sexy.

THE *SPARKLING EMERALD*, DAY THREE

"Excuse me, are you the woman in the video?" A trainer approaches while I'm on the elliptical machine.

I nod.

"That was really cool. I'm Mark." He extends his hand.

"Yeah, I'm Samantha," I say somewhat breathlessly. "Thank you so much."

"I've always wanted to get into voice-over, but being from Phoenix, Arizona, I just didn't think it was possible. I never knew there was an academy, a school like yours. You are my living, breathing dream come true. I traded shifts with my colleague so I can attend your lecture today at 3:30."

"You are so kind, Mark. I hope I don't disappoint you today."

"I'm sure you won't! Hey, if you need any help here with the equipment or if you have any questions, I'm your guy."

I smile. "I will definitely bug you if I need some help, thank you." I turn back to my machine and continue my workout. I'm so nervous about this afternoon. I hope what I'm planning will be okay. I only have forty-five minutes. Since my lectures with first-time people are always three hours, I'm worried about how I'm going to cram three hours into forty-five minutes.

I rehearse the lecture in my head.

Okay . . . no time for people going around the room introducing themselves. I'll introduce myself and thank them for coming. God, I hope people will attend. Then a brief explanation of what I do, what voice-over is, and actually how universal it is. That voice-over is a part of everyone's lives and affects every living being on this planet. People just don't realize that. And then I will jump in and show them how it's done.

After encouraging their inner six year old to come out and play, I will start with the placements. I mean that's universal . . . everyone has been six . . . nobody actually ever forgets how to play, do they? I brought plenty of pictures of cartoon characters. So, the plan is to have people coming up, giving them each a picture, and then I will teach them how to sound like their characters.

I'll show them that just merely standing like, or making the face of, the character, they can create a voice. That always gets a laugh, when grown adults make funny faces. I'll show them that just by laughing like you imagine the character would laugh, you can create a voice. It can be so much fun!

Oh, but what if they don't like it? What if they don't want to play? What if my methods are too "loud, brash, American"? Or worse, too "totally, oh my gawd" Californian? What if this is a flop? What if it's not what Sparkling Ocean was expecting at all? What if I'm fired?

Wait . . . how can they fire me? I mean, they can't exactly throw me overboard.

Or can they?

Outside the big windows, the ocean is showing whitecaps. The display on my machine shows that I'm in an intense hill climb mode, peddling and pushing faster than ever. I have to slow down.

Relax, Samantha. Relax. Stop with the "stinkin' thinkin'!"

What do I always tell my students? "Don't think, just do. Come from your heart. Don't over-analyze." That's what we adults do. We over-analyze everything to death, which drains our creativity. It drains our souls. I just have to be myself. Just come from love, and it will be okay.

I notice the ocean is rough. There are whitecaps everywhere and it's beginning to rain. Wow. Mother Nature is really amazing. Yesterday, she was dressed in diamonds, light and sparkly, peaceful and alluring. Today she's strong and clearly not going to take shit from anyone. She is in control, demanding respect.

Take your cue from Mother Nature.

That's it! She's sending me a message. I simply need to be a little of both of her sides today. I hop off the elliptical machine, nodding my head. Since I left on this journey, the universe has been sending me so many messages.

Is the universe this busy with me when I'm at home?

8:45 a.m.

I slide my tray past the pastries, meats, and cheeses along the buffet toward the fruit, which looks sensible.

"You do realize that breakfast is the most important meal of the day."

I turn and see Kent decked out in all his cruise ship whites and name badge.

"Good morning," I say a bit tentatively.

"We haven't officially met, Samantha. I'm Kent." He extends his hand.

"Yes, it's nice to meet you. I figured I'd be seeing you today at my lecture."

"I'm looking forward to it. That video of yours is quite compelling. We should have a nice turnout."

"How many people do you think we can expect?" I ask, holding my breath.

"We have you on the seventh floor in what's called 'The Study.' It holds about thirty people."

There's no way I'll get thirty people.

At least it's not a big room that'll have me speaking to a lot of empty chairs. "That sounds comfortable. Do you mind if I ask you something? I was going to call Bonnie after breakfast, but because I'm standing here"—I drop my voice several octaves— "talking to the big cheese," I say as Kent smiles, "I'm wondering if I can meet with your audio/visual guy. I have quite a bit of set-up to do."

"Sure, Samantha, what do you need?"

"Well, besides all my scripts, I brought my computer and a

microphone so I can record people, and I've got all these different cords that hopefully I'm going to remember how to connect."

Kent starts to chuckle.

"Yeah, you're laughing, but I'm serious. I haven't a clue how to do this stuff. I have wonderful worker bees back home who do it for me. Anyway, I'm assuming I can plug into your speakers. Oh, and I need to borrow a music stand."

"Anything else?" he asks with a playful smirk.

"Judging from your expression, I think it's best to say, 'No, that's it,' but in reality, one never knows!"

I can tell Kent finds me amusing.

"Are you going to your stateroom after breakfast?" Kent asks.

"I think so. It's not exactly sunbathing or paddle tennis weather."

"Alrighty then. I'll have Gary give you a call in about an hour. He'll set up a time for you two to meet."

"Great! Thank you, Kent. It's nice to have finally met you."

We shake hands again and he glances subtly at my chest where my name badge should be hanging. Either he's being fresh, or he's just making a mental note of the fact that I definitely have an issue with rules.

Too soon to tell.

9:30 a.m.

I enter my stateroom and let out a sigh.

Jesus, six hours until the lecture. What in the world am I going to do?

I don't feel like reading the novel I brought, nor do I feel like learning needlepoint. The phone rings.

"Hello?"

"Hello, Samantha, it's Carolyn."

"Oh, hi! How are you?"

"I'm fine, but what dreadful weather," Carolyn groans.

"I know, John was right. No paddle tennis today."

"No, not today. But we are looking forward to your lecture. I'm calling to see if you'd like to walk around the shops with me a bit this morning."

"Oh, that would be great! Thank you so much. I'm just waiting for a phone call that I expect any minute, and then after that I should be free. Shall I call you back? What's your stateroom number?"

"We're in 9052."

"9052? You're kidding me."

"No, it's 9052. Why? What's the matter?"

"Carolyn, hang up the phone and walk out into the hallway."

"But I'm in my nightdress."

"It doesn't matter. Just do it. Trust me."

I hang up the phone and walk out of my room. Ten seconds pass, and she opens her door. "Surprise! I'm in 9050!" I exclaim.

"Samantha, this is quite something! Here we are on a 900-passenger ship. What would the odds be that we are right next door to each other? It's amazing."

I give her a hug. "Good morning, neighbor!"

Just then my phone starts to ring again. "That's my call. I'll ring you back when I'm done."

"Or just knock on my door," Carolyn adds, slipping back into her stateroom.

I rush to answer my phone. "I bet this is Gary."

"Why, yes, it is! Am I speaking with Samantha?"

"Ding, ding." We make a plan to meet at 1:00, which gives me plenty of time to get set up. I hang up the phone and dial Carolyn. John answers. "Well, hello, neighbor!"

"Hi, John, I know, isn't it crazy?"

"I think it's absolutely marvelous. Carolyn is just finishing getting dressed and told me to tell you she'll be ready in fifteen minutes. Just tap on our door."

"Great! I'll see you in a few." I know it's no coincidence that this lovely couple I just met by chance is right next door to me. I close my eyes to drink in all the gratitude I'm feeling.

Thank you, universe, for making me feel safe and not alone.

Then the universe sends me another message, this one more like a reminder, about the Sparkling Ocean rules I left on my desk at work. Unread.

Shit! I forgot to text Vicki.

I pray my phone will get a signal. I see the three bars pop up. The universe at work. I do my part:

Hi, honey. Hope all is okay. My lecture is today at 3:30. Cross your fingers. The Sparkling Ocean rules are on my desk. Please tell me what they mean by the two-feet rule? Text me back. Love you. Give my love to Chuck.

I inspect my reflection in the mirror to find a bad case of bedhead Sammy.

I've been walking around the ship looking like this?

I make a futile attempt at fixing my hair, but I know it's silly. I will shower and attempt to make myself look presentable for the lecture later. I cross over to the full-length mirror and smile. At least my workout outfit is cute. I grab my room key and exit my room, ready for another friendly chat and some retail therapy.

1:45 p.m.

I hop into the shower. Gary was terrific and helped me set up everything. We even did a silly recording/sound check, where I taught him how to do a couple of voices. He loved it and said he was coming to the lecture himself.

If he's not BSing me, that makes six.

This new shampoo I bought while shopping with Carolyn smells really nice. I smile, thinking about Carolyn. She's the definition of nice. When we walked around the ship after shopping, she talked a lot about her daughter, with whom she is extremely close.

Does it make me long for a relationship like that with my own mom? *Absolutely not.* I have never allowed myself to miss something I never had in the first place. For me, that sense of longing feels more like self-pity, and I don't see a positive benefit in that.

I rinse the shampoo out my hair and start to think about the people I've trained who share with me why they feel miserable, why they aren't successful, why they drink, or why they're overweight. While feeling sorry for themselves, they blame others and keep telling themselves old stories over and over, which holds them back. This frustrates me. If only they could find the power within themselves to change things and not be victims of their stories.

For every student like that, I've had twice as many students in similar situations who do turn their lives around, who *find their bunny*, and move happily forward. But what can I possibly accomplish in forty-five minutes?

I run through the lecture in my head again, hoping the final moments in the shower will inspire me. I know I'm making a way bigger deal out of this than I need to. I'm not exactly getting ready to emcee the Academy Awards. I'm doing a voice-over lecture on a cruise ship. Jesus. Thinking of it that way doesn't make me feel better, it makes me feel pathetic, because people in the entertainment industry who "do cruise ships" are usually—but not always, I keep telling myself—old and washed up or were never talented enough to make it big.

3:15 p.m.

I'm ready, name badge and all. It's a good hair day and my makeup looks great. So do my clothes, shoes, jewelry, and nails. And yet the same thought enters my head that always enters my head when I look in the mirror before I go out anywhere.

You're fat and ugly.

I know it's just bad programming, but it's in there. I remember the diet pills and my pickle-eating days.

Talented, but too fat. That was from my soon-to-be first agent, when I was fifteen.

The casting director thinks you're a terrific actress, but you're just not pretty enough for the part. That was when I was auditioning for parts on TV. Those words cut deep. They're initially one of the reasons why I got so good at voice-over. It was out of spite, so I could still earn my living as an actress and not have to worry about relying on my looks. I would be judged only on the basis of my skills. I decided to become better at voice-over than anyone my age, because becoming great at voice-over made me feel in control.

Images of Nina Foch and Johnny Truffa are demanding my attention, but I'm not going to give in. I have a lecture to give.

As I start to make my way down the stairs to the seventh floor, I reach into my pocket and feel the smoothness of my calm stone from Andre that I brought with me.

Knock 'em dead. Once again, I hear Andre's voice. Then I think of my other beacons of positive light: My "mother" Janet, Vicki, Chuck, and Nancy . . .

"Okay, guys, I'm ready to do this," I whisper aloud to myself.

As I approach the room, I see a few people hanging out by the entrance, and a few more people hanging out down the hall.

"Hi, guys. I'm Samantha. What's going on? No chairs yet?"

"Oh, there are chairs, there are just no chairs *left,*" a woman says.

"What?" I poke my head in to see it's standing room only. These folks weren't waiting to come in, they actually *can't* get in.

"Oh, my gosh, guys, I'm so sorry. Let me squeeze in and see what I can do."

I make my way to my table and see Frank and Lilian in the front row. I look for John and Carolyn, concerned that maybe they didn't get a seat. I spot them in the back row and nod toward them. I look for Bonnie or Kent, but don't see any sign of either.

"Hi, guys, welcome. I'm Samantha." I have to fully project over all the talking. "I see we have a bit of a problem here with seating. There are still a few more folks outside in the hall who would like to come in. Maybe if we organize our standing guests a bit more, we can accommodate everyone." I look around and guesstimate that there are sixty to seventy people here. "Are you all here because of the rain?"

A flurry of unexpected responses follows. This crowd is psyched up.

"No!"

"Your video was so interesting."

"Sparkling Ocean has never offered anything like this before."

"You seem like so much fun!"

I organize the room a bit better so everyone can fit comfortably. Some men give up their chairs so that other people who need to sit, can.

"This is quite a turnout," Kent says, as he comes into the room. "I guess we should have given you a bigger venue."

"Who knew, right?" I shrug. "I guess it won't be too horrible for the people standing, seeing how it's only for forty-five minutes. I better get going." I raise the pitch of my voice and sing out, "Quiet, everybody! Well, you're all so chatty, you probably don't have a problem with your communication skills, so maybe we'll just call it a day!" Several people laugh.

"Thank you so much for coming. I'm truly honored. As my name badge here says"—I wiggle my fingers at it—"I'm Samantha Paris, and I own a company in Sausalito, California, called Voicetrax, where for twenty-two years now I have taught thousands of people the art of voice acting. I'm thrilled you all watched the video, so you have a bit of an education already on what voice-over is. It's everywhere! It's in our homes, our cars, our computers. It's part of our telephone communications, our toys, games, movies, and more. What you probably don't know is how we create these performances and also how studying the art of voice acting can simply help you in your everyday life. Back home, I have students from every walk of life and every age category. Ten year olds to folks well into their eighties."

I look at Lily and smile. "I have stay-at-home parents who want to be able to read a better bedtime story to their children, people in corporate America who want to feel more comfortable making a presentation, trial lawyers who want to be more engaging in front of a jury, and some people who are just so painfully shy it's nearly impossible for them to leave their homes. I work with doctors, construction workers, high-tech folks, priests, ministers, and therapists. Heck, I even had an honest-to-God rocket scientist! I also have a lot of retired folks who always dreamed of doing this and now that they have entered a new chapter in their lives, they are setting out to do the thing they always wanted to do. They all love studying this; they have benefitted from it personally and professionally. And yes, several have gone on to be successful voice actors as well."

Long pause.

"Several hundred."

That snags a few smiles. Everyone appears to be engaged, but what's the deal with Kent? Why is he standing off to the side, leaning against the wall with his arms crossed like that? Maybe he's concerned that there are too many people in this room and it could present a hazard?

"During the course of these four lectures I'll be giving on the ship, I will explore with you some of the different styles of voice-over. We'll work in the world of narration, which really benefits people in the corporate world. If there are any doctors in the house, I've got some great medical narration copy. Monoamine oxidase inhibitors, anyone? Say that three times really fast!" I start to get some giggles.

"We will explore the world of commercial acting, where learning to be totally honest and connected to your audience can be a bit challenging when you have to say, 'Stock up on Pepsi, pork loin, and panty liners.'" The laughter grows. "Today we're going to start by exploring the world of character voices for cartoons, animated films, and video games. Ready to get started?"

"We're ready!"

"Let's go, Samantha."

"Let's do it."

"Okay then, let's!" I slowly gaze around the room and squint to create a feeling of tension, of seriousness. "Now," I say slowly, "before we jump into this, I have to ask you an important question. Honest. It's really important." I stare at the whole class. "How many of you have ever been six years old?"

As the lecture continues, I feel like I'm having an out-of-body experience. First, there I am working with these people, drawing things out of them that they never knew existed within them. I am encouraging them, pushing them, laughing with them, hugging and kissing them, and singing with them. And then there's this other me in the back of the room, who is watching me, marveling at how I do what I do.

Where did all this come from? Why do I tell myself that I hate teaching, when clearly, I don't? How can I hate something that makes me feel such intense joy and love inside?

Forty-five minutes ago, this place was an uncomfortable, crowded room of strangers. Now we are all singing The Wizard of Oz *song like Munchkins, in all sorts of accents and in three different languages. It's astounding and I can't believe my time is up.*

"Wow, guys, that was glorious! You are really something! When was the last time you sang that song? You are all so incredible, and I hope to see you at my next lecture."

‖ How many of you have ever been six years old?

Then the thunderous applause starts. "Oh, thank you so much, but you should be applauding yourselves, not me!"

"Wait, that's it?" says my new Italian student, Paolo.

"Dinner's not for several more hours," his brother, Carlo, jumps in. "Can't we do more?"

Others chime in. Nobody seems to want to stop.

I look at Kent.

"It's entirely up to you, Samantha. This room is available the rest of the afternoon."

I turn back to the class. "Okay, well, we've done forty-five minutes. How about we go for another hour? That will still give all of us ladies time to freshen up before dinner." My suggestion is met with more applause and so the class continues. The hour flies by, and then it's time to say goodbye. "Guys, thank you so much. I hope you enjoyed this as much as I did."

"When is your next lecture?" asks the French woman with the scarf.

"I think I'm scheduled to speak every other day. You'll have to check the daily program for the times, as I don't know myself."

Everybody starts gathering their belongings.

"Samantha, you were marvelous," a woman greets me. "My husband and I thoroughly enjoyed it!"

"Yes, we really did!" he adds. "My wife, Meg, has been wanting to write a book for years. I've been trying to encourage her, but unfortunately she has been doing what you talked about today—always believing the negative things people say and pushing away all the positive things," he says, as Meg nods in agreement. "She had one teacher in high school who told her she couldn't write."

"I had an acting teacher who told me I couldn't act, so I can totally relate. Meg, get going on that book!" Smiling, I give them both a hug.

"Samantha, I loved when you said, 'talent can be taught,'" exclaims a late-forty-something gentleman.

"And why is that? I mean, I truly believe it, but how does it resonate with you?"

"Well, I'm a weekend golfer, and for years I've been frustrated with my game. I just don't seem to get any better and I figured it was because I lacked talent. I've been telling myself, 'I'm never going to be Tiger Woods, so just accept it.' But what happened with me today takes me back to my teens and early twenties. I wanted to pursue voice-over work, I always dreamed of doing cartoons, but didn't think I had the talent, so I gave up on the idea."

I nod my head understandingly, knowing where he's going with this.

"The way you took us through your techniques," he continues, "teaching us how it's actually done, I realized that talent has nothing to do with it. It's schooling. I just wasn't schooled."

"Exactly! So, what are you going to do with all this newfound knowledge?"

"Golf! At my age, living in Dallas with a wife and family, pursuing that dream of voicing cartoons isn't practical. However, taking up golf lessons is. I've never had one. I can't wait to get home and take some lessons."

"And what are you going to do if you suck at first?" I ask playfully.

"I'm going to think sucking is super sexy!"

"Ding, ding, ding!" We both start to laugh as another participant, Warren, approaches.

He extends his arms and we embrace. "Samantha, I cannot thank you enough. You have lit a spark in me that I cannot describe. My soul has literally felt dead and now I feel reborn!"

I whisper, "Happy birthday, Warren," and give him one last squeeze.

The adorable Italian brothers approach me. "Thank you, Samantha. That was great!" Carlo says.

"Back home in Italy, I'm a musician, so I obviously hang out with a lot of artists. I have a buddy who speaks English and does dubbing in Italian for English-speaking films. I've been thinking it would be cool to do that, so I'm now going to check it out."

"Oh, that is fantastic! You'd be great at it." Then I look at Paolo. "What do you do back home?"

"I design shoes," he says rather proudly. "Hey, Samantha, I'd like for you to meet our parents. This is my mother, Daniela, and my father, Sergio." They are full of smiles. Then they start talking to me in Italian.

I turn to the boys. Carlo offers, "They don't speak English." I give a little giggle. I find it so strange that they would come to this, and yet I remember seeing them doing the placements and pulling the word "hello" out of their heads, their noses, etc. They were laughing away.

I turn back to Carlo. "Well, thank them in Italian for coming and tell them I think they are absolutely delightful! I'll see you guys around." I make a mental note to ask the boys, the next time I see them, how they came to speak English so well. I try to connect with everyone in the room, give them a hug, and say goodbye.

I come to Lilian and Frank. "Oh, Samantha, you haven't changed a bit," Lilian gushes.

I smile and we embrace while I'm looking at her husband. "Hi, Frank. It's really nice to meet you." I warmly take both of his hands in mine. "I'm looking forward to our dinner tonight."

"Yes, Samantha, you've worked up quite an appetite, I suppose."

"Ah, this was nothing. Ask Lily. Sometimes I go seven to eight hours like this, but I must say I am feeling a bit peckish. What time shall we meet for dinner? It's 5:30 now."

"How about we meet down at The Emerald Cove for drinks at 7:00, and then we'll have dinner after that?" Frank suggests.

"That's perfect, I'll see you then."

I make my way to John and Carolyn, who have patiently been waiting for me up front by all my equipment.

"Hi, guys," I say shyly, smiling.

Carolyn immediately gives me a hug. "Miss Paris. We've only known you a few days, but we feel like proud parents! That was so enjoyable and inspirational. Your own parents must be so proud." I give her a smile, ignoring the comment, and turn to John for a hug.

"You did a fantastic job, Samantha, and to think you were worried about your attendance."

"Yeah, I know, you guys were right. That video of mine did the trick."

"Being neighbors and all, how about we help you break down all this and carry it back to your room? That way you won't have to make two trips," John offers.

"Really? That is so nice. You just made me an offer I can't refuse."

As we begin to collect all my stuff, Kent approaches. "Hello, Mr. and Mrs. Baker. It's always a pleasure to see you."

"Nice to see you, as always, Kent," John says, shaking his hand.

"You two are friends of Samantha?"

"Well, no, we only met her at The Rodeo Club the first night, but we feel like we've known each other for ages," Carolyn shares lovingly.

"You did a great job, Samantha," Kent says, turning to me. "I don't think I've ever seen a group so enthusiastic. You offer something rather unique to Sparkling Ocean."

"Thank you very much, Kent. It was certainly my pleasure." I turn to help John and Carolyn pack up my stuff.

"I've got one more activity to oversee. I wish the three of you a pleasant evening," Kent says and heads out.

"I think we're all set," John says, his arms filled with equipment.

I look around the room one last time. "Yep! We're good! Let's blow this popsicle stand!"

John and Carolyn both look at me and chuckle. "Blow what?" John asks.

"Sorry. American for 'Let's go.' I might have been married to a Brit for twenty years, but for better or for worse, I am an American."

We chat all the way to our neighboring staterooms, with John changing up his voice every two seconds. I tell him that his potentially new career as a professional paddle tennis player looks brighter than that of a voice actor. He laughs at that one. I thank them both for helping me with everything and close the door behind me.

"Whew," I let out a sigh, glad to now have quiet. I plop down on my couch and see that I have a text from Vicki.

Hey, Sammy, Hope the lecture went well. The two-feet rule came under the heading of sexual harassment, and means you are to stay a healthy two feet away from everybody. A handshake is okay, although they don't recommend it, as it can spread germs.
No bodily contact whatsoever.

I giggle, knowing I broke that rule within a few hours of boarding the ship.

Another incoming text dings on my phone. It's Vicki again.

We know you won't be seeing this until after your lecture, so Chuck just said, "Too late, Sparkling Ocean, Sammy must have hugged and kissed every student there!"
XOXO, Vicki.

I appreciate those two so much. I check my phone. The universe comes through with three bars, so I dial. After a lot of radio silence, Vicki magically answers the phone.

"Good morning, Voicetrax, this is Vicki."

"Good morning, Voicetrax, this is Sammy."

"Oh, my God, Samantha, did you get my text?"

"I did and, like your text just said, I not only broke the two-foot rule, I shattered it. I hugged and kissed everybody to death."

"So, the lecture went well, I take it."

"It was fantastic and I'd have to give it a ten!"

"Wow," Vicki says. "You never give yourself a ten. I wish I could have been a fly on the wall!"

"It's funny you should say that, because I kind of felt like a fly on the wall while I was teaching. Like there were two of me— one doing and one watching. I won't bore you with all the details, and this roaming is going to be expensive but—"

"Samantha Paris, you are never boring," Vicki says. "Hey, Chuck, pick up the phone, it's Sammy." I hear another click.

"Hello, darlin', Chuckie here."

"Hi, babe, so I was telling Vicki that the lecture went great, but I had kind of an out-of-body experience. I've been a nervous wreck about doing this, because I just didn't think it would translate."

"Yeah, we know, but Vic and I never understood why."

"Because when people come to Voicetrax, they start to study, they work hard, they have a great time, and spend all this money to learn, but in my mind, it's okay, because eventually they will earn it all back when they start booking voice-over jobs."

"Okay—" Vicki says in a way that tells me she's not really following my train of thought.

"What I mean is, our school is in the Bay Area, so there is plenty of voice-over work. We are also next door to Los Angeles, where there's a ton more work. Why would people on a vacation, on a cruise for Christ's sake, want to study voice-over if they had no real prospect of getting work?"

After a long pause, Vicki says again, "You do have a point, but only to a certain extent. You know that every student here, including Chuck and me, has benefitted in all sorts of ways that go way beyond just booking. What do you think all your darn thank-you notes are about?"

In that split second, I feel as if all the blood has drained from my body. All those notes filled with such gratitude and love, pushed or filed away . . .

"I guess that's what I'm kind of getting at here." A massive lump forms in my throat. "As the me who was watching me today, I saw for the first time what I actually do—that what I teach is so much more." The tears fall and I can hardly speak. "I love you guys" is all I manage to get out. The phone line is crackling and I'm losing my signal.

"Sammy, Sammy!" Vicki shouts over the static. "Thank goodness, you are finally beginning to see what we all see."

"I guess—" I begin, making a futile attempt at composing myself. "I think I might have just had my first sip of . . ." and the phone goes dead. I remain glued to the couch in the silence, looking out at the rain mixing in with all the salt of the ocean.

I think I just had my first sip of the Kool-Aid.

THE *SPARKLING EMERALD*, DAY FOUR

My phone is ringing as I walk back into my stateroom, still sweaty from the gym.

"Hello?"

"Good morning, Samantha, this is Bonnie. How are you today?"

"I'm doing well. Yoga this morning at the gym was rather interesting with the ocean being so rough. I was just about the only person who didn't fall over in the Downward Dog position."

"The weather is quite nasty today, but apparently good weather is ahead of us."

"Well, that's great news. It's funny, I was just about to call you, as one of the passengers at the gym this morning stopped me to ask if I would be willing to work with him privately. You know, do private lessons. Is that what you are calling about?"

"Actually, I'm calling because we have had several requests from passengers. A few are interested in having you work with them privately, but most are simply requesting that you do more than the three lectures you are still scheduled to do."

I take a deep breath, simultaneously touched and exhausted by the notion of bringing my crazy Voicetrax life onboard the ship. I'm supposed to be taking a break. "I see," I say, stalling for time.

"You do realize we can't pay you, as we don't pay our speakers," Bonnie continues. "Your free cruise is the payment, so I guess you would have to look at this as donating your time."

"I understand completely and, to be honest with you, I wasn't even thinking about money. I'm just trying to sort out what would work and what I'd be comfortable doing. I do know for sure that I'd like my presentations to all be ninety minutes or even two hours, rather than the scheduled forty-five minutes. Is that possible?"

"I'm not sure about two hours, but that is so generous of you."

"Also, if they could all have that 3:30 start time that would be great." I request that because if the weather is good, the paddle tennis is always from 11:00–1:00.

"That's totally doable," Bonnie chirps.

"Let me digest this and get back to you. I'd like to see how many people actually show up tomorrow for the second lecture. As well-received as the first one was, I can't imagine everybody returning, because now they will all be twice as long, and I'm sure some people won't want to commit to that much time with so many other activities onboard."

"You might be right, Samantha, which is why I'll have to run the ninety minutes versus two hours by Kent."

"Okay, but in any case, if there are fewer people, I can get a lot of folks up to the mic actually performing, so maybe private lessons wouldn't be necessary. I do know that I'd be willing to do a couple of more additional lectures, but I need to think about what I'd actually do with them."

"Wow! Okay, so just to be clear, you want to make them all twice as long, plus do two additional ones?"

"Yep, but let's see what takes place tomorrow."

"That's fantastic. We'll talk soon."

"Bye, Bonnie."

What did I just do?

I'm actually staring at the phone and talking to it. "Samantha Paris, you said 'Let me digest this,' and then in the same breath you immediately committed to doing two more. You are crazy as a loon!" I toss my room key onto the desk and decide that a shower is definitely in order. I do the math in my head as the water warms. *If my second lecture is day five, and I'm now going to do five more lectures, then I'll be working nearly every day. Is that what I want to do?*

I cannot keep doing this anymore, but how can I not keep doing this?

Wait. Why do I say that? What does it really mean? I know what it used to mean or what I thought it used to mean before I boarded this ship.

I cannot keep doing this anymore.

Twenty-two years of teaching when I never wanted to be a teacher in the first place. I hate teaching. Don't I?

How can I NOT keep doing this?

I would let down so many hundreds of people. Not to mention the fact that if I closed the school, how would I support Andre and myself? I no longer have the acting career I once had, because Voicetrax took over.

Andre. Goddamn him. Why did I allow him to take advantage of me like that?

As I begin to rinse off, I rinse that last thought about Andre from my mind. I can't undo what's already been done and wallowing in it will serve me no good. It actually doesn't really matter, because I know something is slowly shifting inside me. Since I fired my mother and walked away from Andre, I feel calmer and happier, but there's more to it than that.

I cannot keep doing this anymore.

That chant is wrong! Teaching is my life. It's who I am. A teacher.

As I step out of the shower I say the words out loud, as if I'm trying them on for the first time. "I'm a teacher."

And what do you do for a living, Samantha? A voice from nowhere asks. I face the mirror and whisper slowly, "I . . . am . . . a . . . teacher." As I stare into my reflection, a soft smile begins to form and my conversation continues. "Sammy, you're worse than Nick Stratton. You've been searching for your bunny all these years, when it's been living inside you the whole time."

I grab my robe, move to the couch, and sit quietly with all this, remembering my calculations from a month ago. If I have spent 52,800 hours teaching in that room, I must be a teacher and a damn good one. I also must really love it and, more important, **it shouldn't be anything to be ashamed of.**

Bam. My biggest revelation ever. "That's it." I say softly. My throat tightens. "I don't hate teaching. I've just been embarrassed all these years to admit that I *am a teacher.*" I shut my eyes tight, fighting back tears. In this instant, I realize that for years, I have been playing the victim unconsciously. Wallowing in it. Fuck you, *Johnny.*" I growl quietly. "I can't believe I've allowed you such power in my life. All these years, worrying if people were going to perceive me as a teacher who taught, because I never really made it as an actress. Or having some kind of scam school like yours and so many others. Go fuck yourself."

I sit there momentarily frozen, listening to the rain. I try to calm myself breathing slowly. In . . . out . . . in . . . out. I get up from the couch to grab some water. "No more, Sammy, you're done." My words float in the air. And in that instant, I know I am. Like with my mother and Andre. Done. I made a commitment to no longer allow drains in my life.

I know I radiate and I only want to be around people who radiate. I happily push the imaginary delete button on one of the biggest drains in my life, Johnny Truffa. And in that instant, he . . . is . . . gone.

I let out a huge relaxing sigh, and I plop down on the couch once again. I pick up the *Sparkling Emerald* daily program, now fully wanting to zone out. Revelations can be exhausting.

I peruse the program in search of activities, knowing it's pissing down rain, and this will now most likely be my only totally free day, because I clearly never know how to say no.

Let's see. I begin to read out loud. "Duplicate and Social Bridge." Nope.

"Odyssey Art at Sea—Create an Exotic Tropical Fish in Pastel Pencils or Watercolor." You've gotta be kidding me.

"Napkin Folding Part Two." I didn't go to Part One.

"Detox for Health and Weight Loss." *Wait, what is this?* "We're exposed to more than two million toxins every day. Come and see how they affect your ability to lose weight and how we can help."

I chuckle, "That lecture will be popular. I'm sure most people would much rather blame toxins than the burgers, fries, and cakes they eat."

I look around the room. "Sammy, who are you talking to? You're mad talking to yourself like this." I laugh meekly. I guess I'm just so used to sound, to noise. It's incredibly still, even with the rain pouring down outside on my verandah. I get up to look outside, as I'm feeling restless.

"Okay, nothing new there. It's fucking rain on your verandah, Sammy," I say, feeling mildly frustrated. I turn and face my room. "What am I going to do today?" Now, I'm whining.

Boy, I really and truly do not know how to simply be.

There must be a real art to not having anything to do and being okay with that. That thought suddenly makes me think of Andre again.

I let out a deep sigh and decide to simply take a walk around the ship and see what happens. Maybe I'll check out the spa and treat myself to a massage. As I get up to get dressed, I see the photos I brought smiling at me. I love the picture of Ollie that Andre drew. Maybe I'll text him later to tell him the lecture was a "ten," because I haven't had a signal on my phone since my conversation yesterday with Vicki and Chuck.

I open my closet and stare at my clothes. "Why am I getting dressed?" The outward conversation continues. "I'm getting dressed for what? I really don't want to walk around the ship. There's nothing to do, nothing to buy, and I can't go outside." I sit back down on the bed and bury my head in my hands.

Am I lonely, or am I merely learning how to be alone?

I sit quietly with that one for a while. My head wants to explode with all the thinking I've been doing this morning. I guess I want to believe the latter. I am simply learning how to be alone. It's new, and like anything that one is first learning, it's not easy. I guess I kind of suck at it, just like my paddle tennis serve. I let out a big sigh and convince myself once again that I'm not lonely. If that were the case, then that would mean I am feeling sorry for myself, which is ridiculous and off-limits. My room is silent. The rain has stopped, and it's suddenly so bright. I open my sliding glass door. It's freezing, but the ocean is beautiful.

"Good morning, Mother N. Are we in a good mood or a bad mood today? You look as if you haven't quite made up your mind." I say aloud. "I'm going to be in a good mood. I'm going to get dressed and be okay with being on my own." I step back into my room where it's warmer.

Nope, being lonely is not an option, I think as I move to my closet. "It's just the motivation I need to get dressed and get out the door. I mean, there's got to be something to do on this ship besides the 'Knitting and Tea Social' or 'Origami for Beginners.'"

THE *SPARKLING EMERALD*, DAY SIX

"Hi, Bonnie, it's Samantha. Sorry to phone you at the end of your day, but I need to talk to you about what is happening with my classes."

"No problem, Samantha. What's up?"

"Well, I did the second lecture yesterday, and I just finished the third one a half an hour ago. It's going off the charts fantastic, and I've now come up with what I want to do for my additional lectures."

"You've got your fourth one tomorrow, right?"

"That's right. So, listen to this." I can't believe I'm so excited to tell her about my crazy idea. "You've heard of *The X Factor* and *American Idol*, right?"

"Of course."

"Well, in my next lecture tomorrow, I'm going to announce a contest. Try this on for size: 'The Sparkling Ocean TransAtlantic Voice Idol!' Groovy, huh?"

She starts to laugh. "Well, by your level of enthusiasm, I'd say yeah, it's groovy, even though I'm not fully sure what you're planning."

"Tomorrow at the lecture I'm going to hand out to each student packets of scripts for the competition, so I'll need to use your copy machine. Is that okay?"

"That's perfectly fine, Samantha. Don't hyperventilate."

I laugh. "Then, the two following days, which are days eight and nine of the cruise, I'm going to hold auditions, and day ten will be the last lecture where I will crown the winner. That leaves day eleven free for them to pack, and then the next morning disembark. What do you think?"

"I still don't fully get it, but it sounds fine. I'm off to a meeting now, but let's talk tomorrow morning."

"That's perfect. Can I come by to copy the scripts at 9:00 and explain then?"

"Great idea."

"One more thing. I will need a more private room for the two days when I hold the auditions. Two to three hours each day should do the trick."

"Wow! Why so long?" she asks.

"Well, each student will have their call time, just like a real audition. Warren will be at 2:00, Carolyn at 2:10, John at 2:20, and so on. I'll record fifteen people one day, and fifteen the next day."

"Samantha, you are going so above and beyond the call of duty. I'll work on getting you another room tomorrow. Oh! Kent mentioned to me today that he would like the three of us to have dinner. Is there a particular night that would work for you?"

I know my dance card is beginning to get full, and I really

don't feel like spending an evening with "the boss," but it's nice for him to offer.

"Can we do it tomorrow night? I think it's the only night I have free."

"I'm off to meet Kent for this meeting, so I will run it past him and get back to you when I see you at 9:00 tomorrow."

"Sounds great, Bonnie. Thanks a bunch!"

THE *SPARKLING EMERALD*, DAY SEVEN

I like being a little naughty.

We all do, I guess. It's not that I've ever done anything major. I am, after all, the girl who alphabetizes her spices. Take my name badge for instance. I wore it to that stupid meet and greet and my first lecture, but that was it. It sits on the desk in my stateroom, and I smile at it, because it's a reminder that I have to live my life a little to the left.

Now I'm in the mood to be naughty as it applies to that snob of a maître d', Zolton. After being told the first night, "there was no table for me," I have dined in the dining room three times, and tonight will be the fourth. The first time was with Frank and Lily. When the three of us walked up to Zolton's counter to be seated, Lily and I were holding hands. I smiled at Zolton and said, "Tonight I feel like a grownup because I get to sit at a table." Lily squeezed my hand gently, as I had told her what had happened.

My next encounter was when I dined with Warren and his partner, Richard. Flanked by two impeccably dressed gay men, with me in my hot fuchsia party dress, was pure fun. That night, I just smirked at Zolton. And then last night, I dined with the Piermartire family, as in the brothers, Carlo and Paolo, and their parents Sergio and Daniela. When we walked up to the counter,

I jokingly said, "Look, Zolton, I have been officially adopted by this wonderful Italian family. They are insisting I must have a place at their table every night!" I enjoyed seeing Zolton's white, pasty face flush. But tonight, I have to have fun with him one more time. The opportunity is just too sweet. I am dining with Kent and Bonnie at the officers' table.

The officers' table.

I pick up the phone and dial extension 10 for the dining room.

"Good evening, *Sparkling Emerald* dining room, this is Zolton."

"Good evening, Zolton, this is Samantha Paris calling."

"Oh, yes, Miss Paris, how may I assist you?" he asks in a painfully polite manner.

"Zolton, tonight I'm dining with Kent and Bonnie. Could you please have a bottle of Billecart Rosé Champagne chilled at the officers' table? We are dining at 8:30, I believe."

"That is correct," he offers.

"You know, we might actually need two bottles, as I'm not sure how many other officers might be joining us."

"Not to worry, Miss Paris, I will see to everything."

"Thank you so much, bye," I giggle at the phone. My hope is that the sommelier, Martin, will be busy with the other guests, therefore leaving Zolton with the honor of having to pour the champagne for the table. *For me.*

My plan set in action, it's time to go upstairs to get my hair done. A special night calls for special hair.

6:40 p.m.

"Hi, I'm Samantha Paris, checking in for my 6:45 hair appointment with Sara."

"Yes, Samantha, please have a seat and Sara will be with you momentarily," says a perfectly groomed receptionist.

"Hi, Samantha," a familiar voice exclaims. I turn to see one of my regular students onboard, the highly strung Beth, looking through her Voicetrax packet of scripts while waiting for an appointment.

"Fancy meeting you here," I say.

"Yes, I'm about to get a pedicure, so I figured this would be a perfect time to go through the packet and figure out which script I'm going to do for my audition tomorrow."

"Don't study these too hard. You're supposed to be on vacation, having fun."

She smiles. "Samantha, this voice-over work is more fun than fun! Not at all like my cutthroat job back home. And to think I'm going to find out what it's like to be an actor tomorrow and audition."

"You're going to do great. You've been one of my shining stars in all the lectures so far."

"Hi Samantha, I'm ready for you," my hairdresser, Sara, announces.

"Okay!" I bend over and give Beth a kiss. "Don't overthink these scripts," I whisper. "Sometimes you try too hard. Remember you've gotta care enough not to care so much."

Beth gives me a thumbs-up as I enter the salon.

7:45 p.m.

I jump up on the bar stool next to John. "Hi, guys!"

"Wow! Look at you tonight. Va-va—voom," he says in that corny way that lets me know that he knows it's corny.

"You look gorgeous," Carolyn adds.

"It's a far cry from what I looked like at paddle tennis this morning. I have to dine with 'the boss' tonight, so I thought I'd make an occasion out of it. It's actually weird. I've never had a real boss before."

"Something tells me that you never will," John says, smiling. "Samantha, this contest of yours is creating quite a stir. You've brought the excitement of *The X Factor* and *American Idol* to Sparkling Ocean!"

"I saw several people practicing for their auditions out by the pool," Carolyn adds. "And Warren has phoned our stateroom twice for advice on what script he should select."

"Oh, my God, that's so Warren. He's such a worrier, bless him. It's funny, I just saw Beth going through her scripts while she was getting a pedicure.

"Carolyn and I are ready with our scripts, but our audition isn't until day after tomorrow."

"Well, don't ask me anything about them, or I will have to disqualify both of you. You know our strict contest rules!" The three of us laugh and then I change the subject. "Hey, what was with that guy today at paddle tennis? He's so competitive, and he nearly tore my right ear off with that blasting approach shot."

"Dimitrios? He's harmless," John says.

"No, he's not! He's a beast and he damn near killed me."

"You're right, Samantha. Some of the men are just that way," Carolyn says sympathetically. "They won't dial it down a bit when playing with women, especially the diehard players."

"You held your own out there today, Samantha, and you didn't have a single double fault." John offers a high-five.

"That's because of your coaching. When I hit the pro circuit, I'm going to have to take you with me," I say, getting up. "Well, I'm off—big dinner date. We're on for sushi tomorrow night, right?"

"Indeed, we are!" says Carolyn. "Just tap on our door about 7:30."

"Are we not seeing you on the courts tomorrow morning?" John asks.

"I'm not sure. With auditions starting tomorrow at 2:00, it might be a bit tight. I'll have to see. Anyway, enjoy your evening. I expect mine to be kind of boring, but duty calls!

As I take the stairs down to the fifth floor, I take stock of how different my life has been for the past week. The highs and lows have been just that: really high and really low, as if my emotional being has been on steroids. I need a break, but somehow, I don't think that the universe is going to let me off the hook. Life lessons seem to be unfolding everywhere.

Is this how my students feel when they take my classes? Sometimes they are utterly euphoric and at other times it's quite the opposite.

"But it's all good," they usually tell me, "I'm really growing, evolving—"

"Hi, Samantha."

"Oh, hi, Bonnie." *Slow down, Sam.* "Sorry, I was deep in thought. You look beautiful tonight. No whites?"

"Thank you. It's so nice when I can get out of my whites and dress like a normal person. It's not often I get to do it, though. I guess I have you to thank."

"Me? Why?"

"Well, because of Kent wanting you to join us for dinner tonight. He doesn't invite people very often. He cut me a pass from my whites, so you wouldn't feel like the odd one out."

"I guess I'm honored." *Thank God, I ordered the champagne.* I had wanted to get Bonnie some kind of thank-you gift, as she has been so helpful, but I couldn't figure out what to buy. Unless you're older than sixty, there isn't anything to buy on this ship. At least now, her special evening has become more special.

"Good evening, ladies." Kent looks more starched in his whites than ever. "You both look lovely. "

Zolton approaches, in full snooty, Zolton-approach mode.

"Oh, I blew it!" Kent suddenly stops. "Bonnie, I left my phone in the office. Zolton, will you see the ladies to our table? I'll be right back."

"It will be my pleasure," Zolton drones. "Ladies?" He extends an arm to each of us and as we walk through the dining room I secretly giggle. I've gone from "no table" to the officers' table, and he has to escort me to it.

"Here you are, ladies." He pulls out a chair for both of us and instead of wisecracking, I smile and simply offer a polite, "Thank you, sir."

Case closed.

"Look!" Bonnie says, pointing at the champagne. "You must have a secret admirer."

Smiling I say, "Actually, Bonnie, it's for you. From me. I wanted to do something special for you."

She looks at me, stunned. "Oh no, Samantha, you shouldn't have. If anything, we should be . . ."

I interrupt her. "Yes, I should have. You have been so helpful, and I damn near took over your entire office today with the copying, the faxing, the printing, and I'm sure there were other "ings" I'm forgetting. Honestly, thank you so much for everything."

Her sweet smile is all the thanks I need.

"How did it go today?" she asks. "Are the passengers excited about the contest?"

"Are they ever! At the end of the session, I passed out the packets and they all had to draw their audition call times out of a Sparkling Ocean hat that I bought. They love the idea of doing an actual audition and it seems like . . ."

Just then two officers join us at our table. "Good evening, ladies."

"Hello, Nicolas, Dimitrios," Bonnie says. "Gentlemen, I'd like you to meet one of our presenters. This is Samantha Paris."

"Didn't I see you somewhere before?" Nicolas asks quizzically, as he sits down across from me. I'm way ahead of him. He was one of the guys I first played paddle tennis with, one of the diehards. He looks so different tonight in his whites.

"Yes, on the paddle tennis court the first day. Doubles, remember? You were really mean out there and we won."

"That's right! You told me you hadn't played in quite a few years. You were great!" Then it immediately dawns on me who his buddy is, now seated at our table.

"And Dimitrios," I say, extending my hands out wide. "I landed on my ass this morning trying to avoid a nasty passing shot of yours!"

A look of shock flickers across Bonnie's face. Dimitrios is the head engineer on the ship; it's possible most people don't usually talk to him like that.

"You look even lovelier sitting up straight," he says with a sly smile. "After you left this morning, I felt quite bad." He stands and offers me a half bow. "I hope you will accept my apology."

"No worries. My mother always used to say to me, 'If you're going to play with the boys—'"

"Evening all!" Kent plops himself down at the dinner table next to me. While they are exchanging pleasantries, a less than pleasant memory invades my mind—

1969

WOODLAND HILLS, CALIFORNIA

"Don't be such a wimp. Pitch it, you wussy!" My brother's friend, Mark, shouts, scraping his feet on the cement, pretending it's the dirt of the batter's box at Dodger Stadium.

"Who you callin' a wussy! Get ready, Schulman. Let's see if you can take the heat!" Larry says, copying his moves and then assuming the pitching position.

Thwack.

Mark takes a practice swing that connects with my temple. I think the sound might be my skull crushing my brains. My brother is now standing over me.

"Bobbi! What did you walk in front of him for? You're so stupid. Are you dead?"

"I'm okay," I say, even though I can't move from the ground. Slowly, I turn myself over and the shock and pain set in. I get up bawling and make my way inside the house into the kitchen.

"Mark hit me in the head with the bat," I scream through tears.

"Stop crying," my mother says, her back to me as she stands over the stove. "If you're going to play with the boys . . ." my mother admonishes, clucking her tongue. "Go to your room and lie down. You'll be fine."

Blurry vision and continuous pain send me to the doctor's office two days later.

"Your daughter has suffered a mild concussion," the doctor says to my mother. "She needs to rest, stay away from TV, and any heavy physical exertion or heat."

My mother glares at me, then turns back to the doctor. "I'm constantly telling her she needs to pay more attention, but you know how kids are. She knows this was all her fault."

I cast my eyes downward, feeling sad and embarrassed. "My mom says I've gotta be tough if I'm going to play with the boys. I guess she's right. I do have to be tough, because playing with girls is boring. I hate dolls."

We walk out of his office, past the lobby, and open the door. A smoggy blast of 97-degree heat smacks me in the face. I want to reach for my mother's hand, but she's busy digging in her purse for a cigarette. I shrug it off. I know I have to toughen up.

"Samantha, you look radiant! Have you met Dimitrios and Nicolas?" Everyone laughs and Bonnie fills Kent in. Then he notices the champagne. "What's with the champagne? Who ordered this?"

"Samantha did!" Bonnie says, beaming at me. "For me. For us."

"Shouldn't we be getting this for her?" Now Kent turns to me. "You are doing such an incredible job. Everywhere I go, passengers stop me to talk about you."

"What exactly do you lecture about?" Dimitrios asks. Just then the sommelier arrives to pour the bubbly. I begin explaining voice-over to my two paddle tennis buddies. They seem amused. The bubbles help. I'm glad I ordered two bottles.

"Tell me about these additional lectures you're doing," Kent says with genuine interest. "Bonnie says there's a contest involved?"

"Hey, mister," I say playfully. "It's not just any contest. It's the Sparkling Ocean TransAtlantic Voice Idol!" Everyone at the table laughs. "The students have been fantastic. So much so, that I'm mirroring a contest that I do back home at my school. The students select a script that is either a cartoon, video game character, commercial, or narration piece. They come in one at a time and audition for me, just like real actors do. I'm going to hold auditions tomorrow and Wednesday."

"So that's it!" Kent exclaims.

Huh? We all give him a look.

"I heard a guy today up on twelve staring at a piece of paper saying, 'Your dog will love it and so will you,' over and over. I figured he was having a senior moment or something."

"Oh, brother." Bonnie laughs. "He was practicing for his audition."

Zolton appears to pour more bubbly all around. He never cracks a smile, even though we are all laughing. I'm beginning to admire his style.

"Yes, they're all practicing for the contest," I say. "I've warned them I'm a tough sell."

Nicolas looks thoughtful. "I heard a gentleman reading something in a strange voice to his wife at the bistro just an hour ago. I thought maybe he'd had one too many espressos."

We all start to laugh again.

"After the auditions," I explain, "I'll narrow it down and send the top ten via MP3 and e-mail to my office. Hopefully the ship will have a signal. My staff will listen and pick the winner."

"What will they win?" Bonnie asks.

"Unfortunately, not much, but the passengers don't seem to care," I say. "It's all in good fun. At home, the winner is 'discovered' by a big Hollywood agent. Here onboard, the winner will receive a Sparkling Ocean hat and T-shirt that I just bought, and if they ever find their way to Sausalito, I'll give them a free class."

"Sparkling Ocean will provide the T-shirt and hat, then," says Kent. I suddenly feel a foot rubbing my foot. "Maybe we could do the same for all the top ten."

How generous. Now the foot is rubbing my ankle as well. It's Kent.

Oh, boy, here we go. Now I know why he's invited me to dinner. I take note of his wedding ring.

"Samantha," Bonnie asks, "how'd you get into voice-over in the first place?"

"Yes, Samantha, and how do you know Karen? She's a great gal," Kent adds. His hand makes its way to my knee.

"So many questions!" I reach for a menu. "How about we order. Aren't you all hungry? I'm starved!"

Bonnie and Dimitrios chime in and pick up their menus. Kent has no choice but to do the same and use both of his hands. The conversation turns to food and we all order. I want to get off the subject of me for a while, and I am about to ask Bonnie what part of Australia she's from when the footsies game starts again.

"Samantha," Kent says, "the head office has caught wind of your popularity onboard, and they have asked me to ask you if you'd be interested in doing our World Cruise next year?"

"Oh! Ahh!" Nicolas and Dimitrios sing in unison, all smiles. "Congratulations!" By the look on Bonnie's face, I can tell she knew this was coming.

"World Cruise?" I ask.

"Yes. It starts next January in Los Angeles and sails the world for four months." His hand is back on my knee. I let out a big sigh and a nervous laugh. Not only because of what's going on underneath the table, but also because there is no way I could or would want to be on a cruise ship for four months.

Exit, stage right.

There's no exit in sight though.

"Wow, this is really something. I went from not having one person come to my table at the meet and greet, to this."

Kent's hand travels north toward my thigh.

"I really am touched," I say. *Quite literally.* "I'm honored. Maybe when I retire, but I could never take off that much time now. My school is incredibly demanding. It took an act of God for me to carve out these two weeks."

"Please at least think about it," Bonnie says. "You wouldn't have to commit for a couple of months yet."

"Yes, please take it under consideration," Kent says, as his foot keeps traveling up and down my calf. Our food arrives and it's all hands on deck again, so to speak, as we dive into dinner and the usual small talk. I learn that Bonnie is from Sydney.

"I love Sydney," I say. "My former husband and I visited twice. It's so beautiful there. We also spent time at Cairns, the Great Barrier Reef, of course, and we flew to Alice Springs and then on to Uluru."

"You've been to Uluru? The outback? I've lived in Sydney my whole life and have never done that." I can tell Bonnie's quite impressed. So is Kent. His hand is back on my knee.

"Not only did I go there, but I also climbed Ayer's Rock." At this point, Kent's hand is climbing up my thigh.

If you're going to play with the boys . . .

I cross my right leg over my left, tightly, crushing his hand. I bear down, so glad I work out. "Kent—" I turn to him, smiling. "Tell me about Charleston. I've been there, but only for a couple of days. I thought it was beautiful, but there was a weird vibe there."

Like the weirdness happening underneath the table.

"Weird vibe?" he asks. "What do you mean?"

"Not to get all political, but it just feels like there are a lot of folks living there really unhappy because they lost the Civil War. They're probably not too happy with our new president either."

Kent's trying to pull his hand free.

My grip tightens as I continue. "Tell me about your family. You're married, right? Do you have any children?" Dimitrios and Nicolas are chatting with the waiter and ordering dessert. Bonnie is reading a text message she just received. I decide to let Kent off the hook and uncross my legs. He appears to be suffering from a loss of appetite and a dick gone limp.

The waiter comes to me for my dessert order, and I order an espresso. Kent passes on everything, but he's all smiles. He shares an inside joke with the guys and checks his phone. I seriously doubt that there's a message for him, but he fakes it and stands.

"Please, excuse me, I'm needed in the theatre. Samantha, you are an absolute delight, and thank you so much for the champagne. I do hope you will give our offer some consideration."

Which offer was that?

"Thank you, Kent. I promise I will."

The evening winds down with coffee and dessert.

"Samantha," Dimitrios says, nodding to me. "It has been a pleasure. We still have a few days left, so I'm hoping you'll join me as my tennis partner one morning."

"Why not? It'll certainly be a hell of a lot safer playing with you than against you!" We all rise from the table, laughing. Two-feet rule be damned, I give each one of them a hug, and they freely hug me back.

"Samantha?" I turn to see Meg, who missed the lecture today, at a nearby table.

"Guys, I'll see you later. Great fun to be with you." I walk over to where Meg and her husband are seated.

"Samantha, I'm so sorry I had to miss today, but I heard about the contest and I'm wondering if it's too late for me to join in?" She really seems concerned.

"Not at all, honey. What stateroom are you in?"

"7009."

"Great. I'll drop off a packet of scripts to your room before I go to the gym tomorrow morning and your audition will be on Wednesday."

"Oh, thank you so much!"

"It's no problem at all."

Out of the corner of my eye, I catch Zolton looking at me and actually smiling.

I give him a smile back and exit the dining room proudly. I start my stair climb to the ninth floor.

Hmm . . . would what just happened be considered sexual harassment? What happened to Kent's two-feet rule? He's such a pathetic dick. It was kinda funny, though.

As I enter my room, smiling, I toss my key onto the desk, knowing that when you're a woman owning a company, you gotta have some balls. "Yep, Sammy" I say aloud. "If you're going to play with the boys, the boys had better be ready for you."

THE *SPARKLING EMERALD*, DAY NINE

I wonder if I'll miss falling asleep to the gentle rocking of the ship when I'm home. It kinda feels like my old waterbed . . . what the fuck was I thinking buying a waterbed? Was it the late 1970s? Oh, this bed feels lovely.

I take in a deep breath, feeling happy. These last two days auditioning, the passengers have been enlightening. Aside from my own personal revelations, I've learned that it's astounding how much someone can absorb when they do it relaxed, playfully, and without a huge agenda. With just four lessons under their belts, these students have now experienced what it's like to audition and compete. Many of them performed better than students who have six months of training under their belts.

They really took to heart my expression that "safety lies in the risk," meaning that when you have to do something, like diving into a freezing cold swimming pool, or you have to do something that scares you, it's much easier to simply dive in. We fool ourselves into thinking it's safer or easier to enter in the shallow end, one, slow, painful step at a time, but that's crazy when we *know* it would be much easier the other way. This is such a great metaphor for life, that it's actually safer to just go for it, for you'll be far less likely to fail. Worrying about failing is crippling.

That's why Andre never did anything with his art. You can't hold back, if you want to be successful. You've got to put yourself out there and take a chance.

I take in a big yawn. *Who are Vicki and Chuck going to pick as the winner? My dark horse, Warren, blew my mind, he was so good, but I have to put my money on Wayne. Carolyn, however, was great, because she picked a travel narration script that was so right for her vocally.*

I roll over on my side. *How many hours will I sleep before my worried subconscious wakes me? Four hours? Five? What song will keep playing over and over in my head? What should I do for the last class tomorrow? How should I announce the winner?*

It's actually safer to just go for it, for you'll be far less likely to fail. Worrying about failing is crippling . . . You can't hold back, if you want to be successful. You've got to put yourself out there and take a chance.

I yawn again, knowing it doesn't matter who wins. They all loved the experience. I feel as though I could sleep for ages. I close my eyes and listen to the distant thrum of the *Sparkling Emerald*'s unseen but mighty engines.

THE *SPARKLING EMERALD*, DAY ELEVEN

"Good afternoon, Voicetrax, this is Vicki."

"Hi, honey, it's me!"

"Oh, hi. How are you? Chuck, pick up the phone— it's Samantha."

"Hey, darlin'," Chuck's voice comes through. "Boy, we miss you around here. You about ready to come home?"

"Yep, after I talk to you guys, I'm off to bed and I'll be off the ship early tomorrow morning for my flight home."

"I can't believe you're flying home immediately." Vicki says. "You sail all the way across the Atlantic to Spain, only to hop on a plane and head back without even looking around."

"Yeah, it's kind of crazy, but I have been here before, and I just don't want to be in Barcelona by myself. Just being on the ship was fine. I really had a great time."

"How'd the final day of the contest go? It was yesterday, right?" Chuck asks.

"Yeah. Oh, guys, it was so cute. I surprised them by not picking the winner myself." I hear the familiar giggles of my two devoted soldiers. "When I told them that I e-mailed the top ten performances to you, and that you selected the winner, they were so impressed. And I'm so glad I did a runner-up and the winner. I thought Warren was going to faint when I gave him his Sparkling Ocean key chain."

"And what about our Texas golfer? What was his reaction to winning?"

"Wayne was so thrilled, it was so sweet. After the class, he and his wife came up to me, and she told me that she was going to make damn sure he would come out for the free class."

"That's fantastic!" Vicki squeals.

"Yeah, it really is. Hopefully after our time together, he'll see that he can realize his dream of doing voice-over, and that it's never too late. Anyway, thank you again for all your help on this. I would have been sunk if you hadn't faxed me those additional scripts."

"Chuck and I had a great time trying to figure out which scripts would be easy for them, because they haven't had the entire beginning student curriculum."

"We couldn't believe the performances you got out of them." Chuck adds.

"I know! Weren't they something? They were so open and receptive to direction. Anyway, we can chat more about this on

Monday. For now, I'm calling to see what my Monday looks like. Chuck, are we still doing Shawn's demo?"

"Nope. He just called an hour ago with a terrible cold."

"And there's very little on your desk, so why don't you just come in on Tuesday? You can sign checks then."

"That's great, Vic. I might want to play catch-up, but I'll wait and see how badly the 'jet lag bug' bites. Okay, I'm going to call it a night. I've missed you guys and I love you."

"We love you too, boss."

"Chuck," I groan, "how many times over all these years have I told you I hate it when you call me that?"

Vicki laughs. "Which is exactly why he says it!"

"Yeah, yeah, I know. Alrighty guys, time for me to hit the hay. Have a great weekend."

"Good night, Sammy," they both chirp, and I think I hear the word "boss" once or twice more through their laughter. I hang up the phone and the soft click puts a period on this entire journey. I'm done and done. I let out a sigh. I'm glad to be going home, but, like any great trip, I am feeling a bit melancholy. I'm not quite ready to let all these experiences become memories. But like Andre once taught me, "It's best to leave the party at its high point." And I know he is absolutely right.

Part 4

Five Months Later

"Gabrielle, you are a sight for sore eyes." As we hug, years of childhood memories fill my heart.

"You are the sight," she says. "My God, singlehood agrees with you. You must be fighting the men off left and right."

I let out a large chuckle and roll my eyes. "Just get in the damn car." As I open the trunk, a security guy motions me to hurry up. He's also smiling at me. I toss Gaby's bag in, shut the trunk, and hop in the driver seat, eager to catch-up with my longtime friend.

"How was your flight? How are Scott and the kids?" I ask, as we head out of the airport, north, toward the Golden Gate Bridge.

"The kids are great." She beams. "They're doing so well."

"That's a fucking miracle with three teenagers. How do you do that?"

"I know, crazy, right? Scott and I are the same, I guess. We're just living our lives. He does his thing, and I do my thing."

I shake my head, fully understanding.

"So how are you, Sammy? You look wonderful."

"Oh, thanks, babe. I'm okay. I'm actually doing really well. Since I moved back into the house it's been a bit of a challenge. I love being back home, but it's an awful lot of house for one person to take care of, and, of course, you know I've never had a clue how to do anything in the garden."

"Of course, you don't know how to garden, you're Jewish."

I turn and look at her and smile, then giggle. "Have I ever told you the story of when Andre went away for a week to a sculpting seminar and I had to take care of the house?"

"I guess not. What happened?"

Every time I tell this story, I can barely finish it, as I end up laughing at my own stupidity.

"So, it was summer and we were having a really bad heat wave and Andre kept drilling into me the importance of watering his tomato plants every day while he was away. He took me out back and showed me where the hose was and how to do it, repeatedly reminding me to water these plants every single day."

"You didn't even know where your hose was?"

I shake my head "no" and try to contain my laughter. "I had to be shown how to clean the pool too, but that's not part of this story. Anyway, he was just so damn intense about watering that I had to assure him. 'Okay, okay, okay. I *get it*. I'll water the tomato plants!'"

"So, did you?"

"Of course, I did. Or at least I thought I did. A couple of years later, when we were at a dinner party, Andre tells the story of me having to take care of the house while he was away, and I'm thinking, why is he telling this story? I watered the plants, cleaned the pool, the house survived, no big deal, right?"

I'm cracking up and now Gaby lets out a laugh of her own. "What happened, Sammy?"

"Well, apparently I wasn't watering his tomato plants. He told everyone there I was actually watering his pot plants."

"What?" she gasps. I'm still laughing.

"Yeah, I was shocked too! He said he went down to the

hardware store and bought little red Christmas ball ornaments and hooked them on the plants, so I would think they were tomatoes! He knew how gullible and unobservant I am, and he also knew I would be totally against growing marijuana. Can you believe how stupid I was?"

"I don't know," Gaby says half giggling. "Unobservant, for sure. If it can't talk or make a sound, Sam, you don't always pay attention. But I think it's more about being trusting. If Andre said it was a tomato plant, then it was a tomato plant."

"I can be too trusting. I don't always question things."

"It's what makes you, *you*, Sam, and you're absolutely adorable. In case you hadn't noticed."

I let out a big, relaxing sigh. It always feels great to have a good laugh, especially with Gabrielle, my only real childhood friend growing up in LA.

"How's Ollie?" she asks.

"He's a bit of a challenge too, but we're figuring it out. When I have to work my twelve-hour days, he's got to come down to the studio with me, and on the other days, I battle the traffic so I can get home in time to take him for a walk. Sometimes it's nine o'clock before I can start my dinner."

"I'm impressed you even bother with cooking."

"Well, I enjoy cooking, but it is lonely. Twenty years is a long time cooking for two."

"Speaking of which, how is Andre? Where's he living now?"

"He's down in Palm Springs, housesitting for his ex-wife before me, Lynda Paris. She only lives in the desert during the cooler months and goes to Norway to live with her boyfriend the rest of the time."

"What's he going to do when she comes back? Is he going to live with her?"

"God, no!" I laugh. "They would drive each other crazy. I think Lynda's going to help him find a place, or I'll go help him."

"Sammy, I think it's amazing how you've managed to create such a loving divorce."

"It takes two, and Andre was quite angry for a while. The divorce isn't final yet. I have to be super patient sometimes, true, but it's worth it."

"Worth what? Not to be taken to the cleaners?"

"Gaby," I tell her, "it's not like that. Andre's not like that. He's actually taking the moral high road rather than the greedy legal one."

Gaby shakes her head approvingly.

"No," I continue, "come on, Gab, you know how I feel. I don't want to completely lose Andre. I spent nearly my entire adult life with him, and I don't want to throw all those years away. I don't ever want to think of those twenty years as a mistake. They're not. When you love someone, you love them. If you end up hating someone you were married to, then you didn't love them to begin with."

Gaby nods. By her silence I can tell she is thinking about Scott. Things have not been that great with them lately.

"Not to change the subject—" I lie, "but let's talk about dinner. We're just crossing the Golden Gate, which means we're still at least an hour, maybe more, to Petaluma in this traffic. Are you starving? We can stop in Mill Valley and eat, or just talk our heads off until Petaluma. It's up to you."

"No, Sammy, it's up to you. You're driving. I'm just so happy to be here."

"Well, I'm thinking I'd just kind of like to get the drive done. That way we can both really relax." "Okay, then let's go home and go to that Italian restaurant that you and Andre took me to a couple of years ago."

"Graziano's Ristorante? Oh, that's an interesting story. Funny you should suggest that. I just went in there for the first time, since Andre and I split, a couple of weeks ago." As I dial my handsfree keypad, my fingers go into auto mode. I have been dialing the restaurant for seventeen to eighteen years now.

"Buonasera. Graziano's," a man's voice answers.

"Is this Mati?" I ask. Graziano's headwaiter.

"Sì, sì! Who am I speaking with?"

"Mati, it's Samantha Paris."

"Ah, bella, how are you? I haven't seen you for some time now."

"I was in a couple of weeks ago, but you had the night off. Any chance for dinner tonight about 7:15, 7:30-ish?"

"Oh, no, Samantha, I'm so sorry. Not tonight. We stopped taking reservations three days ago. We're overbooked. How about tomorrow night?"

"I don't know what our plans are yet, but I'll call back shortly if we can do tomorrow," I say. "It's nice hearing your voice, we'll speak soon."

"Okay, bella. I'm so sorry. Ciao. Ciao."

"Ciao. Ciao, Mati."

"Busy place," Gaby says.

"It's always packed on the weekends, but usually they could squeeze Andre and me in. How about that Thai restaurant you and I went to in February?"

"I did love it, but do you remember how much food we ordered?" Gaby groans. "We had those spring rolls and let-tuce cups as appetizers, and then you insisted on three different curries."

"But it was you who insisted on that banana flambé thingy," I say accusingly. We both giggle.

"Okay, Thai it is, but I'm doing the ordering this time. So, tell me, what happened at Graziano's?"

"Well, up until last night, I'd been casually dating this guy, Adam, for about a month or so."

"You didn't tell me you were dating!" Gaby interrupts. "Let's talk about him."

I roll my eyes. "Trust me, there's nothing to talk about. It was a mistake from the beginning, but just let me tell you this story. Adam wanted to go to Graziano's because he'd heard about the vodka bar."

"What vodka bar?" Gabrielle scrunches her nose.

"Graziano put in this additional bar that's actually a room that's 28 degrees. You put on faux mink coats and go in there and do vodka tastings. It's actually really cool."

"Cool as in below freezing?" Gaby fakes a shiver.

"An-ny-way, I didn't want to go there, because I knew the minute I walked in and Graziano saw me with another guy, he would ask about Andre, and I didn't want to have to deal with that."

"But you obviously did go there, right?"

"Of course, silly, or else there's no story!"

Gaby laughs.

"So that's exactly what happened. We put off checking out the vodka bar until after dinner, and while we were having appetizers, Graziano saw me and came to the table. He made a big deal about not seeing me for so long, and I introduced him to Adam and then he asked about Andre."

"Was it awkward?"

"I made it less awkward by asking Adam if it was okay if I excuse myself from the table for a few minutes to talk privately with Graziano. I had warned Adam ahead of time that I was probably going to have to do that."

"So? And?" asked Gaby, wanting me to fast forward.

"He took me to this small private table just around a corner, and I told him that Andre and I had been separated since January and that we were getting divorced. Graziano was shocked and seemed quite sad."

"But why? I mean, he owns a restaurant. I'm sure hundreds of his customers get divorced."

"That's true, but it really threw him. He said he had no idea, because we always seemed so happy. I then proceeded to tell him *everything,* which I wasn't really planning on doing, and, of course, I ended up crying too."

"Of course," said Gaby squeezing my hand, which was on the seat between us. "What exactly does *everything* mean?"

"The truth—that I'd been unhappy for years, that I supported both of us and how Andre always acted entitled. Graziano was shocked. He thought, like most people, that Andre was my sugar daddy."

"Did he say that?" Gaby asks. "Did he actually say *sugar daddy*?"

"Yeah, and it stung, but I've been dealing with people having that assumption for years."

"You know, Samantha, Andre leads people to that conclusion. It's not just your obvious age difference."

"Well, I wouldn't exactly say he *leads* people to that conclusion. People are all too happy to judge. He would simply, as he calls it, 'lie by omission.' He knew all the time the stereotypical judgments that people were making, and he never chose to correct them because he liked it. It painted him in a positive light. Sadly though, it didn't matter to him that I was being painted in a negative one."

Gaby softly sighs. "It's really sad, isn't it? It was always all about him."

"Yeah, whatever. Anyway, it was kind of strange confiding in Graziano that night, because he was always way more engaged in Andre when we would come to the restaurant. He'd sit with us for a few minutes, maybe share a glass of wine, and the men would talk, usually about soccer or Graziano's love life."

"I'm trying to remember Graziano," Gaby says. "Did he have a ponytail?"

"Yep, he still does. He's always had it."

"And an accent?"

"Of course. And it's a thick one, but his English is good, and he's also fluent in Spanish and French."

"Wow! I think I remember him being really handsome in a short, sexy, Italian sort of way."

I laugh and the phone rings. The familiar number beams up at me from the screen. "Speak of the devil, it's the restaurant. Hello?"

"Ah, ciao, bella, it's Graziano!" he says in a loud and animated voice. "Mati told me you a' wanted to come in tonight. I will make sure you a' have a table."

"Oh, that's so sweet, Graziano. You don't have to do that."

"Well what's a' matter wit choo? I told you a couple of weeks ago, I'm gonna take care of you. Whenever you want, you just come in and I a' feed you.

Gabrielle stifles her giggles with her hand.

"Graziano, I have a girlfriend with me, so there are two of us," I tell him.

"That's a' fine. I see you soon. I have to run. Ciao, bella."

I look at Gaby and shrug. "I guess we're going to Graziano's tonight after all."

"Super-issimo," Gaby jokes. "Hey, is Graziano single?"

"Yes, he's always been single since I've known him. He always has these different hot blondes hanging off his arm. He used to complain to Andre that he just couldn't find the right one." I can see Gabrielle grinning ear to ear. "I know what you're thinking and you can just stop it."

"What? Me, thinking?" Gabrielle says, not so innocently. "I'm not thinking anything."

"Bullshit, you're not!" I say, laughing. "Graziano and I have known each other for ages, but I've never thought of him in that way. I was married and we are friends."

"Okay, okay. So, what else happened that night, the vodka bar night? You didn't finish."

"It was actually a little uncomfortable. We talked longer than I realized, and Adam was at the table waiting."

"Ouch."

"Ouch is right. Anyway, Graziano did say to come in any time, and he would take care of me. I told him I felt uncomfortable, because it's quite a bar scene, and I wouldn't want to deal with men annoying me. He just said he would take care of me and not to worry. He was really nice and it was a tender conversation, but I knew I would never go in there by myself."

"And now here we are two weeks later."

"Exactly. But getting back to Adam, I must have been gone at least half an hour and he was not happy. He could see I had been crying. He told me that I shouldn't care so much about Andre, and I just shook my head. I had been wanting to dump him and was going to do it that night at Graziano's. Unfortunately, he'd already had too much to drink while waiting for me, and so I decided against it."

"And so, you dumped him this morning? What took you so long? And what was wrong with him anyway?"

"Well, I just told you, didn't I? From our first date, I tried not to talk about Andre, but it's kind of hard when that's who I'd been with for twenty years. Adam made it clear that once you break up with someone, that's it. You move on and don't look back. But I knew then, as I know now, in my heart of hearts, that Andre is always going to be a part of my life and whomever I end up with, *if* I ever find someone, is going to have to accept that. I guess you could call it a deal breaker."

"Good luck, Samantha. That's one hell of a deal breaker," Gaby warns. "Most people think like Adam."

"But why? I really don't understand that. Do you think like Adam and most people?"

"I'm really not sure how I would feel if I was dating someone who was so loving toward their ex," Gaby frowns. "I don't think I would like it."

"I never had a problem with Lynda Paris," I say, mentioning Andre's ex-wife. "I never felt threatened by her and I love her. Not to mention the fact that her family is my family! Remember I told you about my Thanksgivings in Dallas?"

"Right, now I'm putting it together again. Sammy, most people are not like you, that's for sure."

"That's a good thing. I find myself utterly exhausting at times." I look over at Gabrielle and she's smiling. "What are you thinking about?"

"Just about when we were kids," she muses. "You always seemed so confident, and you always knew what you wanted."

"I might have always known what I wanted, but I'm not so sure about the confident part. I always wished I could be you, Gaby. You were so beautiful and skinny, and the boys followed you everywhere. Remember when we would go to the beach? The boys always wanted you to ditch your chubby friend."

"You were not chubby," Gaby protests.

I think about those painful growing-up years. I grab her hand for a squeeze. "Thanks for not ditching me, babe."

"You're un-ditchable, Sammy," she says, squeezing my hand back. "I love you."

"Yeah, I love you too." After a sweet moment of silence, our conversation continued for the next hour, all the way up 101 to Petaluma. She reminded me of what life is all about when you've been married for more than a couple of decades.

Better the devil I know, than the devil I don't. That's what Andre's mother always used to say about her husband and their sixty-year marriage. It's the same thing I'd repeat to myself in living with Andre.

It's different with Gabrielle. Although things are rough between them right now, she and Scott will find a way to make it work because of the kids. Kids are so often the glue in those vows of "for better, for worse." For worse, as in, you try everything possible to make your marriage work. When it doesn't, you're still willing to stay together and remain miserable for the rest of your life. I really can't imagine what it would be like to sacrifice my entire life, my own happiness for my child. Never having loving parents or a child of my own will do that.

"I always love coming here, Sammy," Gabrielle says, as we turn off the highway into Petaluma's little downtown. "It's so quaint—the river, the boats."

"Yeah, and our wonderful, crazy 'Petaluma Pete,' who's been pounding away on that same old upright piano on the sidewalk for all the years I've lived here.

"Hey, Pete," I call out, giving him a nod and throwing a dollar into his basket as we walk by.

We enter the restaurant, diving into a sea of people. It's a madhouse. Gabrielle motions to me that she's off to the restroom, as I make a feeble attempt to get us a seat at the bar. My mind is still fixated on the discussion in the car. I know several couples in unhappy but long-lasting marriages.

Am I throwing my life away with this divorce or taking a chance on a new journey?

"Samantha, bella, ciao!" I'm thrust back into reality with Mati's warm but piercing voice. He kisses both of my cheeks as Italians do. "Graziano gave you his table tonight," he says, pulling menus and urging me to follow him.

"That's so sweet of him," I say, as Gabrielle joins us. "Mati, I'd like you to meet my girlfriend, Gabrielle. Gabrielle, Mati."

"Mamma mia!" he exclaims. "How am I going to be able to concentrate serving two such beautiful women?" He pulls out each of our chairs. "Can I get you a cocktail?"

Knowing Gaby is a total lightweight, I say, "I'll bet a million dollars that my beautiful girlfriend here would like hot tea."

"Samantha would be right." Gaby laughs.

"I, on the other hand, will have a Stoli elit straight up, really chilled with an olive."

As Mati quickly disappears into the madness, Gaby opens her menu. "Yum! Do I want the gnocchi or the lasagna?"

"Are you talking to yourself or are you asking me?"

"I know how you used to tell Andre what he wanted to eat all the time, so I thought I'd give you the pleasure."

"I'm sure you remember you had the gnocchi here the last time and loved it."

"Did I have the pesto or the meat sauce?"

"You had the pesto. However, you can order it fifty-fifty, which is actually what I think you should get!"

She laughs as Mati appears with our drinks and bruschetta. He remembered that it's my favorite. "Thank you, sweetheart. What's the special tonight?"

"Tonight, we have halibut with white wine, sun-dried tomatoes, and capers. It's beautiful," Mati answers.

"Great. We'll have Caesar salad for two, Gabrielle will have the gnocchi fifty-fifty, and I will do the fish with vegetables and no potatoes." I hand the menus to him and can see by the look in his eyes that Graziano must have told him about Andre. He gives me a loving, understanding smile and heads toward the kitchen.

"I think he's got a crush on you," Gaby says, making sure Mati is out of earshot, "and doesn't realize he's going to have to wait in line. First, it was the security guy at the airport, now we're sitting at the owner's table, and you have one of his employees after you, and I've only been with you a couple of hours. I wish I could have your life, but I guess I'll just have to live vicariously."

"Ha, ha," I say in a singsong voice, like I did when we were kids. "Very funny. You're so funny, I forgot to laugh."

"Okay," Gaby says, laughing and looking at me only the way someone who has known me for forty years can, "I'll stop teasing you, but honestly, you look like a completely different person since I saw you last February. Your entire aura is different."

I look down at my bruschetta and shrug my shoulders. "I don't think I look any different, but I do feel kind of different. As I said in the car, my life is more challenging now, but I feel more at peace."

"How so?"

"Well, you know how I've always felt about Voicetrax—I didn't want it. Andre always used to say it grew in spite of itself."

"I often wondered how you dealt with running the business and not acting as much," Gaby says.

"Not so well. I was living with a lot of anger and frustration inside. I've always loved my students, that's undeniable. But, for all these years, I've been so conflicted with helping all these people realize their dreams when I wasn't living mine. Or so I thought. You know, I used to want to put a bullet to my head."

"Sammy, that's an awful thing to say. You didn't mean that." I shoot her a glare.

"Don't dismiss me, Gabrielle. That's what Andre used to do when I would tell him this. He'd say, 'Oh, you don't mean that,' and then he would walk out of the room. That used to make me want to kill myself even more."

Her eyes widen.

"What? Don't look so stunned. We're sitting here eating. I didn't do it. I'm not dead!"

"Yes, but you never said anything. Why didn't you talk to me? Did you ever talk to a therapist?"

"Yeah, I tried a couple. I lasted two visits with each one. I just felt like it was crazy telling these strangers my problems when I knew I could and *would* figure it out on my own. Like I always do."

"Here you are, ladies," Mati says, arriving with our salads. "Can I offer you some vino?"

"No, thank you," Gaby demurs. "I'm going to stick with tea tonight."

"I'm still nursing my martini," I say, "so I think we're good. This looks great."

"Mangia!" Mati says before bustling off to take care of another table.

Gaby appears sullen, as she picks at her salad. Even sulking, she's still beautiful. Sometimes I think she grew up, became the mother, the responsible adult, and I'm still my twelve-year-old self.

"Hey," I say, poking at her side. "I do feel different now. I've come to the realization that my real purpose in this life wasn't to act, but to teach. I've just been fighting it for so long. Like I was desperately trying to hold on to my Plan A, when Plan B fit me so much better. It's so much more fulfilling."

Now Gaby smiles, but wanly. "We both know I've been living my Plan B from the moment I married Scott and had three kids. If you remember, I was never going to settle down."

"Oh, I remember all right," I say, laughing.

"Buonasera!" Graziano exclaims. Here he is, ponytail and all, approaching our table with his arms out wide.

I stand to hug him. "Graziano, thank you so much for your table tonight. We feel so spoiled." I turn to Gaby. "I'd like for you to meet one of my dearest friends, Gabrielle."

She extends her hand and he kisses it. "Such a pleasure to a' meet you. Welcome to my ristorante."

"I've been here once before. Samantha and Andre brought me here when I was visiting a couple of years ago. I had your gnocchi, and my daughter had your lasagna. It was heavenly."

"And what you a' eat tonight?"

"The gnocchi!" We say in unison and laugh.

"What about you, Miss Samantha? Please no a' tell me the feesh. That's a' all I ever see you a' eat."

"And that's what you're going to see her eat again," Mati says, setting our dinners in front of us.

"Mamma mia!" Graziano grumbles. "What's the matter with the rest of the menu?" he says, pinching his fingers together.

"What? I love your fish. Pasta is too fattening. My girlfriend here can afford it, but I can't."

"What are you a' talking about?" Graziano says, pinching his fingers together again. "You are so beautiful." He beckons to Mati. "Bring them a bottle of Kistler Chardonnay."

Gaby and I exchanges glances—she an eyebrow, me a smile—that gives away nothing.

"Ladies, enjoy your dinner. I be a' back later. The kitchen, it has needs."

"Thank you, Graziano," I say warmly, as he hurries off. "This looks yummy. I didn't realize how hungry I am. Are you hungry?"

Gaby picks up her fork and points at me accusingly. "Samantha Paris, Graziano likes you. I can tell. And he's gorgeous and such a sweetheart!"

"Didn't your mother tell you it's not polite to point?" I playfully lower her fork. "Look, Gaby, I know he likes me. We've been friends for about seventeen years. But we're *friends*. That's it."

"You might feel like that from your perspective, but he's looking at you like something more than friends." She takes a bite of gnocchi and her eyes roll heavenward. "Oh, my God, Samantha. This is even better than I remember. This tastes like a cloud that dissolves in your mouth. It's unbelievable."

"He's quite a chef. That's why this place is always packed."

Gabrielle is tracking Graziano's movement around the dining room. "You know, he has this majestic quality about him," she says. "He's also cute and he's perfect for you." She licks her fork, in a trance, like the pesto is some magical potion.

"Stop it! You're thinking again. I can't go out with Graziano,"

I say adamantly. "It would be too weird. We've been friends for way too long."

"That, my dear friend, is about to change. I'm telling you, he's the one and nobody would know that better than me. I mean come on. I've known you longer than anyone."

I'm searching for a way to change the subject when Mati rescues me, arriving at our table and opening the chardonnay. He pours me a taste.

"It's delicious. I hope you will join me and pour yourself a glass. I cannot drink this on my own." I'm relieved when he takes me up on my offer. We toast and he excuses himself to take care of his other customers.

"As I was saying," I continue, once he's out of earshot, "I'm so much happier now because I'm not fighting with the universe anymore. I have not only accepted my role in this life, but also I feel tremendous gratitude."

Gaby finally takes her first break from eating. "If I lived here, I would be in here every night. I don't know how you stayed away from this place for so long."

"Are you even listening?"

"Yes, of course, I am, Samantha. You said you feel grateful, which I think is kind of strange. You have always been grateful for what you have. Not to mention the fact that you have worked your butt off for everything in your life. Even when we were kids."

I shake my head. "Yes, of course, I've always appreciated the life I have: my 'trappings,' the traveling I've done, and having my business. There isn't a day goes by that I'm not grateful. But that said, my 'trappings' have also served as a reminder of a career I didn't want—one I said I hated. So, I probably didn't fully appreciate everything, which has made me feel incredibly guilty."

"I am so full, I cannot eat another bite. Would it be weird to ask if we can take these last two gnocchi home?"

"No, sweetheart. It would not be weird to ask for a doggie

bag." I look at my watch and think of my sweet Ollie at home, alone all afternoon and evening. "We probably should go because of Ollie. Do you mind?"

"Not at all!"

I signal to Mati for the check. Gabrielle is craning her neck in search of Graziano, but I'm focused on leaving a proper tip, because we weren't charged for the appetizer or the wine. I know Graziano isn't coming back to the table. He's always so busy and never has time to visit with the same customers twice. On second thought, with Andre and me, he would share a little wine with us at the beginning, and then later he'd always bring over some lovely port on the house, and then he and Andre would chat some more.

"Okie dokie." I finish signing the check. "Let's blow this joint."

"Thank you so much for dinner, Sammy. It was wonderful."

We make our way through the crowd and then Gabrielle spots Graziano at the end of the bar near the front door. We walk over to say goodbye.

"Oh! You ladies are leaving so soon. It's a' Friday night!"

"Yes, it's Friday night, but tell that to my little nine-pound doggie who's been alone nearly all day and night. It's been wonderful, but we have to go. Thank you so much for everything." I lean in for the Italian double-cheek kiss.

"Graziano, thank you so much for this amazing dinner. Samantha was chatting away, but I could only concentrate on my food. I think I fell under some kind of spell; it was so good."

"I'm a' glad you enjoy. I hope you come back soon." He kisses her hand. "Samantha too, of course."

"You know, Graziano, I think you should ask Samantha out," Gaby says.

I freeze in my tracks, wishing a hole would open and swallow Gabrielle.

Graziano eyes me slowly up and down, as though I'm a big salami he's considering purchasing. He shrugs and smiles. "What are you a' doing next Tuesday?"

"Ah, Tuesday?" I'm fairly sure I have to teach. Gabrielle kicks my ankle. "Um, Tuesday? I think I'm free." I feel so strange and embarrassed.

"Good," he says. "I will pick you up maybe about seven o'clock. Do I have a' your phone number?"

"You called me this afternoon, so, yes," I say teasing.

"Well, then I will a' call you Tuesday morning to let you know for sure the time."

"It sounds wonderful. I'm looking forward to it," I say somewhat touched but still so embarrassed. I notice both Gabrielle and Mati are grinning and, surprisingly, so is Graziano. Now my face is beginning to turn red and I hear in my head "Snagglepuss" beckoning me to exit, stage right. "Okay, Gab, come on, let's go. Thanks again for everything!"

As we walk out into the beautiful, balmy September evening, Gaby reaches for my hand and I let her take it. I should be annoyed with her, but somehow, I'm not. But I am just a' wondering what next a' Tuesday will bring.

Three Months Later
7:00 p.m., December 31, 2010

PETALUMA, CALIFORNIA

Next a' Tuesday turned into next a' Wednesday, Thursday, Friday, and then every day of the week. And then October, November, and now December. New Year's Eve. Gabrielle was right. Graziano was The One. My life was suddenly filled with a love that I had never known. It was the same for Graziano. Some of his friends and family members felt it was all happening "a bit fast," but, for us, finally finding true love at ages fifty and sixty-nine, respectively, wasn't too fast at all.

Unfortunately, though, the words "gold digger" and "sugar daddy" swirl around the restaurant, like it's yet another sauce coming from the kitchen. I should be used to it, of course, but it's always been so damn hurtful, because it couldn't be further from the truth. What am I supposed to do? Wear a sandwich board and walk around the restaurant ringing a bell saying that I'm my own woman with a successful business?

I inspect my reflection in the mirror, as I wield the mascara wand. I'm meeting Graziano at the restaurant at nine o'clock. I know firsthand that it will be a zoo, as Andre and I had celebrated there a few times in our twenty years together. A lump forms in my throat.

Damn. Why is life so complicated?

I'd like to say that since we've been separated just a few days shy of a year and the divorce is nearly final, that I go days without thinking about him. I'd *like* to say that, but that would be a lie. I think of him every day. I worry about him. He's seventy-nine years old and all alone. His life did not turn out the way he thought it would, and I know he holds a lot of regret.

"Oh, Andre," I sigh aloud. "I need to tell you about Graziano but I don't want to hurt you."

I look in the mirror and can see the pain behind my eyes. *Sammy, it's not going to be easy but you gotta do it. You have to tell him. Until you do, none of this is even real.* I do feel a bit dishonest at this point as hardly anyone from "my side" even knows about Graziano—only Gabrielle, Chris, Jeff, and Cathy. Not my staff, not my students, not even my "mother," Janet. Only these four know until I tell Andre.

Ollie is growling at my feet.

"What, Ollie?" I look down and discover three different toys he has placed by my feet as a request to play. "I'm sorry, sweetheart, Mommy's been distracted." I pick him up and head into the living room to sit by the fire. "Ollie, why am I so happy, but feel sad at the same time?" He cocks his little head to the left, then the right, and then licks me. "Why? I love Graziano so much, and he's so good to us. Huh, little guy? Why do I feel sad?" He licks me again. "You don't even eat dog food anymore. It's fresh chicken or salmon or filet mignon for you!"

He jumps off my lap to fetch me a toy. I heave a sigh. Graziano's sensitive. He understands my sadness. I know he's carrying some of his own private pain, as it applies to Andre. They were friends. Ollie drops his toy at my feet and stares at me. "Okay, Ollie. Tomorrow's the day. It's the first day of the new year, and I'm going to start it out right."

Ollie takes off like a rocket when I throw the toy, and I fear he's going to crash into the wall. "Slow down, Ollie," I say a bit concerned and get up from the fire. "Ollie, tomorrow I'm going to sit and write your papa a letter. Does that sound like a good idea?"

Ollie barks in response. I know it's because he wants me to throw the toy again, but I take it as a yes in response to my question. "Yep," I whisper to him, "tomorrow is the day. Andre needs to know."

1 January 2011

Dearest Andre,

This will certainly be the most difficult letter I will <u>ever</u> have to write. I fear it's going to create such pain for you on several levels and since I love you it makes it so difficult.

You once said to me many years ago, "Ask me any question but be ready for the answer." I loved when you said that and not only did I live by that with you, but I have used that expression and lived by that with my students. Oh How I have learned so much from you . . . The problem now however is that I have never had anything to hide. You haven't asked me what I've been doing outside of working and still trying to support us, and I haven't told you. I have been (here comes another of your famous quotes) "lying by omission." This of course pains me to no end as I have never lied to you on any level ever. So why now? Simply because I didn't want to hurt you and I wanted to make absolutely certain that what I needed to tell you was <u>real</u> . . . that it wasn't just a passing moment. The truth? I am in love with Graziano . . . When Gabrielle was here in September we went to the restaurant and she met him. When we were leaving she went up to him and said, "I think you should take Samantha out." <u>I was shocked</u> and so was he. Nevertheless, on September 21st we went out on our first date. By our third date we were in love, and during Hanukkah with his friends and family here at the house for dinner, he took me completely by surprise and got down on his knees and asked for my hand in marriage. Through my tears I said yes . . .

There is so much more I could say right now . . . One thing being the awkwardness and empathy Graziano feels for you as you are reading this. How neither of us wants to hurt you but we know that <u>you</u> <u>are</u> <u>hurting</u>. But let's leave him out of this. This is a <u>painful</u> moment for me because although I am happy with him, you have been <u>MY</u> <u>LIFE</u> for nearly 23 years and there is a part of me that will always love you . . . because A) I want to. And B) because you are embedded in my soul . . . Through my sobbing and shaky hand right now I pray you will forgive me for keeping this to myself these last few months and know I just didn't want to hurt you. Ultimately, I hope you can find it in your heart to accept this graciously and lovingly and that you and I can move on to a new chapter.

So process this right now. It's why after tons of careful consideration I opted to write you a letter rather than be face to face. I felt it would be much easier on you. When you are ready to talk, please call and we will get together. I pray it will be soon . . . I need a hug.

With love,

S. xoxo

Part 5

Three Years Later
June 22, 2013

"And so, like I said, the best advice I can give you as an agent is to be authentic and just do what you do, because that's what producers are going to buy. The minute you start trying to be something you're not, it comes off phony and today, especially in commercials, *they want the real thing.* If they want a pygmy who sounds 2-foot, 8-inches tall with a Spanish accent, they're going to find a real, 2-foot, 8-inch, Spanish-speaking pygmy."

The students laugh, hanging on Jeff Danis' every word. A few are beginning to get antsy. They want to get going with the competition, even though they know that Jeff is one of the biggest voice-over agents in the business, and that these pearls of wisdom are priceless.

"What you guys are doing here is great," Jeff says. "Training is vitally important, because there is a lot of technique involved. It's not easy and a lot of actors can't do it."

A hand goes up. "Oh, you mean, read the copy in thirty seconds, be authentic, be rhythmically right, utter ridiculous copy points after copy points, and sound completely natural in your approach?" Steve says with playful sarcasm.

A few giggles erupt. Jeff silences them.

"That's absolutely right. We have to trust you and trust what you're saying by *how you say it,* or we're not going to buy it. And because your goal is to sell products, if we don't buy what you're saying, you're not going to book. It's as simple as that. And one other thing. You have to trust your agent. Just because maybe you haven't booked in a while doesn't mean you should change agents. If he or she tells you to shut up and keep going, then shut up and keep going. Don't argue with me or second-guess things."

I see half the room smile, as they have agents here in the Bay Area and know the frustrations of being in a booking slump.

"There's a reason why DPN is so successful. And it's not because we don't know what we're fucking talking about! Lighten up, relax, and go with it. It's not going to happen overnight. It's a fun business if you let it be fun."

Time for me to step in.

"Okay, guys, we have time for one last question. I don't want to stop Jeff, but I need to make sure we have enough time for the task at hand. Nick?"

"Is it true that your agency is not known as a starter agency? In other words, if we want to be represented by you, we have to already have both a healthy résumé and a healthy voice-over income?"

"It used to be somewhat like that, but not anymore. I love taking on new people. I *have* to take on new people, because that's what producers want nowadays. New, new, new! The biggest myth is that it's hard to break into voice-over. It's easy to break in, actually. There is such a huge demand for voices today compared to ten years ago. It's astounding. What's difficult is staying in, *maintaining* the work, because producers always want new and the next and the next. That's one of the reasons I love coming up here to Sausalito and have done so for years. We've found great fresh talent here at Voicetrax."

"Yeah, Jeff, but you also love coming up here because Graziano cooks for you," I tease him. All the students, frequently the lucky recipients of fantastic lunches lovingly prepared by my husband, laugh.

"You're right about that," Jeff laughs. "Last night's pasta was incredible!"

"Thank you for all this, Jeff. Now it's showtime, everyone!"

Jeff touches my arm. "Hang on, Sam, I want to make one more point I don't think I covered. I've got time. My flight isn't until four o'clock."

"Great, the floor is yours!" I say, smiling. My heart is glowing with love for Jeff. He's been my agent for more years than I can remember, a huge supporter of Voicetrax, and he's the big brother I never had. I've always looked up to him, admired and respected him, and although he's tough, in my mind there's nobody like Jeff Danis.

"So, guys, listen. Just remember, you're never more than an audition away from a huge account. You're just as likely to book a car account as a radio commercial for IHOP. It's the same skill set. I've seen lives change overnight, after five years of trying, with one simple audition. And it's so exciting for me. Watching clients go from fifty-thousand dollars a year to solid six-figures-a-year incomes that last more than six or seven years with one account. And for women, it is especially exciting! You are doing more than ever before. It used to be that for every ten jobs, one of those was for a woman. But now I can hear five, six, seven spots on the air and hear lots of women. Women, women, women!"

I can see the six women competing today glowing.

"Don't get discouraged," Jeff cautions, "just keep auditioning. Do a good job, don't be a pain in the ass, don't overthink, and be a good little soldier. It's an exciting time, it really is, in voice-over."

"And today is an exciting day," I add, "because one of you is going to be selected to go to LA to audition at DPN for a week."

As if everyone here didn't know that.

"That's right, Sam, so do your best today, guys, but *relax*. This is supposed to be fun."

I hustle all the students out into the lobby, so I can have a moment alone with Natanya and Jeff. "Hey, Jeff, thank you so much for your talk. As you must know, they hang on your every word." I turn to Natanya. "Of course, they also hang on your every word, Natanya, because you're such an amazing animation agent and one of our most beloved instructors here. Too bad we ran out of time for you to talk!" I give her a wink, and she flashes a huge wide smile at Jeff, which beams, *Sammy is right, Jeff, so why do you always go on so long?*

"No problem, Sammy," she says with a slight chuckle. "I talk a lot about the animation business in my classes, and I've worked with all these students several times."

"Okay, well, it's time to get going." I turn to Juliet, now the booth director for DPN, but also one of my former students-turned-employees from years ago. She is running the auditions this morning. "Are all the scripts ready, Jules?"

"Yep, I put three commercial scripts for the women and three for the men on the counter. They can pick which one they want to do." Then she hands me the huge pile of animation and video game scripts for round two.

"Great, I'm going to put these across the courtyard for them to look over and decide which character they should do and start rehearsing."

"Sammy?" Natanya jumps in. "Please tell them to choose wisely. It's going to really hurt them if they pick an inappropriate character. I don't want Anthony trying to do a forty-year-old prison guard when he naturally sounds like an adorable prepubescent kid."

"I'll tell them," I say, "and hope they listen." Too many actors think they're right for everything. I walk back out to the lobby.

"Okay, guys, remember what Jeff said. Try to relax and have fun. That being said, I know some of you are really nervous, which is okay too, because being nervous means that you care."

I put my free arm around Stacey, who looks like she's about to crawl out of her skin. "But you also have to care enough *not* to care. Got it?"

I can tell by Stacey's nod that she doesn't, not quite. Oh, well, nobody ever said it was easy.

"A few other quick points: First and foremost, this is just supposed to be another Voicetrax *class*. Granted, there's a huge carrot attached to it, but it is a class. You've been through the preliminaries, made it here to the finals, and have done the prep labs for this day too. All along the way you've been learning and growing from this experience. This just happens to be the last phase of this class. You will grow tremendously today if you remain receptive."

I point to the studio door. "Jules, Natanya, and Jeff will be directing you and giving you valuable feedback. Nerves might be a factor for some of you, but that's okay because, believe me, it takes practice to be able to perform while nervous. I know!"

"Me too!" Diane adds. "The first year I did this competition, I was so nervous I could barely get anything to come out of my mouth. I was devastated, but I got back on the horse the second time, made it to the finals again and was a lot better. Still somewhat nervous, but better for sure."

"And how do you feel today with this being your third competition?" I ask with pride, because I know her answer.

"I feel cool as a cucumber, a room-temperature cucumber anyway, and I'm going to go in there and have a great time."

"Good for you, honey! See, it just takes practice. One last thing—I know this is going to sound corny but it's really true. I am so proud of each and every one of you and in my heart, there isn't one winner, because you are all winners to me. You didn't just work hard to make it through the prelims, you've been working hard from the minute you first walked through this door and took your first beginning class. And look at where you are now! I love you so much and just know I'm pulling for you."

Broad smiles greet me. "Now, I'm going to go put all these animation scripts across the way for you to sort through, and, for God's sake, pick the right one for your voice. Natanya is going to have a cow if you don't."

"Okay," I say to the chorus of bobbing heads, "we're going to start with the commercial auditions, and for round one, we'll go in alphabetical order."

"What will we do for round two?" Gary asks.

"I don't fucking know, Gary! Maybe we'll start with you men and see which guy can pee the farthest." Everybody starts to laugh. "I hope you know I'm teasing you. Anyway, I don't know yet. I'm going to be in the studio with them, listening to you and taking notes. When they leave, about one o'clock, I'll know the winner. We'll eat pizza and decompress—go around the room to discuss what you got out of this experience, how you felt you did, and I'll share how I felt you did, and then I'll announce the winner. Capisci?"

"Capisci!" they answer in unison, and I can tell they're raring to go.

"Now don't forget how much I love you, and knock 'em dead!"

And so went another T.O.P. Voice finals morning. There were a few surprises, as always. One person didn't do nearly as well as I thought he would, but three people performed at their personal best, which is thrilling. One might think my favorite part of the day is when I get to announce the winner, or, in this case *winners,* as Jeff and Natanya picked two this time, but it isn't. My favorite point happens in the two seconds immediately *following* the announcement.

First, comes the shocked response from the winner, who usually shakes his or her head in disbelief. Then I see the rest of the students experience their one-second wave of disappointment, but by second number two, they are applauding enthusiastically, hugging and high-fiving the winner. It's so genuine and beautiful—it's a magical moment that beautifully reflects twelve exquisite human beings, Voicetrax-style.

July 20, 2013

STAFFORD LAKE, NOVATO, CALIFORNIA
VOICETRAX TWENTY-FIFTH ANNIVERSARY PICNIC

"Sam!" Nathan calls, jogging toward me. "Sammy! Roni wants to know when you want to call lunch. The schedule says 12:30, and it's just past that now."

He reaches me, out of breath. "Jesus, Mr. Perry, you're out of shape. You're sitting behind a microphone too much," I tease him.

"Tell me about it," he says, panting. "Anyway, Graziano is ready with the food, and it's probably going to take some time to get everyone served, so we should get going."

"Okay, go ahead. There are plenty of people up there by the food area, drinking away, so start with them. Tell Sterling to wind down making his gigantic bubbles with the kids, and we have one more inning of softball here to play. After I have my go at bat and drive in our two necessary runs, I'll tell the volleyball folks to finish up."

I kiss his sweaty forehead and turn back to the game in progress as he lumbers off.

"Come on, Aaron, you can do it!" I call, turning back to the game. "Let's see a homer, so we can have lunch!"

Nick pitches a strike. "Wow! Mr. Smoking Stratton. You're serious." Nick gives me a nod and throws a second pitch.

It's a grounder, right down the third base line. Laura fumbles the ball, and Aaron makes it to first. Now, the bases are loaded and it's my turn.

"All right, Nick," I say, wrapping my fingers around the bat. "Show me what you got. Strike me out, and I'll give you a free private." I step into the batter's box and execute a practice swing.

"No way! If he strikes you out, he should pay double for his private," Michael calls out. The pitch comes, and I hear the crack of the wood against the ball, a high fly ball to center field. I take off like lightning toward first base. Anthony, one of the only guys who brought his own glove, catches the damn ball, and all the runners return to their bases.

I'm out. Just as well.

"Sorry, guys!" I call out to my teammates. "They're beginning to serve lunch, so finish out this inning and come up." I start my trek over to the volleyball area.

It's a beautiful 85-degree day and the perfect way to celebrate Voicetrax's twenty-fifth anniversary. I take in a deep breath and shake my head. For the majority of the people here today, this is their first Voicetrax picnic, as the last one was probably held in 1999 or 2000. We did them for about seven years straight, but then they started to fizzle out. Just like me.

"Hey, guys!" I yell to the volleyball folks. "You've spiked your last ball. Lunch is ready. No dilly dallying!"

My long-beloved Andre has made two banners that are hanging beautifully above the lunch area. There are 150 people gathered under a huge gazebo, and there are another 50 or so approaching. I marvel at how my true love, Graziano, makes feeding all these people appear effortless. I wave to him and blow a kiss, which he catches expertly.

Thom Pinto, my first husband and voice-over teacher

extraordinaire, approaches. "Well, Samantha P., you've done it again. Another great picnic and another great turnout." The familiarity of his hug both warms and astounds me. We've been doing this hugging thing since 1981.

"I saw you out there playing volleyball. You look as good in your shorts now as you did thirty years ago," I tease him.

"You never were a great liar, but I'll take the compliment," Tommy groans. "I just wish my knees could function like they did when you used to hold these picnics."

"We all get older. Hey, remember Mom at Martoni's when she turned fifty?"

"Hey, everybody," Tommy says, launching into an impression of my drunk mother, "I'm fifty years old today. I know I don't look it!"

"Actually, mother—" I begin, pointing to my head to indicate it's what I was thinking at the time but not saying aloud—

"You do!" Tommy sings in unison with me.

Both grinning wickedly, we head up toward the feed tent. So many memories. I don't have a blood family to share history with, but my family of friends and past loves suits me much better.

"Hey, Thom," Tim Moran approaches. "I booked a great narration gig last week, thanks to your new 'Invitational Colors' class." Both Tommy and I are all smiles. "I just zoned in on my blue read, and it did the trick."

"Oh! You mean you channeled your logical, cool, objective, calming, centered read?" I say in a dropped tone to *sound* blue. I look at Tommy and he smiles. "It's nice to know all these voice-over techniques that we teach you work!"

The three of us laugh, and I squeeze Tim's cheeks. "I'm so proud of you! Gotta scoot, guys!" I set off in search for Roni, as she is in charge of everything and I've forgotten what's planned. I find her over by the bridge chatting with the psychic we hired for the afternoon fun.

"Hi, ladies. Sorry to interrupt. Roni, you've done an amazing job with everything. I could not be more pleased. So, what's on tap? I know when everyone has their food, I'll make some kind of speech and then we'll move on to the awards. Where are the huge cardboard checks that Andre made?"

"I've hidden them behind Graziano's food station. But wait, Sammy, before you speak, Pinto is going to say a few words."

"A few?" I start to laugh. "It's virtually impossible for Tommy to say only a few words." We both giggle, knowing how long he can keep me on the phone. "Okay, so after lunch, what?"

"We have Rainbow here to do the psychic readings, and Lucia just arrived to do face painting and temporary tattoos for the kids. We've got the water-balloon toss to do after lunch, because it's really hot. Colin just went out on a beer run, and to get more ice, because that margarita machine has been going nonstop since 11:30. Oh, and, my God, have you seen how much food your sweetheart of a husband has prepared? I'll be surprised to see who still has the energy for anything after this meal."

I shake my head, feeling both fortunate and mildly uncomfortable at all these coordinated efforts on behalf of me and the school. "By the looks of the line, I'd say there's probably a good twenty to thirty minutes before everyone is seated, so I'll just see you up there. And Rainbow, thanks for coming today. I'm sure you're going to be quite popular." I jog away toward the lake chuckling to myself at her name: *Rainbow the Psychic.*

I pause to drink in my environment and take a "slow, Sammy, slow" moment. This Marin County park is stunning. Although the lake has receded in the past few years, the glistening water and beautiful trees remind me that I live in one of the most beautiful areas in the world. With the birds communicating overhead, it makes me wonder what they are talking about. Shit. What am I going to talk about? What am I going to say?

That mouth of yours is going to get you in trouble. Another one of my mother's famous expressions.

Personally, I think my mouth has been rather successful, but I worry about what will come out when I speak to the group. There are a few key points I know I want to make, but other than that . . .

I breathe deeply and turn my back to the lake to face the gazebo. Wow. There are so many people who have all come to celebrate this important milestone. They're all celebrating twenty-five years of Voicetrax, but I feel as though I am celebrating only the past three, as all the years before that were a struggle, to say the least.

Where have those twenty-five years gone?

I ponder whether or not I should share with everyone my bathroom key story. When Andre first built the studio and made keys for the staff, we were one bathroom key shy. I decided to go without one. It was no big deal, because I figured I'd be teaching for a year or two and that would be it. It wasn't until I came back from teaching on the cruise ship three years ago that I made a key for myself. That's when I finally felt "all in." I shake my head, watching the sight of my three husbands among the crowd—Graziano cooking, Andre's decorations, and Thom on the Voicetrax staff. It feels so natural to me to have all of them here with me. There's no way I could or would want to celebrate this day without them.

The din of 200 people chatting and laughing away is wonderful. I'm so proud, which is a new feeling for me. I have actually built something—a company based on dedication, devotion, integrity, loyalty, and love. I'm grateful my students, staff, and instructors seem to have all my positive qualities, rather than my negative ones that I'm not so proud of—such as being controlling, demanding, and impatient. I know I'm still a work in progress. I glance at my watch. I still don't know what the hell I'm going to say, but I guess I shouldn't worry about it. What do I tell my students all the time?

"Safety lies in the risk. Just dive in and don't overthink."

"Don't worry about being perfect. Perfect is boring."

"Only worry when you're not being honest. When you're not being authentic."

A flurry of greetings and hugs envelop me, as I make my way around the picnic tables.

"Hey, Sammy," James calls out.

"Glad you could make it!" I tell him.

"Wow! This husband of yours is quite a chef," Angela exclaims.

"Thanks for such a great party, Sam," Larry Smith from my early days calls out. "Congratulations!"

I blow Larry a kiss.

"Samantha," Nick calls out, "I'd like for you to meet my wife and kids!"

I go over and hug Nick and his entire family. "I bet you guys are proud of your dad!" I get huge smiles from all three of them. "How about that, Nicky? What is this, your third video-game booking?" I squeeze his cheeks.

I then spot Thom Anderson, one of my first students and later one of my first employees, and my eyes fill with tears. I plop down on his lap and throw my arms around his neck. "Can you believe this, Thomsky? Who'd a thunk back then that we'd be here twenty-five years later?"

"Oh, Samantha, I'm not surprised in the least. The only person who never believed in you was *you*!"

Safety lies in the risk. Just dive in and don't overthink. Don't worry about being perfect. Perfect is boring. Only worry when you're not being honest. When you're not being authentic.

I give his beard a loving tug and then feel a tap on my shoulder. I turn to see another Tom, Tom Appelbaum, my first student.

"Holy fucking cow, you made it!" The years have been kind to him, as he still has that wonderful boyish quality he always had. "Did you see Andre?"

"Yeah, I did! I'm sorry you're not with him anymore, but we toasted with a beer."

"Come with me. I want you to meet Graziano." I take him by the hand, and we make our way through the crowd. I see my sweet husband wiping both his hands and his brow with a towel.

"Ah, my love!" he says to me, grinning from ear to ear. "Do you a' think everyone is enjoying the food?"

Both Tom and I laugh. "Honey, are you kidding me? I seriously doubt anyone has had food like this at a *picnic*. You and the food are amazing!"

"Couldn't agree more, Graziano. This food is incredible," Tom adds.

"Well thank you very much."

"Babe, this is Tom Appelbaum. He was my *first* student."

"Ah, bravo!" Graziano says, pumping his hand. "It's so nice to a' meet choo. You are numero uno!"

Out of the corner of my eye, I can see the line for food is dwindling. "Guys," I excuse myself, "I love you both dearly, but I have to keep this train moving forward."

I spot Roni sitting with Vicki and Chuck.

"Madam chairlady, I think we should start now with Pinto and me and then the presentations."

"Roger that," Roni says, as she stands to go find Tommy.

"This is really so amazing, guys," I confide to Chuck and Vicki, "but I'll be glad when it's over. I kind of feel like a politician, shaking hands and kissing babies."

"Samantha," Chuck laughs, nearly spitting out his food. "I don't think I've ever seen you shake anyone's hand."

"I know you feel uncomfortable with all this attention," Vicki says, "but remember we all love you," Vicki adds. "And besides, heavy is the—"

"Head that wears the crown," "Yeah, yeah, yeah," I add, as the three of us finish together.

I make my way to the front and discover Andre, Jeff, and Max front and center. I'm still sad Cathy isn't here, but her out-of-town work commitment with her dance company made it impossible. I spot Graziano speaking Spanish with his three assistants and enjoying a well-deserved glass of ice water off to the side.

"Hola, Gonzalo. *Muchas gracias f*or everything!" My Spanish stinks, but I get the sentiment across.

Gonzalo gives me a nod.

"Honey," I say to Graziano, "how will I ever be able to thank you for all this? You've worked so hard." I stroke his cheek with the back of my hand. "How did I ever get so lucky to have the most wonderful husband on the planet?" I give him a kiss.

"No, I am the lucky one and I am a' so proud! I have met so many of your students. They all a' say such wonderful things about choo."

"Yeah, but they don't have to live with me, right?"

Graziano chuckles.

"All right everybody, it's time to quiet down." Roni's voice fills the air. "We're going to start the presentations, quiet everybody!"

"You're going to ask a couple of hundred voice actors to quiet down?" someone shouts from the peanut gallery.

The laughter ripples through the crowd.

"Yep, that's a tall order all right, Mr. Larsen," Thom Pinto says, taking the mic, "but now I have the floor." And magically there is silence. "A couple of months ago, I was asked by the committee if I wouldn't mind making a few comments today. And so—"

Tommy turns to me. "Samantha P., congratulations." A wave of applause echoes his words. "Owning and running any successful business for twenty-five years is no small task, and you have done it all on your own. Then, on top of that, creating a one-of-a-kind business—the largest and only true voice-over academy in this country—is something that not only should you be proud of, but also you have the respect and kudos from all your voice-over colleagues, both here and in LA." Tommy continues. He is so well-meaning and beloved by the students—he is, by far, my most popular instructor.

"So, Sam," Thom finally concludes, while Graziano gives my shoulder a squeeze, "thank you so much for providing me with the opportunity to teach all these years and, to you students, I thank you for continuing to enrich my life."

As the applause and whistles swirl, I take the mic from him and we embrace. "Thank you, Tommy," I whisper. "Not just for that introduction, but for everything."

Showtime.

"How am I going to follow that?" I say to the sea of joyful faces. I want to keep their love in a bottle and reserve it for a day when I'm feeling low. "Mr. Pinto, thank you! And thank you all for coming out today to celebrate this crazy milestone. Before I go any further, I'd like Roni Gallimore to stand, along with her ten amazing volunteers who put this whole event together." They rise to accept their well-deserved applause. "I'd also like to thank my wonderful husband, who has worked tirelessly the past three days to bring us this spectacular feast." He waves in response to the chorus of whistles and cheers. "From the bottom of my heart, I thank each and every one of you."

I now wait for the quiet. "You know, driving out here today, I was trying to formulate in my mind what I would say standing here. My mind was a jumble of thoughts. I guess that's understandable, because there are twenty-five years of Voicetrax memories living within me. Each and every one of you here lives within me. Anyway, the one word that has been ringing in my ears the loudest for months now is *gratitude*. Mine, for you. For your dedication, devotion, integrity, loyalty, and love. Those are the words that best describe Voicetrax. All of you students here show such dedication to learning the art of voice acting, whether you've been coming to Voicetrax for one year or ten."

Several jaws drop.

"Don't worry, you newbies," I tell the newest students. "It's not going to take you ten years to make your demo, but it ain't gonna happen in one year either. Just ask 75 percent of this crowd here."

Gales of laughter spread through the crowd.

"Now let's move into those words, devotion, integrity, and loyalty, and talk about some of your amazing instructors here today. As I call out your name, please stand."

And so, one by one, I thank them all. *From the bottom of my heart.* Former students turned successful voice actors, other iconic voice actors, casting directors, and talent agents. All have stood by my side for years, some for decades, and have given so much of themselves to the students. I come to my final two.

"There are two other individuals here today who I must point out, because their roles are significant in my life and also to a certain extent in yours. The first is Tom Appelbaum. Tom, will you stand so they will know who you are? Guys, this is Voicetrax's first student!"

Shock and excitement fill the air as everyone begins to applaud again. Tom, the ham he is, soaks it up. "Talk about 'safety lying in the risk,' well, if it weren't for a fateful phone call initiated by Thom Pinto and placed to me by Mr. Appelbaum, I don't think any of us would be here today. Tom, I cannot thank you enough for coming."

Tom raises his arms and encourages the group to clap more so, of course, they do.

"All right, all right," I say over the noise. "You've had your moment, Appelbaum, now sit!" I tease him. "And last, I have to thank Andre." I look over at him tenderly and smile. "Andre was actually there in my home, while I gave that first lesson. We were then married for twenty-two of Voicetrax's twenty-five years, and Andre has endured, for better and for worse, living and breathing Voicetrax with me and still does to this day. It was he who taught me one of my most important life lessons and it has forever been Voicetrax's mantra. *Enjoy the journey.* Honey, can you please stand?"

Knowing Andre the way I do, I can read his look clearly, silently, crying: *For heaven's sake, Sam. You know I hate this attention. I thought being divorced would let me off the hook, but here I am, once again having to be a good sport.* He sheepishly stands while everyone applauds, and then he does a quick wave and immediately sits.

"What many of you don't know," I continue, "is that Andre built Voicetrax with his own two hands and, yes, he is the one responsible for the air conditioning not working in the booth!"

"Can we kill him now or later?" someone calls out from the crowd and laughter erupts.

"He is also Voicetrax's resident artist, as you all enjoy the colorful murals that are painted everywhere around the premises." My former husband receives more applause, and I give him a wink.

"And while we are on the subject of husbands, I again want to thank you, Graziano." He now gets my most tender glance. "I know you didn't realize what you were getting into when you married me. I guess I had you fooled! You thought you had met a low-maintenance woman—one with no real family to speak of, no children, totally financially independent, and yet here you are today cooking for more than 200 of my family members!"

I turn and blow him a big kiss and, immediately, he sends one back. I turn back to the crowd, "Which now brings me to the rest of you. My beloved students." I hear the birds above again, and my heartbeat pounds in my ears.

How do I tell them how much I love them?

How do I express that the reason I never found anything in the Wizard's bag is because, just like Dorothy, I had it all along?

"We all know it is far better to give than receive, and for twenty-five years now that is what I've done. I have tried my best, to give you my best. It is what each and every one of you deserves: unparalleled instruction and a safe, supportive, loving environment in which to grow. I made a vow to personally guide each and every one of you on your journey. That's what I gave, and I did it with no intention of receiving anything. It is after all, my job; it's what you have paid me to do. But we all know that magic happens when we least expect it and believe me, you are all *my* magic.

"You are all *my* mentors as you taught me far more than I ever taught you. You have given me more than I ever gave you. Through the years, I have marveled at your dedication, have been blown away by some of the tremendous sacrifices some of you have had to make, and have been so moved witnessing how you all love and support one another. It is so apparent that by lifting others up, we lift ourselves. You are in one word, extraordinary."

Heads nod and people exchange warm glances as the instructors start to applaud.

"A few months ago, Graziano and I gave a dinner party at our home. I didn't know the guests well, as they were all friends of his before me. At one point, I wanted to kill him—" I turn to him and say, "Not really, honey." I turn back to the crowd. "But it was really embarrassing, because he was bragging about all my past 'accomplishments.' Namely, when I was living and performing in LA, doing all my on-camera work, voicing the cartoons, et cetera.

|| By lifting others up, we lift ourselves.

"Anyway, this one woman asked me what I felt was my most favorite role or greatest accomplishment. Now if this had been a few years ago, I'm not sure what I would have said. But at this dinner, I knew. I told her my most favorite role was that of a teacher and that my greatest accomplishment was the school I had built. I told her I had approximately 300 active students and that I loved each one of you profoundly.

The dinner table then became eerily quiet, and I know they all thought I was crazy or full of you know what. I mean, come on. How does one genuinely *love* 300 people, right? I tried to explain a little bit about Voicetrax, what I do, what we have. But how do you really describe this place? I didn't even attempt to explain my dots to her. Can you imagine?"

I make a feeble attempt to laugh at myself to keep my tears at bay. "But you know what, guys? When I sign each and every dot form, 'My love as always, Samantha,' or 'I love you so much it's not funny,' it's true. And the beauty is that I know that *you know I do.*"

Andre's head is bowed. I know he can't stand to see me cry. I'm not sure what he's thinking, but what I'm thinking is that for nearly twenty-two years, I said, "I hate teaching," "I hate Voicetrax," and "I hate my life." I was so conflicted and, of course, what I ultimately realized was that regardless of where my deep-seated pain came from, he was indifferent to it.

"I really didn't want to cry, I'm sorry," I confess. "Anyway, I do love you with all my heart, and I admire you more than I could possibly express. With your help, you might say I have found my bunny. You know, I might be the founder of Voicetrax but *we all have built Voicetrax.* This place on Bridgeway that we love and support is *our place* and this is *our* twenty-fifth anniversary. Happy anniversary, everyone! Will somebody please hand me a Kleenex? And now on to the awards!"

From the time she was five years old growing up in Los Angeles, Samantha dreamt of nothing but becoming an actress, 1968.

Before Samantha changed her name, she booked heavily doing on-camera commercials and episodic television, as well as voice acting, as Bobbi Block, her given name, 1978.

Samantha's first students in her home office in Mill Valley, 1988.

Samantha directing a group of students, 1990.

The first *Stars Wars* video game being recorded with former Voicetrax student turned successful voice actor, Roger Jackson, circa 1996.

Samantha with her young, blind, voice-acting student, Dionne Quan, who soon thereafter went on to become globally known for her starring role in the hit cartoon series, *The Rugrats,* circa 1997 at the Voicetrax Sammy Awards.

Ollie, the Voicetrax mascot, 2009.

Samantha and her chosen mother, Janet Mann, at her bridal
shower before marrying Graziano, 2011.

Samantha and Graziano enjoying the traditional
wedding walk, Torre di Palme, Italy, May 2011.

And the crowd goes wild at the Voicetrax 25th anniversary picnic,
Lake Stafford, Novato, California, July 2013.

Samantha with her two right hands, Chuck Kourouklis and Vicki Baum,
at Voicetrax, 2013. Photo by Lisa Keating Photography.

Samantha coaching Maureen O'Donoghue, who exemplifies many students
who come to Voicetrax seeking to start a new chapter in their lives, 2013.
Photo by Lisa Keating Photography.

Happy "Will Read for Food" contest winners, who won a free class taught by Samantha and a gourmet lunch with Graziano, July 2016.

Peter Coyote and Samantha at Voicetrax for his workshop,
"Unmasking Your Infinite Potential" for advanced students, 2017.

Andre, Samantha, and Graziano enjoying the
BNP Paribas Open in Indian Wells, California, March 2017.

Andre, while in town visiting friends and staying with Samantha and Graziano in August 2017, stops by to do a touch-up on the 1992 mural he painted at Voicetrax.

Samantha with first student Tom Appelbaum, back nearly 30 years later
to record his part in the audiobook version of *Finding the Bunny*, August 2017.

Epilogue

This song in my head is driving me crazy.

I roll over to my other side, gently rubbing Graziano's arm so his light snoring will cease, though truth be told, I find it rather comforting.

What was that?

The silence in the room is piercing, but I have to listen closely.

Did I remember to check if the front door was locked? Did I set the alarm last night?

A rush of anxiety washes over me. Ever so carefully, I get out of bed to see if the alarm's red light is on, and it is. I feel relieved, but continue to listen as I slide back under the covers. Ollie is also snoring away on my pillow above my head. I bring the covers up all around me perfectly, as I have done for so long, minus the one foot out I've been allowing myself for years.

After a few silent moments, Bruno Mars' hit song, "Uptown Funk," starts playing on repeat in my head.

> *Don't believe me just watch*
> *Don't believe me just watch*

A tear gently rolls down my cheek. Then another, and I wipe them away.

When is this ever going to stop? When am I not going to feel afraid anymore? Will I ever truly feel safe? I have everything in life I could possibly want.

I turn to Graziano, who looks so peaceful when he is sleeping. I draw in a deep breath, exhaling slowly as I gaze at the ceiling. I am bathed in love by this man. I tell him every day how much I appreciate him, how much I love him and how safe and comforted he always makes me feel.

I hear a noise again. I am paralyzed with fear. *Jesus! What is that sound?* It happens again; my body tightens and then, suddenly, relief washes over me.

Ah, that's the icemaker dropping ice cubes on the kitchen floor again.

I let out a gigantic sigh, close my eyes, and shake my head. I know I had better get up and go pick them up, because it's not good for the hardwood floors.

"My love, where are you a' going?" Graziano calls as I get out of bed.

"The icemaker is at it again. I just want to pick up the ice cubes."

"Are you okay? Are you sleeping?"

"Not too good tonight, but I'm okay. Go back to sleep, I'll be right back." I go out to the kitchen, pick up the ice, and as I return to bed, the symphony of both "my men" snoring plays on.

8:00 a.m.

"Hi, babe, how are you?"

"Well, good morning, I'm wonderful! I just finished breakfast, I'm on my second cup of tea, and I'm reading the paper."

"Did you have the leftover frittata from New Year's Day?"

"God, no, I ate that the moment you guys left. Then I fin-ished the lasagna last night. You should tell Graziano not to cook so much, because I only eat it."

I giggle.

"Okay, well what did you have this morning?"

"I had my English fry-up, and it was delicious."

"Andre, how can you do that? You're eating eggs, beans on fried bread, and tomatoes and mushrooms? You've gotta stop!"

"You forgot the bacon, and I promise to go back to grapefruit tomorrow. Anyway, do you want to hear your horoscope?"

"Okay, shoot."

"Okay, Gemini . . . Gemini . . . Ah! Here goes. Don't be a pain in the ass all your life—"

I finish the sentence for him, "Take the day off. Yeah, yeah, very funny, Andre. You've only said that to me a million times. You're not even on the horoscope page, are you? I betcha you're reading sports."

"If I told you I just read that Rafa won yesterday, would that put a smile on your face?"

"I actually knew he won, because I watched the match. Do I sound crabby?" There's a pause on the other end of the phone.

"Well, maybe tired."

"Yeah, I am. I didn't sleep well, which you know is nothing new."

"Voicetrax stuff?" he asks caringly.

I sigh. "Of course, but other stuff too. How's your knee?"

"Much better today. I iced it all day yesterday after pickle ball."

"You know, honey, I keep telling you it's not necessary for you to play four or five games. You can go there and be social with everyone and play one game."

"I know you're right, Sammy, but I just can't help myself. I love playing," he says sheepishly. "I did, however, remember to take your tennis racquet to the clubhouse to be restrung so that must count for something."

"Well, that's sweet of you, but it still has nothing to do with this knee conversation. Also, there was no rush to do my racquet, because we aren't going to be coming back down there until March."

"Ahh . . . but what is our most famous Paris expression?" he asks leadingly so we say it together.

"N.T.L.T.P."

"Good girl! I would have thought you'd forgotten it."

"What? Oh, Andre, don't be silly. Look, speaking of N.T.L.T.P., I hear Graziano upstairs watching TV, so he's awake. I want to take him his coffee. Can I call you later? How about I check in with you before *60 Minutes* tonight?"

"I will be waiting for your call. But Sammy, you know you don't have to call me all the time. I love it that you do, but you don't have to. I really am fine."

Now the pause is on my end, as I know I will never be able to *not* worry about Andre.

"I know I don't *have* to call, honey, but I *want* to, and you know that." There is silence once again. There are 545 miles and a six-year divorce that separate us, yet we will be forever attached. We say our goodbyes, hang up, and I look at the phone knowing I simply could not have had it any other way.

As I stare out at the pouring rain, I begin feeling melancholy and a little unsettled. Being so much older, Andre always used to talk about dying before me. He would say things like, "Now when I'm dead and gone, you're going to have to learn how to pump up your own bicycle tire." Or, "When I'm dead and gone, you're going to have to know how to trim this bush." I used to roll my eyes heavenward. But he also made a promise similar to Nanna's that he wouldn't die until he was sure *I was ready for him to die.* That I would be strong enough to let him go.

I know I will *never* be ready for that moment. We've been

through so much, and our divorce made us both better people. Andre is much more giving in all aspects of his life now, and I can more fully appreciate all the incredibly valuable life lessons he taught me, many of which I have passed down to my students. These are the kinds of big-picture lessons I should have received from my parents, but, thank God, I had Andre. I take in a deep breath and close my eyes, trying to imagine my life without him. It's such an unpleasant thought that I immediately shake my head, push the thought from my mind and walk into the bedroom where I find Ollie sprawled out on the bed, next to Graziano, getting his tummy rubbed.

"Good morning, honey. Boy are you spoiled, Ollie." I grab my robe and put on my slippers.

"My love. Where are you going?"

"Outside to get your paper."

"No, you are a' not. It's raining," he says, as he extends his arms for me to come over and give him a cuddle. I cross over to the bed and sit on the side near him and lean in.

"Oh, you feel so good."

Ollie turns over and licks my forehead.

"You tired?" he asks, as he gently strokes my head.

"Yeah, I woke up about 3:00 a.m. and, as usual, I couldn't fall back asleep."

"I know. You kept turning and I can a' always feel you thinking."

"I know, I'm sorry. I should really just get up and go into the other room but I know that would upset you."

"You're right. I would be upset. So, what were you a' thinking about this time?"

"Just a million things like usual. I was trying to remember when Lorenza's birthday was, what the theme should be for the new Voicetrax website, and I had this Bruno Mars' song in my head, and I kept trying to quiet the trumpets. Plus, I told Cathy that for Super Bowl we would go over to her house, so you could finally teach her how to do the chicken in the pot, but I started to worry last night that maybe that's not such a good idea, because she and Jeff are going to have a few other people there, and I don't think that is something you would want to cook."

"No! I think bollito will be good, and you shouldn't worry about a' my job! Who is a' the cook around here?"

I let out a slight giggle.

"I know, but you wanted to know what was in my head. Plus, I'm worried about Andre, so that was playing on me too."

"Did you talk to him this morning?"

"Yeah, we just hung up."

"Darn. I wanted to tell him that his team, Arsenal, is a' playing right now, and I think Manchester City is up next. We can't miss our Sunday morning soccer."

"Well, as soon as you stop stroking my head, which I hope is never, I'll bring you your coffee and then I'll call him back or you can call him."

"Has he decided when he's a' going to do his knee surgery?

"That's what I'm worried about. I don't think he should do it. Not at his age. And his last knee replacement was a disaster." I sit up and let out a sigh. "And do you know what else I was thinking about last night?"

"There's more?" Graziano says, teasing me. I just shake my head.

"I feel guilty saying this, but we have spent the past three Christmases with him in the desert, and I'm just not sure I want to do it next year."

Graziano looks surprised. "But why? We love our home, and the weather . . . and you two love your bike rides every morning and playing tennis. Plus, we had a wonderful time in Vegas!"

"Yes, we did, and I still can't believe he won that $4,500, but I was worrying last night that maybe I'm being a bit selfish. We are always with Andre in Rancho Mirage, but your family in Italy is constantly begging you to come home for Christmas, now that you sold the restaurant."

"Babe, please a' stop your worry so much." He looks a bit distraught.

"I'm sorry, I just can never shut off my brain." I get up from the bed to go get the coffee. "Come on, Ollie boy. Come with Mommy, and I'll give you a treat." And like a rocket, Ollie is off the bed, leading me to the kitchen

Filling Graziano's cup, I realize that although I'm so tired, I am fulfilled. My soul is smiling with the knowledge that I really did find my bunny in life. I have never known such happiness. I am married to such a loving, supportive man, who is undeniably the love of my life; I have a wonderful business that I'm really proud of; and I'm grateful for the loving relationship that I managed to carve out with Andre.

I return with the coffee and see that Ollie has once again joined his papa on the bed. "Honey, I'm going to go give you-know-who a bath and then, if the rain has stopped, I'll go get your paper."

"Ahh, no, babe. Please just come here and a' lie down. You look a' so tired. *Please.*" He taps my side of the bed, and, like Ollie, I obediently do as I am told. "Why don't you crawl back under the sheets and really try to a' sleep?"

"No, this is okay. I know I couldn't fall asleep at this point." I give Graziano another snuggle, as I lie in his arms and then close my eyes.

Don't believe me just watch
Don't believe me just watch

Holy cow, not Bruno again.

I draw in another deep breath. Now Rafa Nadal invades my quiet, but he makes me smile. I was so excited yesterday, watching him win the first tennis tournament of the season, especially since he had such a miserable season last year. I always love thinking about Rafa, because he is such a great motivator for me. I love his strength, his work ethic, his "I will not quit, no matter what" attitude. I also love that he is vulnerable and not afraid to show it.

I wonder how Rafa sleeps at night? Does he only allow one foot to stick out, like me?

Maybe. I mean, we all have fears. The key is not to let those fears paralyze you, and do your best with the hand you've been dealt. Maybe the cards I was initially dealt weren't the greatest, but they certainly were nowhere near the worst. I've learned through the years that it's *what you do with those cards* that matters. And although I'm much better now, I might not ever graduate beyond my one-foot-out syndrome. Maybe that's one demon I'll never be able to chase away for good.

Sure, the demon disappears come morning, when it's a fresh new day full of promise. I force him into a dark corner, where I know he can't get at me and I can feel safe. I simply will not allow him to take over my life. After all, I'm on a journey, and I really want to enjoy the ride.

The End

ACKNOWLEDGMENTS

First and foremost, this book would have *never* happened without the unyielding love, support, and dedication to this project from my dear friend and publicist, Nancy Balik FitzGerald. She knew this book was inside me, long before I did, and I would have never typed one word without her. I could simply stop there.

However . . . because it really did take a village for me realize this dream, there are others who also must be thanked. I call it my "three degrees of separation." The first degree is my voice-over agent, Jeff Danis. His support of me and my academy through the years is staggering. Because of him, thousands of Voicetrax students have had the good fortune of studying with the voice-over industry's elite.

And certainly, at the top of that elite list, is our beloved Voicetrax guest director, Peter Coyote. From the moment we met, I was so taken by his expansive and inclusive nature. I had long been an admirer of his work, and his voice is one we all know and love. However, I have had the great privilege of getting to know this special human being, and I can attest to the fact that his voice is truly a reflection of his soul—deep, warm, beautiful, and abundant. He has enriched my life and the lives of my students in so many ways, and we are all so infinitely grateful.

I'm also profoundly thankful to Peter for introducing me to his book editor, Terry Bisson. Terry is a brilliant, supportive, and sensitive editor who was incredibly patient and nonjudgmental with me when he had to take on the work of this first-time writer. I smile every time I think of Terry being such an acclaimed science-fiction writer and me insisting that because this was my memoir, every word had to be truthful. What a wonderful mismatched pair we were!

And speaking of truth, *Finding the Bunny* is my life story, as I recall my memories and experiences—although, at times, some timelines had to be changed for storytelling purposes, and some names had to be changed for legal purposes. I chose to insert the names of friends and loved ones whenever possible.

I also wish to thank my "Book Sherpa," Gail Kearns. Just when I thought my book was done, the universe said, "not so fast, Sammy" and she entered the project. Thank God! She pushed me to go deeper, and in the end, it was her prodding that made this book be all it could be and finally made me feel proud to utter the words, "I am now an author."

And finally, I thank my first-rate cheerleading section—those of you who donated your time and voices to our "Bunny" promo pieces and those of you who willingly took on the task of reading *Finding the Bunny*. Throughout the early stages of the book, you were all there to encourage me, offer suggestions, and even throw out some tough opinions at times. But I knew it was always done in the name of love, support, and friendship.

Lucia Antonelli
Carolyn Baker
Vicki Baum
Ralph Caulo
Peter Coyote
Jeff Danis
Roni Gallimore
Caroline Gelsman
Devin Glischinski
Nina Greeley
Chris Green

Jeff Gustafson
Max Gustafson
Jon Hyman
Edie Keller
Scott Kessler
Chuck Kourouklis
Gerry Mandel
Karen Mann
Damian Marhefka
Dan Noyes
Elizabeth O'Neill

Graziano Perozzi
Thom Pinto
Cathy Pruzan-Gustafson
Sam Pond
Deborah Rothenberg
Gabrielle Russell
Scott Russell
Brian Sommer
Tom Sipes
Robert Snyder
Chuck Wedge

To all of you, my love and gratitude.

ABOUT THE AUTHOR

Samantha Paris is an award-winning voice actor, educator, entrepreneur, and founder of Voicetrax San Francisco, the largest and most respected voice-over academy in the United States. Born Bobbi Block in Southern California, Samantha began performing at the age of five. After landing a commercial agent at the age of 16, Samantha enjoyed a career that included nearly 1,000 national and regional commercials and roles in nearly 200, half-hour, animated, television, cartoon shows, including the megahit cult series, *Jem and the Holograms*. She appeared in several episodic television roles, a starring role opposite Michael Landon in a two-episode storyline on *Highway to Heaven*, and in a CBS Afternoon Playhouse episode, *I Think I'm Having a Baby*.

Yet with all her performing success, including three CLIO Awards, Samantha yearned to live near the iconic Golden Gate Bridge in San Francisco. So, at the height of her voice-over career success in Los Angeles, she moved to the Bay Area.

It wasn't long before Samantha was unwittingly thrust into the teaching profession. Before she knew it, Samantha had unconsciously created a groundbreaking training program and a flourishing business. Voicetrax San Francisco was founded in 1988, with its studio built soon thereafter in Sausalito.

Throughout the years, Samantha has successfully trained more than 10,000 aspiring and working voice actors in the Bay Area. Her students represent people from all walks of life and backgrounds—many of whom have gone on to book voice-over jobs regularly to supplement their incomes, and many others who go on to make voice-over their full-time and handsome living.

With a fierce commitment to the philosophy that *talent can be taught*, Samantha built a hugely successful business, strictly through enthusiastic word of mouth and substantial media attention.

Above all, through Voicetrax, Samantha has helped transform the lives of people through the process of helping them find their voices and, ultimately, find their bunnies.

In the process, she found *her* bunny.